To my long lost sister Mary,

The Hitchhiker's Guide

To Jack Kerouac

On the (Red) Wings of Jack

The Adventure of the Boulder '82
On The Road Conference —
Finding Kerouac, Kesey and
The Grateful Dead
Alive & Rockin' in the Rockies

Thanks for the reads and posts and comments and support and humor and passion and play! ☺

[signature]

May 4, 2017

On the writer and the writing ...

"Your article sent me into raptures. I just LOVE the way you write. Your wit and turns of phrase and insights are so unique and beyond compare. You must write many books!"
> - Carolyn Cassady
> (wife of Neal and love of Jack's life)

"Jack would've *loved* you!"
> - Edie Kerouac Parker
> (Jack's first wife)

"This is an exceptionally fine piece of work on your part. Marvellous dissertations and mightily written rapportage!"
> - Henri Cru
> (Remi Boncoeur in *On The Road*)

"I like your distinctive narrative voice. You are a great stylist."
> - Sterling Lord
> (Kerouac & Kesey's literary agent)

"Hombre, let me say right off – you are a hell of a writer! This piece you wrote is just wonderful. I love it! It felt like I was there.....what a treat."
> - Walter Salles
> (director of *On The Road*)

"You're not an *On The Road* scholar — you're an *On The Road* character!"
> - Teri McLuhan
> (Marshall McLuhan's author/filmmaker daughter)

"You can write your ass off!!"
> - David Amram
> (Kerouac's principal musical collaborator)

"If it's happiness you want, Brian Hassett seems to have found it."
> - Bill Sass
> (*Edmonton Journal*)

Early praise for *The Hitchhiker's Guide to Jack Kerouac*

"What a fresh light you're shining on the Beat Scene. And in a loving, lyrical style. Showing, in a way no one has before, how those around Jack influenced him and helped preserve his work for us. Your book will be an important addition to the ongoing Saga of Jack."

- Cor van den Heuvel
(America's foremost haikuist)

"It reads wonderfully. The stories of your adventures are always intriguing and fun. Despite what's going on in the moment — you have an outlook on the world that is just joyful. And I love your play with words "

- Jerry Cimino
(founder & curator of The Beat Museum)

"This is top level. It's breezy and friendly and fun to read. It's naturally gripping stuff, full of personality, and it works. There's a nice rhythm – chunky, meaty, bouncy, like a good Grateful Dead road song. Plus, the book is offering valuable original material."

- Levi Asher
(Beat scholar and founder of the globally renown LitKicks)

"This excerpt and news is great! I can't wait to get a full copy of the book!! You are such a good writer!"

- Carolyn Cassady
(Neal Cassady's wife and Kerouac's lover)

"This is very rich, vivid and informative. It tells me things I didn't know – and is definitely another chapter in the music/Beat nexus that is so worth airing."

- Simon Warner
(Beat scholar and author of *Text and Drugs and Rock 'n' Roll*)

"You nail Herbert perfectly. I can hear him say those lines in my mind's ear. And nice job on Edie and Henri. This book might help give them the credit they deserve."

- Tim Moran
(Huncke's friend, & executor of Edie Kerouac & Henri Cru's estates)

Later praise for *The Hitchhiker's Guide to Jack Kerouac*

"The book is a youthful memoir with all the never-to-be-recaptured frantic zest of a young man. Everything is wonderful in Hassett world, even bad luck. Every cloud he sees has a silver lining. This attitude takes him far. It's the sheer unbridled enthusiasm that pours from Hassett that is so engaging. This is a brilliant read."

– Beat Scene magazine
(world's premier Beat magazine in print)

"This is an excellent book about Uncle Jack, and also a heartfelt outpouring of love for Mom and Dad, and the Grateful Dead, too. Thank you for writing this."

— Jami Cassady
(Neal & Carolyn's youngest daughter, and "Jack's favorite")

"It's a remarkable tale of getting yourself going to goneward. Made me laugh, and overstand your estimations of the so manys I've known. Very glad you got it in print and I have it in hand."

– Gerd Stern
(poet & multi-media artist – who did NOT lose Neal's letter)

"You are a worldwise, lifewise storyteller of the highest order. This rocks with diamond halos and rolls with musical glee. A Beat bridge between then and now, and now and then. On the road, mad to write, mad to live, and everyone goes awwwwww ...."

– S.A. Griffin
(L.A.'s foremost Beat poet & performer)

"A tremendous author. The writing in this book is fantastic. It's a phenomenal work. If you're wanting to expand your consciousness and you're trying to become more enlightened, I can't recommend a better book."   — Jake Feinberg
(The Jake Feinberg Show, PowerTalk 1210 AM)

"This reads like a breathless telephone call or letter, a cassette-tape transcription, an annotated bibliography – because it's all of these — utterly at home with thinking aloud reportage, fast & free, both street talk & literature, a textured ear, humorous, true, however knowingly comic, without obscuring the candid, naked, generous moment!"

— Kris Hemensley
(Collected Works Books, Australia)

The Hitchhiker's Guide To Jack Kerouac

•

The Adventure of the Boulder '82
On The Road Conference —
Finding Kerouac, Kesey and The Grateful Dead
Alive & Rockin' in the Rockies

Brian Hassett

Gets Things Done Publishing

ISBN: 978-0-9947262-0-9

First Edition — Pranksters in Wonderland (100 copy print run)
Second Edition — Earth Day 2015
Third Edition — Beat Museum Shindig in San Francisco and
                    Grateful Dead's 50th in Chicago
Fourth Edition — Lowell Celebrates Kerouac! 2015
Fifth Edition — Christmas 2015
Sixth Edition — Pranksters In Space – summer 2016
Seventh Edition — Summer of Love 50th Anniversary 2017

Front cover photo by Barry Floch — in the famous Jack spot in front
of the Kettle of Fish on MacDougal Street, 1982, wearing the S.S.
Doric t-shirt from the oceanliner I stowed away on, and carrying my
dad's WWII gas mask sidebag.

Cover design and production: the Michelangelian David Wills.

**The book's large 12 point font and open space is intentional.
Books should be fun and easy to read and not a chore.
You're welcome.**

Brief quotes used under the Fair Use laws of Section 107 of the
Copyright Act of 1976.

For more information and to stay up to date go to . . .
BrianHassett.com
or email . . . **karmacoupon@gmail.com**

Dedicated to my two late great moms,
Enid Hassett and Carolyn Cassady,

and to Jack, Jerry, Ken,
and all the guiding lights in the darkness

CONTENTS

DESSERT

EXPLANATORY

Perception is like snowflakes. Of the roughly 30 featured performers, 300 full-time participants, and 3,000 or so who were there for part of it, no three stories of this Wild West Adventure would be the same. There were simultaneous workshops and panels and readings and concerts and gatherings and hang-outs and road-trips and no one could be everywhere at once. I mean, so much happened — who knows what *you'll* take away from it.

What you're reading was prompted by unexpectedly seeing in an online forum a photograph of a group of people taken at a gathering I was part of in 1982. Some friends who weren't there asked about it, and what I thought would be a quick remembrance grew into what you find here. In the process, I uncovered numerous thought lost cassettes I'd recorded while *on the road*, and notebooks written as it happened, and photos that somehow survived, and reports others wrote or filmed or photographed that jogged still more memories — and it became proof of how much is inside our floating organic hard drive that we thought was erased but with a little effort and joggers can be retrieved.

And to be sure, I ran the various parts of the book by all those who appear in it that I had a Beat on, or their estates if they've passed, so this is as close to the heart of the matter as possible.

The Great Rememberer, indeed. Heaven's holy notebooks. Jack was right. It's all in there. And it's fairly out there.

Introduction
by
John Allen Cassady

My mother Carolyn and I have gone on the road on many adventures with the author of this book, Brian Hassett. New York City, Northport, Amsterdam, San Francisco, you name it. The thing about Brian is, well, Carolyn put it best, in a line she used ever since we were first blessed to go traveling with him ... "Brian gets things done!"

Depending on how big a problem he'd solve or new thing he'd come up with, my Mum would stress the "done" to different degrees. It became a running joke in our family whenever we were with him. Somehow he could always get us into wherever we wanted to go, and get us out of whatever jam we were in. This was a happy occurrence for all of us, and Getsthingsdone basically became Brian's name in the Cassady family as we traveled together through the years and cities of Jack and Neal celebrations.

As the wheel turned, the Prankster footage of when my Dad was driving Ken Kesey's bus back in the sixties finally got made into a movie called *Magic Trip* a couple years ago, and although we'd seen some short clips and still pictures, seeing the footage was as new to us who weren't there as it was to everyone else. Imagine our surprise when we were watching this, and right next to Dad at his driver's seat, one of the Pranksters had taped up a big sign: "Neal gets things done!"

For some reason, Brian ended up in the middle of our family, and we were never sure why, but maybe he reminded us of someone who was always part of it. Besides getting me off my ass and "on the road" more times than I can remember, he also went and lived with Carolyn in England for several months when none of the rest of us kids could be there. The guy is always on a mission, whether it's taking care of my mother, or his own, or getting me to sneak past the Do Not Enter warnings to climb up to the Hollywood sign.

Or maybe it was getting me to the Rock 'n' Roll Hall of Fame for the Grateful Dead show, or to go on the road with him and *On The Road* director Walter Salles, or to go to L.A. for The 50th Anniversary of Jack Writing On The Road Show he put on there with S.A. Griffin, I don't know what it is, to tell you the truth, but somehow Brian gets things done. He even gets me to get things done, which is even more amazing!

The exploits chronicled in this book happened before I was on the Beat circuit, but then this was really the first one. Naturally, my mother was there, and charming the pants off him from what I hear. Well, not literally. At least I hope not. But I've been hearing about this thing ever since it happened. Every time any two people who were both there were in the same room they'd talk about it like they'd taken some wild trip together. That's why I was so "chuffed" to hear there was finally going to be a book on it ... and who was writing it.

You will soon meet Brian through his words, and I think you will know right away why we like traveling and doing things with him. It's not just what he does, but how he does it. You'll see. And it's how he describes it. He writes the way he talks. And he lives the way he writes. Which also reminds me of my Dad and Uncle Jack.

This Kerouassady fascination has done nothing but grow during my lifetime. We thought it was a big deal when some famous writer would come to visit, or Dad would take me to Grateful Dead shows, but it's gotten nothing but bigger since then. There's more biographies about my Dad and his friends than I could ever read, and now we go to premieres of Hollywood movies with actors playing him with surround-sound and images bigger than life. Which is appropriate for Neal.

Something else I was reminded of while reading this was how Allen Ginsberg was always front and center for any big event, and how he kept coming to visit us in the '70s when a lot of Neal's friends had fallen away, and that here he is in this book, in the '80s, still being so Allen, organizing this whole thing that wouldn't have happened if he didn't do it. Come to think of it, "Gets Things Done" would work for him, too.

I regret not being able to attend in person, but between my mother Carolyn, our friend Brian, and all the others who knew or loved my father Neal, I feel the family was indeed well represented.

Keep the Beat!

John Allen Cassady

"We had come from all over
the country, from all periods of
Kerouac's life, and more of us
were together than had ever been
in one place at one time before."

John Clellon Holmes
"Envoi In Boulder" in
Representative Men

Let me take you there, cuz I'm going too . . .

The Sequence of Synchronicity

My first year at NYU I met my hero, concert promoter Bill Graham, and worked my way onto his Rolling Stones Tour in 1981. By this second summer "abroad" in '82 it seemed like time to return to the grounding homeland and city that launched me into America — Vancouver, Canada — with the summer's great notion to meet my second biggest hero, Ken Kesey, come hell or high kool-aid.

First I stopped half way in hometown Winnipeg and stage managed the largest No Nuke concert in Canadian history on the steps of the Manitoba Legislative Building, then two daze later a buncha friends threw me a surprise 21st birthday party at our cottage in Gimli just before I lit out for the coast. Ultimately I'd travel over 10,000 miles that year adventuring around the continent — but here's the best part —

I had the greatest girlfriend in the world. Sue was a smart strong art-centric cool-grooving makeup-free wavy-haired Swedish blond ballet dancer who was the first girl I ever asked to go out with me, start of grade 12 — the fair Maid Marian to my gallant Sir Galahad in a fairy-tale romance we lived for years.

She'd just moved into a princess's cottage in the same coolsville Vancouver West End neighborhood we were living when the first New York adventure was launched — San Francisco North, the soul base, the laid-back hippie hipster heart of homeland Canada — so I had to return to the old-growth roots that my new New York was flowering from.

Turns out, that month her little sister was turning 18, and I thought it high time big brother-in-law gave her some grown-up books to help her on her way, so I went out to pick up *On The Road* and a couple others. No Hunter Thompson, mind you, but Jack ... Jack's love of the Earth and Life and The Journey ... that was what her just-blossoming soul was in need of at this fertile time.

I made a quick run to the nearest cool bookstore in West End Van, went to the fiction section and grabbed an *On The Road* and ... wait ... what? — "There's no Jack? ... *At all?!*" I went to the counter and asked, and they looked him up, and ... "Nope" — they don't have *any* books by him. ... Huh?

I shook my head, thought, "No problem," and went to the next bookstore. Over to the K's, ... Kael, Keller, Kennedy ... and ... no Kerouac!! *What?!* Find the information desk again, "Um, do you guys have *On The Road* by Jack Kerouac?"

"Who?"

And again I walk out shaking my head at Canada, grumbly reminding myself why I'd left in the first damn place. But since New York and Bill Graham taught me No is not an option, I persevered, on to the next store.

Damn! . . . You gotta be kidding me!

After a couple hours of this I was a little too familiar

with every author from Kafka to King, so by at about the sixth place I just skipped the fiction section and went straight to the help kiosk — "Do you guys have ..." — and as I looked up at the young man and woman behind the counter, right in between their heads I saw this giant poster on the wall —

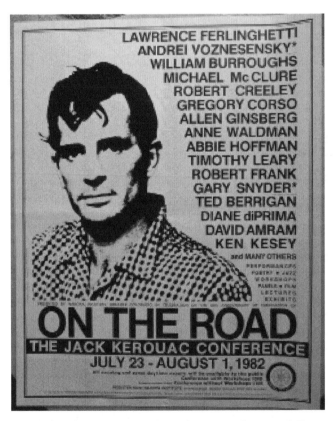

The poster that changed my life

And there in large print — "KEN KESEY"

And in tiny print at the bottom — "Partially funded by **the Grateful Dead**." !!!

WHAT?!?!

If I had gone straight to the bookshelves in this store and found the copy they had instead of going to the help kiosk, I never would have seen the poster!

Right away I got on the phone before I got On The Road. The conference cost about $200 or something, which is like two million today, so I told them I was a show person and could help them stage it from a production standpoint, and the coordinator said, "Yeah, we could use you. Come on down."

Done!

Only catch was — I didn't know a freakin' soul in about a ten state radius of Boulder, Colorado — no base to land on, no grounding for this Groundling. But in Major Fate Factor #2, as in, if any of those first bookstores had *On The Road* I never would have gotten to the sixth sense store to see the poster, and now ... just that month, as part of the great migration of 'Peggers to the West Coast — as in Winnipegers who had the Road pull strong enough to break free from their deep prairie roots and travel across the barren wheatfields and over the massive Rocky Mountains to the land of free spirits — in this energy-powered Network of the Motivated, was a Brother of Adventure, who, between the time I'd arrived out West and had some insane trips with on Vancouver Island and the time I saw the poster ... *had moved to Denver!!*

Track down his number, "Hey Cliff! There's gonna be this writers' conference in Boulder, could I crash at your place?"

"You kiddin' me?! Mi casa su casa! Come on down!

This'll be great!"

Boom!

If ol' Cliffy had moved to any other city in the world, this trip never woulda happened. But suddenly I had a base camp at the foot of the mountains, and a waiting sherpa at the peak who promised that somewhere along the line the pearl would be handed to me if I could just make it to Boulder's Pearly Street gates.

Hit The Road Jack

Much like a certain Jack trip, I hit The Road with a bunch of reality sandwiches — crispy veggie mothers made by mother Sue, angel of health, and overseer of mine. In fact, as she was sending me off, she knew more than I did how big this trip was going to be for me. How is it women know these things?

And like Jack, I took the bus to begin The Road — all the way from Vancouver, B.C., to Portland, Oregon. There I bought a fat black elMarko felt pen and hunted down a big perfectly fresh cardboard box to open up into a large sign

Hitchhiking Schedule – Vancouver to Boulder July 20th-23rd 1982

9:30 say goodbye to Sue
7:00 board Trailways at Sandman Inn
10:30 into Seattle
12:15 leave Seattle for Portland after offer from wacko to store guns for his car
4:45 into Portland
5:00 get hit by car, buy felt pen, phone Marty, take local bus #5 w/ nice bus driver to outskirts of city – To Dallas
7:05 Amy on highway 84
7:35 first ride – "Easy Does It" bumper sticker, Archie Bunker/Jack Nicholson + trail mix, 70mph to The Dalles
9:00 on edge of highway again
9:09 notice graffiti on girder "Oh won't someone please stop. Will I be here forever?"
9:10 Ride 4 nice guys, unmarried, Rathgunale scans, M. Howard
10:20 take quick hit of acid/speed at gas station
10:35 drop me off on pull back highway in my dale of nowhere
11:30 get too scared to sleep on side of road, walk to campsite area
12:15 am naked + ready for bed – well cleaned up, sleeping under stars till sun up
7:30 AM woke up, had thought wash
8:20 on the road
8:32 pick up by parts truck driver, to Pendleton
8:55 dropped off out of Pendleton   wrote Sue letter
9:10 picked up by Cadillac with Idaho plates, BT like, quiet, too quiet, carly Baker Oregon – police training center learning to be australian – slow down
3:40 dropped off at Mountain Home Idaho after a Coors light at Brew + Burger in Boise
3:45 picked up by paraplegic – one leg – got high for first time – Snake River Canyon – came back here
5:00
5:35 old man in camper, drove 40 mph, first camper
5:45 dropped off nowhere
6:05 young guy in sports car
6:15 dropped off at Salt Lake City highway
6:18 sheriff in patrol truck "You see 2 guys going the other way?"
6:55 off in middle of nowhere – eat last sandwich for dinner
6:55 old man in semi – first semi – 55 mph, bumpy as shit
9:00 Ogden Utah, "Bad vibe state", stuck on freeway ramp got Police warning, walk long way to other ramp
10:25 young guy in pickup drinking red wine + Sprite
10:35 off at major Salt Lake I-84 intersection
10:50 3 young guys, driving too fast, scared
11:15 middle of nowhere – Morten, looked like for the night
11:40 guy waiting, in pick up, surprised anyone stopped, dying of thirst
11:55 off under last lights in Utah, looked like there for the night, 45 minutes to border
12:10 Semi maker amazing stop, cold goodies, goes to Denver (!!) laugh Like Phantom Ice – middle of night, wide smile – whoop it cold
6:10 got into Cutlass Supreme at last stop, 4 hours from Cheyenne
10:05 off at I5
10:07 asked away/guy in van with wife problems
10:50 off at exit 27$

1
2
3
4
5
6
7
8
9
10
11
12
(13)
14
15

on which I wrote in huge block letters SALT LAKE CITY — the half-way target point of this half-continent crossing. From the bus depot I caught the local as far East as she'd go, Troutdale, Oregon. Friendly bus driver, too, on this desolation run. But a braking whoosh and a door open swoosh, and I'm on my own, no direction home, standing alone, on the shoulder of a whizzing interstate.

    21 years old, 1982, 7:00 at night.

A half-hour later the first car stops — with an "𝕰𝖆𝖘𝖞 𝕯𝖔𝖊𝖘 𝕴𝖙" bumper sticker, driven by a kindly old Archie Bunker but talking more like Meathead about how Ronald Reagan was a crazy dictator screwing the country and destroying the environment, all the while driving about 20 miles over the speed limit along the winding Columbia River and eventually to a place called The Dalles. Everything had been looking so good ... and suddenly I was standing back out on the road again, all alone on a racing interstate — and now it was getting dark. In the carless quiet, I looked down at the girder next to me and somebody'd written, "Oh won't someone please stop. Will I be here forever?" Not exactly a good road sign.

    But about a minute later this nice old farmer in a nice new pick-up stops! I'd already seen other hitchhikers on the trip and they were bearded and scruffy and disheveled looking. I was a clean-shaven college boy wearing white jeans with elastic cuffs that Sue sewed on and brought to a nice dust-protecting puff at my ankles, and a bright striped Pranksters' t-shirt.

    Besides dressing like Ken's krewe, I was following

Jack's words with more than just the sandwiches and the bus. As he instructed in his confessional *"Origins of The Beat Generation"* in *Playboy* in 1959, which I'll tell ya about more and importantly later, it's a cardinal rule of hitchhiking to look presentable. And he's right. Between me and my big cardboard sign, and staring intensely into the eyes of oncoming drivers, we made great time the whole way. But when the friendly old farmer blissfully dropped me off at the corner of his country lane in the middle of Nowheresville, Oregon, in the middle of the night, neither was much of an advantage. Luckily I spotted the lights of a campground up ahead, managed to walk to it in the dark, found the campers' bathrooms, had a complete refresh, so essential On The Road, then rolled out my sleeping bag under the stars and had a solid night's roadsleep in dreamy America.

In the morning I pulled the same running water refresher course — all the comforts of home — and two minutes after I stepped on the highway a car-parts truck stopped and right away we were whizzing through the sun-beating orchards and wheat fields of rich organic breadbasket Oregon until we got to Pemberton on the edge of the Blue Mountains, where the partsman had to make his next drop-off, including me.

And again I'm on the side of the highway barely long enough to get myself sorted and take a nice half hit of easily-smuggled acid in keeping with the good energy of the day when a shiny new Cadillac boat pulls up to the dock. Run up, toss pack in the back, jump in the front and it's some cowboy Neal goin' all the way to Idaho! Suddenly we're crossing the mountains together, with cassettes of New Riders of The Purple Sage, Willie Nelson, and The Byrds blasting through the high-end sound system.

The Blue Mountains, green fields, rolling grey highway, dark green pines with dark brown trunks under a deep blue sky fading into a hazy powder blue horizon, with grey rocky roads leading off mysteriously, and yellow caution signs guiding us around the fast winding highway — it was a most colorful day and these Irish eyes were poppin'.

Everything was coming together as cowboy started warming up to this wayward Canuck and began sharing tales of close encounters with rattlesnakes and the advantages of rifles over shotguns and how he stayed out of the army cuz that's for people who like to follow orders ... and I'm realizing this is the still-Wild West of America where guns are fun and fads are for fools. As we slowed down in a town and passed a police training center he looked at it, shook his head, and said, "Learning to be assholes."

He asks me where I'm going, and I tell him about the Kerouac conference and he Bangs! the wheel with his palm — "Damn!! That's where I should be goin'! You read *On The Road*?" he looks over at me, and I give him the "You kiddin' me?" look back. "Oh yeah," he says, as we're driving on the road to the *On The Road* conference. "That's my favorite book. Or ... one of 'em anyway. Can't believe it! They're really having a whole conference for it? In *Boulder?*"

"Yeah, it's some big summit. I can't believe it. Like,

Ginsberg, Kesey, Abbie Hoffman ... uhhh," as I'm trying to remember all the names on the poster. "Oh, and it's partially funded by The Grateful Dead."

"*What!!* You're fuckin' kidding me!! They're not *playing*, are they?" and I gave him another popped-eyebrow affirmative. "Shit. *When* is this?! ... Well, hell, I can't go to Boulder, anyway," he caught himself. "But, *damn!* An *On The Road* <u>conference</u>. That's great! They should have one of those everywhere. Especially Boise. ... I read it in 12th grade. Then me and a buncha friends drove up to Banff that summer — your neck of the woods — non-stop crazy the whole way there and back. What a trip," he said, drifting off in reverie for a bit. "Damn. An *On The Road* conference, well I never ...."

"Maybe you should sometime."

After about six hours of cushy Caddy cruisin' he finally let me off in Mountain Home, Idaho, where he started heading north. And once again, in less than five minutes Brian & His Sign are picked up. I'm meticulously charting this shit and know I'm so far averaging about seven minutes on the roadside between pick-ups!

As Bob Weir once cracked from the stage, "What do you say to a one-legged hitchhiker? . . . Hop in." Which I did, only to find a one-legged driver! The guy lost his left leg in a farming accident but he could still drive, and loved to get high, and I smoked my first joint of this American Adventure, as he's telling stories of the great Snake River Canyon and describes it so vividly I could see it from the car and knew I had to go there. He tells me how the locals all hate "that phony Evel Knievel" for bringing attention to their secret sacred river, but he has no problem sharing with me the details of hideaways and unmapped waterfalls that we visited together without ever leaving the road.

After this trip of a trip, he drops me off, and again I get the next ride in five minutes of being another roadside attraction — an old man with a camper on the back of an old pick-up, who drove along at about 40 miles an hour with cars whizzing past us at twice the speed but he just wanted some company and was in no hurry for his life to end. "It all goes by too fast, sonny," he said. I had no idea what he was talking about, and kinda didn't believe him ... ... at the time.

He slowed down at some gravel road to nowhere — well, it was to his road to Somewhere — but he dropped me off in the wilds of wide-open Idaho and I was suddenly "uh-oh." But sure-damn-enough, 15 minutes later some hotshot in a tiny sports car stops, and we peel off like we gotta make up time. And this fancy light fixtures salesman is talkin' twice as fast as ol' pops drove about how you've gotta make your own way in life and not "sit around like some asshole," as he motors me all the way from the mountains to the Mormons, just inside the Utah border.

I'm not there three minutes when a sheriff pulls up to hassle me — a clear sign we're not in Cool Country anymore. 'Cept it turns out this guy's in a real hurry. He barely slows to a stop, and with the window rolled down yells, "You seen two guys goin' the other way?"

"Nope."

"Thanks." And he squeals a u-ey and peels off in the

other direction.

And finally in lonely desolate Utah I got a roadside wait, first time all trip, so I ate the last of Sue's Super Sandwiches, and dreamt in the immensity of it, no idea how far I'd come or how far to go, but just knew I was On The Road to Jack.

In the downtime, I flipped over the still-in-good-shape cardboard sign, and on the clean backside wrote the second half destination — DENVER – BOULDER in big bolder letters, so I was ready for whatever comes next.

After about an hour, the first semi of the trip finally stopped, and I climbed up the mountain into the big rig, and these things are about the most uncomfortable way to travel since the covered wagon — non-stop bouncing like you're driving over railroad ties the whole time. The driver's a big burly redneck type and ya wonder why he stops for a scrawny longhaired hitchhiker, but he sees us as both trying to beat The Man. Anyone who's operating outside of the system is awright by him.

A couple of bouncing hours later he dropped me off outside the very town Dean Moriarty was born in in the first paragraph of *On The Road* — Salt Lake City. Stepping out of one those rumbling tractor-trailer beasts is like getting out of a helicopter onto terra firma that feels way too firma and your legs too terrible. Imagine getting dragged and bounced down the stairs like a cartoon character — for two hours — and you're getting close to the rubber legs that riding in these giant blenders is like.

Then Boom sure enough right away another Utah sheriff comes up, and I go to tell him, "No, I haven't seen two guys goin' the other way," except he's not asking that. He's telling me to get the hell off the freeways, there's no hitchhiking here. And I'm like, "Aw geez," and have to walk a long scary way in the dark to another on-ramp.

And suddenly I start flashing on *On The Road,* like *I know this place* — Yeah! — Dean falling asleep in the car on the hill overlooking the city when he and Sal and the tourists are driving from S.F. to Denver. He wakes up so excited looking over the city of his unfathomable birth that it brings tears to poor Sal's eyes.

Then, in the state with the most restrictive liquor laws in the country, I get picked up by some guy drinking red wine and Sprite (!) ... then by three kids drinkin' beer and who weren't particularly good at driving. But they loved to talk, and couldn't believe I lived in New York. "Hey, have you seen MTV?" the guy riding shotgun turns and asks.

"No, we don't get it in New York. I think we are in the fall, though."

"No way!? *You don't get it in New York?!* That sucks."

Some voice in the dark says, "I heard it's all Adam Ant and Rod fuckin' Stewart anyway. Who cares?"

"It sounds like a cool idea," I said. "As long as they play good music."

"Yeah? Like what?" somebody asks.

"I don't know, Neil Young, the Dead, Alice Cooper..."

"*Ahhhh!*" they scream and laugh. And the guy beside me in the backseat goes "Ha!" to the guys in the front and pointing at them like they were wrong. "Alice!!! See?! Put 'er there, partner," he says, giving me the old thumbs up soul handshake.

Things were going so well they invited me back to their mom's house to party. "She's asleep — she'll never know. We got the whole basement to ourselves, man." But they were just kids, and I knew there were much better parties ahead if I could just stay On The Road.

They got me to the far side of desolate Salt Lake, and finally The Midnight Special I'd been waiting for arrived as another big rig whooshed to a stop — and was goin' all the way to Denver!

I made it from Vancouver to Cliff's in 2 days, 6 hours,

and exactly **17** rides — that magic number that's followed me around my whole life from the back of my hockey jersey to the age I was when everything changed to the first street I lived on in New York after the Village to the number of submissions I made before I first got published. I mean, *you're reading* page 17 for gosh sakes! And now — it was 17 rides to Jack!

Keep your Neal on the wheel
seeing old Denver at last
the eagle landed

3

Dancin' To The Boulder Boogie

Driving into Boulder is one of those magic experiences on the American Road — where you wind your way up through the gradually growing foothills of the Rocky Mountains, surrounded by endless spaces and evergreens and dreams and buena vistas of adventures and rock outcroppings of dangers, until you crest the final peak and tip down and suddenly splayed out before you is this hidden unexpected mystical mountain plain like a flat calm green oasis with the mirage of a Rockwellian American mountain town framed by the magnificent jutting grey Flatiron cliffs, and you can hear a thousand drivers go, "Awww!"

Right away I went to the conference production office, which was happening out of the Naropa building on the grassy (in more ways than one) Pearl Street, the non-vehicular main drag in downtown Boulder — the college town built around the University of Colorado, a half-hour from Denver. About the only thing I knew about the place was Mork & Mindy lived here. So it's gotta be cool.

Naropa is a small Buddhist-inspired school that only formed about eight years earlier, and right from the beginning, Allen Ginsberg & Anne Waldman ran the Writing Department, calling it The Jack Kerouac School of Disembodied Poetics.

The deal was: it was summertime and the living was easy. I mean, it was summertime which was off-season for the U of C, so Naropa could rent their main auditorium and classrooms and theater and such to hold the conference's readings and workshops and movies and such.

After a quick howdy-do at Naropa headquarters on the second floor, the producers decide we should retire directly to Tom's Tavern across the street, and right away I'm thinkin' — I like the way these guys work!

Tom's is this big old neighborhood corner bar n burgers joint with crumbly brick walls on one side and big windows on the other, all under a wonderfully wrinkled tin ceiling there since it opened in the appropriately dated 1950s and positively reminding me of ol' New York. Except the place was crazy with (non-hippie) Boulder girls in Jordache jeans and headbands around poofy hair workin' the jukebox and singing loudly along with The Go-Go's and Pat Benatar and especially Joan Jett's "*I Love Rock n Roll*," the ubiquitous hit of the summer they played over and over, singing it louder every time. Shyly watching out the corner of their eyes were various clusters of 18-year-old poseur boys in nylon parachute pants and short New Wave haircuts who seemed way more "*My Aim Is True*" than "*Sex Drugs and Rock 'n' Roll.*"

So, we're hoistin' a few, and before long Steve, the overall coordinator who told me to come on down, says, "Hey, go let the rest of the staff know we're over here." So I run back through the low-rise pedestrian mall, which is very not-pedestrian, lemme tell ya, with its endless ongoing carnival of patchouli peasant dress hippie circles of guitars and dreams and songs on the lawn and the benches where the road used to be, and I burst through the doors and start up the creaky old stairs to the second floor, and Boom! There's **Allen Ginsberg** coming down all alone right in front of me! First time I ever laid eyes on him. And boy did he lay eyes on me!

"Hey, Allen! We're all across the street at Tom's. Steve sent me over to let everybody know," and he's all wide-eyed stopped-in-his-tracks – Who-are-YOU?! Suddenly this cute-faced barely-legal fresh prospect was in town and right in front of him and he couldn't be happier! And right-away I'm thinkin', "I dig *Howl*, but speed is the better part of valeting," and kept flying past on my mission as I could hear him *not* continuing down the stairs as my young ass in short shorts climbed them two by two.

This was the first time I met any of my literary heroes. I'd already toured with one of my favourite rock groups, Yes, at age 17, and met Bill Graham and toured with The Rolling Stones by 19 — but these were more the heroes of adulthood. And it was so cool knowing, "I'm not *meeting* them, I'm *working* with them." There would never be, in all these adventures' twists and turns, that awkward fan distance. From the first moment in Beatsville I had a purpose, was on the inside, and we were producing the same massive ten-day event together.

Allen never did come to the bar, but a lot of the other staff did, and as we're pounding cold ones courtesy of the conference, ol' Steve proceeded to grill me on my background even though he'd already hired me. Even by then I had a crazy-long list of credits — assistant production coordinator on the Stones tour, assistant stage manager on the summer pier concerts in New York, touring Western Canada with Yes, Rush, Cheap Trick, Charlie Daniels, Dr. Hook, Steve Forbert and so on, stage managing big folk festivals from Vancouver to Bear Mountain, running the NYU concerts in Greenwich Village, working for the biggest promoters in every city I lived in, producing our own multi-band all-night Acid Tests in Winnipeg — and after he listened rather gobsmacked he introduced me to the rest of the staff with, "Brian here, is something of a show-producing prodigy ..."

BOOM! Never forgot *that* intro! — Here I am, a thousand miles from home, barely 21, at this summit with every living non-rock 'n' roll hero I had, and *these* Masters of production are calling *me* a prodigy. (!) As John Cassady would later say a million times, "I'll take it."

Then along came Arthur and Kit Knight! I'd actually hung with them at a book fair at NYU the year before — and suddenly there was somebody I knew! They're this husband & wife publishing duo who do all these amazing Beat books under the banner "the unspeakable visions of the individual" — from the line in Jack's *"Belief & Technique for Modern Prose."* I quickly tag-team from the stage crew to the book crew and was most pleased to be learning that drinking was still a much enjoyed pastime in Beatlandia!

In a heart beat I was falling in love with cute blond Kit who's vivacious and perky and happy and upBeat and curious and passionate and playful and we just started zoomin' and I tell her about how I was born in Calgary and my artist mom used to carry me into the mountains on her back in a papoose while she painted the Rockies, and how the first time I drove back into those same Alberta foothills a couple decades later I had an overwhelming sense of being "home." And Kit knew *exactly* what I was talking about and went off on her own riff about the power of "the air you were born in" and how our internal compass is pointed to Home and how it grounds us and how Jack kept returning to Lowell for his spiritual refuelling.

"And other kinds of refuelling," I added, as we both drained another pint in his honor.

These two were a hoot! Arthur was extremely friendly as well but also had this super-serious side. Archaeologists are heroes to me, the real rock stars (sorry, just a little archaeologist humor), and I thought one day I'd like to be one. Arthur seemed like the head of the team discovering Tutankhamun's tomb — giddy that he'd finally arrived at the sacred secret magical place of legend — this gold mine gathering of the Beats. He'd alternate between an ENORMOUS smile that would look for a while like it was his permanent expression, then when Kit and I would be riffing I'd glance over and he'd be deadly serious, meticulously checking some notebook schedule or something he was keeping.

Kit was curious about my notebook and what I was writing in it, so I just handed it to her. "Here. Read it." And that was the kind of vibe already flowing in Boulder. Just hand your private diary to a virtual stranger to read. Jack would be proud.

While she was reading it, I asked Arthur what he was writing in his and he started gushing breathlessly about all the conference attendees he was hoping to meet, but sometimes leaning forward all quiet, sharing some secret of a scheduling discovery he'd made.

I guess I haven't mentioned yet **who all was here**.

This was the biggest gathering of Beats and their various spiritual progeny ever assembled in one place — before or since:

Allen Ginsberg (and his brother Eugene), Jane Faigao, the tai chi instructor at Naropa who was the main make-it-happen organizing producer following Allen's lead, William Burroughs, John Clellon Holmes, Gregory Corso (and his daughter Miranda), Lawrence Ferlinghetti, Michael

McClure, Carolyn Cassady, Jan Kerouac, Edie Kerouac, Herbert Huncke, Robert Creeley, Robert Frank, Robert LaVigne, Diane di Prima, David Amram, Peter Orlovsky, Carl Solomon, Ray Bremser, Joanna McClure, Joanne Kyger, Joyce Johnson, Anne Waldman, Ted Berrigan, Al Aronowitz, Jack Micheline, Andy Clausen (with his son Jesse), Larry Fagin, Michael Brownstein, John Steinbeck Jr., early Kerouac biographer Charles Jarvis's son Paul, who was I think the only person from Lowell to make it, Randy Roark, David Cope, Maria Livornese, Jeff Nightbyrd, Jay McHale, Kush, the funny-cool Naropan Judy Lief who some people said the conference was her idea, Bill McKeever, Todd Colby, Patricia Donegan, Eliot Katz, Dan Shot, Dan Barth, Sam Kashner, Henry MacWilliams, Eliot Greenspan, & Joan Dobbie up at the Chautauqua lodge...

As well as the leaders of the generation that followed, Kens Kesey & Babbs, Abbie Hoffman and his "running mate" Johanna Lawrenson, Timothy Leary, Paul Krassner, Pranksters George Walker and Jane Burton ...

And then loads of scholars like Ann & Sam Charters, Lawrence Lee, Dennis McNally, Doug Brinkley, John Tytell & Mellon, Gerry Nicosia, Joy Walsh, Tom Clark, Tim Hunt, Clark Coolidge, Jay & Fran Landesman the ex-pats who flew back from England, Nanda Pivano from Italy, Arthur & Kit Knight as you know, organizer Jane Fiagao's husband Bataan, Henry Allen, Regina Weinreich, Ronna Johnson, Albert Huerta, Warren Tallman (the only other person I know of to come from Canada), Jaap Van Der Bent from Holland, James Grauerholz, Jose Arguelles, environmental activist Peter Warshall, writer/photog

Lance Gurwell, radio alchemist Len Barron . . .

And a bunch of the nearby Denver crew, probably the #3 city in Beat history after New York & S.F., including Justin Brierly (the catalytic source of the Denver–Columbia connection, and who sounded exactly like Walter Cronkite when he talked), journalist Ivan Goldman, Ed "Sketching" White, and Jim "Poolshark" Holmes, as well as a crew from the Denver Union of Street Poets including Les Reed, Padraic Cooper and Carolyn Reed . . .

Plus the actors Paul Gleason (*The Breakfast Club, Trading Places*) who hung with Jack in Florida in the early '60s and decided to become an actor only after seeing *Splendor In The Grass* with him in a theater, and longtime Beat Max Gail (*Barney Miller*'s Wojo, and Chief Bromden in various productions of *One Flew Over The Cuckoo's Nest),* invisible but ever-present photographer Chris Felver, and lots of filmmakers besides Robert Frank, like Janet Forman, John Antonelli, Richard Lerner & Lewis MacAdams, and Doug & Judi Sharples running around capturing it all, as well as Jerry Aronson who came up with his concept for *The Life and Times of Allen Ginsberg* at the conference.

Oh, and a little rock group you may have heard of, The Grateful Dead, were playing just down the road at Red Rocks for three nights, with roving ambassadors John Barlow, Wavy Gravy and Mountain Girl reconning Camp Kerouac and asking respectful questions of the masters just like all the other students.

It was every major Beat figure alive at the time, except Gary Snyder who was officially off building a zendo (a Buddhist meditation hall) in California, but history tells us he's long avoided these attention-getting beatnik gatherings — and as he says, he never saw Jack again after their *Dharma* adventure ended in May of '56. But with his regrets he sent a nice letter to Allen saying, "Jack Kerouac was the wandering scholar troubadour storyteller youngest son of the Jack tales in us all. ... **The voice of the water going over the edge of the waterfall itself.**"

Also, LeRoi Jones (as Allen still referred to the poet known since the '60s as Amiri Baraka) was invited, but he was spending weekends in jail on Rikers Island at the time. And Ted Joans had just been feted at Naropa a couple of months earlier. Surrealist poet Philip Lamantia was invited several times, but as Ferlinghetti said, "It's a long way over the Rockies, and he's a city boy." And another guy who just missed it was Kenneth Rexroth who had sadly passed away only the month before we gathered.

A couple other interesting people Allen invited who didn't make it included Leonard Cohen who had to decline because he was spending the summer in France with his family; William Buckley, who admitted in his regret that "Kerouac was a very special guy;" Norman Mailer who begged off because he was finishing *Ancient Evenings*, (which Burroughs would later admit was an influence on his own novel *The Western Lands*); and Norman "Putz" Podhoretz who famously and viciously attacked Jack in print. It's proof of Allen's sense of inclusion that he'd invite these contrary voices ... but, really, some of them might've just been bring-me-downs at an otherwise unceasingly joyous celebration.

And the other thing to remember is — they were all so fuckin' *young* then. But look who's talkin'! Other than 30-year-old Jan, the youngest of them was still more than twice my age!! Babbs & Tytell were 43, Abbie & Ann Charters 45, Kesey & Joyce Johnson 47, McClure 49, Gregory 52, Allen 56 ... they were in what we now know of as their midlife prime. And while they weren't necessarily producing their early ground-breaking poetry and prose, they had adopted the Cassady and then Kesey concept that your life is your art. They were, to a man and a woman, better *people* than they were in their explosive youth. Better performers, better teachers, better organizers, better tempered, better conveyors of their inner vision. And at this event, thanks to the Bill Graham of the Beats, Allen Ginsberg, they were collectively staging the biggest Woodstock of Jack since he first played the Cavern in '57.

And this whole thing had Arthur positively apoplectic in joy and scholarship! "There's never been anything *like* this," he's gushing. "You're really lucky — the first thing you show up at! Don't take this for granted. The closest thing to this was the Salem State Symposium in '73 — but that was only a handful of them compared to this. Jan is going to be here!" he suddenly blurted with the explosive joy of a parent. "Robert Frank. Edie. Ken Kesey. I've never met any of them — and I've been publishing Beat books for ten years."

Meanwhile, Kit's still completely engrossed in my holy notebook. "We just did our 12th book, *Beat Angels*," Arthur went on. "Honey, can you pass me my bag?" And without looking up, she handed it across the table to him, and he pulled out a copy to give me! Here was this little book with letters by Jack and Burroughs and Corso, and short stories or whatever by Carolyn Cassady and Huncke and John Clellon Holmes — and man, I knew I was homes! Here in the Rockies. A man hands me a book fulla Beats across a Big Table in a Western bar and says, "Here. You should have this."

Home, home on the cool Colorado range . . .

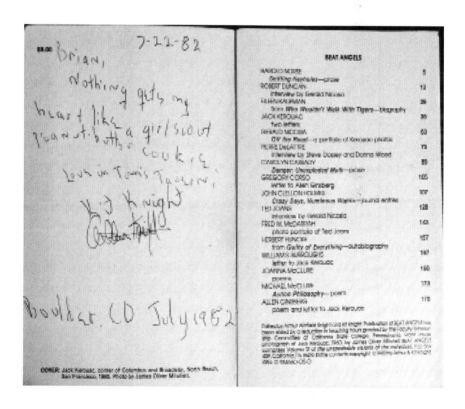

ON THE ROAD

THE JACK KEROUAC CONFERENCE

C/O NAROPA INSTITUTE

1111 PEARL STREET

BOULDER, CO 80302

BRIAN HASSETT

STAGE

4

Meeting Your Heroes 101

From here on out it was a flurry of madness.

One of the first and forever impressions I had was — being on the inside and hanging with Allen and his loopy longtime lover Peter and Beat badboy Gregory Corso and cigarette-chaining novelist John Clellon Holmes in their little homes, just watching these guys, these old friends who'd been brothers of the night and the light since they were the age I was as I was meeting them, and now here they were much older, full-grown MEN, who were still pranksterish, still plotting cool adventures, still finishing each other's sentences, still knowing what the other meant by just a gesture or a silence, and making each other laugh, constantly, but all within the context of productivity, doing things, writing things, working things out. They weren't sitting around talking about sports or half-baked pontifications about politics or trying to prove they were up on the latest band like so many people my age. No. They'd been playing this poetry game forever — and probably *never* noodled in those foolish things — but were talking about philosophy and spirituality and writing and writers and quoting themselves and quoting others and talking over each other and as excited in the moment as little kids.

Allen was definitely the professorial boss, the accepted (but not to say unchallenged) ringleader. He was always carrying around this cloth sorta Guatemalan over-the-shoulder bag full of papers and schedules and books and god knows what, and usually wore some stray suit jacket a couple sizes too big for him with some tie a couple sizes too small. He was gentle, but vibrant; soulful, but lascivious; clipboard following, but constantly poetically improvising. He was sort of the one and only father figure keeping an eye on everything, yet was always fun to be around. He had no problem correcting or admonishing someone, but did so with love and a tender demeanor.

He was like a referee in a pick-up game — making sure we played by the rules, but knowing the whole game wasn't too serious.

Gregory seemed to always have on this black leather vest looking like a slightly older Dylan from "*Street Legal*," like a hot happening sexy dude, with a full head of bushy black hair. He would definitely have been the (and probably only) lady's-man of the group. Or at least fancied himself as such. He didn't give a damn about the outcome of the game, he just wanted to score. He was the Puck, the imp, the joker, and the one most likely to be called to the principal's office. And thank god he was in with the principal or he woulda been expelled fer sure!

And a neat thing I loved — the long-form novel writer **John Clellon Holmes** had a slower cadence than the rest, and a softer voice, and when he'd solo on his *Horn*, the rest of the band laid low. There was an unspoken respect — perhaps still stemming from him being the first of any of these soon-to-be-famous young men to have a Beat book published — his gone novel *Go*, in 1952.

He wouldn't speak too often — whereas Allen and Gregory were like Dizz and Bird, constantly playing off and over top of each other — but John would come in like the organ and lay down these thick slow chords that would then totally alter the next round of soloing. He was Zeppo, the thoughtful straight Marx Brother who didn't really fit in with the others, yet was one of them, and there was nothing he could do about it.

What was extraordinary was that they were exactly like I dreamed and imagined they would be — and as they conveyed themselves from the '50s. Close friends just hanging out, but always up to sumpthin.

And I thought back to the fluke of seeing that poster, the karma / fate of that, and how it was the phrase "Partially funded by The Grateful Dead" that tipped the scales from "I should" to "I'm going" — but whatever the hell it was, I'd somehow made my way here and was now studying

Hangoutology with my heroes. And unlike hanging with rock stars, writing was my art form of choice and practice. Instead of being in private circles of master musicians, I was now sitting among the masters whose music I played.

And another guy who blew me away early and often was **Herbert Huncke.** I'm not much one for these junkie guys, but Huncke was *a trip.* He was SO nice, so friendly — the most personable people-loving people-person you could ever meet. But it was the guy's cadence, *how* he spoke — it's no wonder Jack & Allen & Company totally dug this guy. I tried to talk to mumbly Burroughs a few times, but he was as freakin' weird and misanthropic as he comes across. The adding machine magnate's grandson in the grey flannel suit may have been a *Queer* and a *Junkie,* but other than that he sure didn't seem to have much in common with the other Beats I knew and loved — not the same celebration of life, joy, optimism and gushing compassion in his heart.

Although Huncke may have shared some of Bill's proclivities, he was personable and *gentle* and open in his own peculiar way. Just a few degrees shy of being locked in a federal pen, he was a total *character* — and that was this constant commonality to most of the people in ol' J.K.'s life. Odd ducks. As a novelist, Jack magnetized to these people as fodder for his fiction. Whereas Allen was sort of a businessman, a promoter, a former market research man, and Gregory was a bit of an aggressive hustler and loose cannon, Herbert was absolutely "one of us," not intimidating in stature or demeanor, just a guy you could sit with for hours who would engagingly listen to whatever your story was, and then share some wild ones of his own. If anybody in this whole batch of aspiring Buddhists was living in the calm sea of nirvana ... it was Herbert Huncke.

And I noticed for the first time at the conference how Beat fans were like sports fans in that they all had their favorite team (person) in the National Beat League, and in many cases really didn't much care for the other teams. There'd be the Jack-heads who were at every Jack-specific event, and then Team Allen who'd you'd see every time he made an appearance, and then there were the Burroughs junkies who were there every time he was scheduled but not at anything else.

It's probably the same thing at a Beatles convention — people there only because of John, others only for Paul, and then there'd be the quiet George-heads going about their business, and of course Ringo is played by Gregory Corso.

Ferlinghetti once said "the Beat Generation was created out of whole cloth by Allen Ginsberg," the marketing wing of the party. Somebody else said, "The Beat Generation was really The Friends of Allen Ginsberg Generation."

And there's some truth to that. They were a bunch of very different people who happened to be friends ... and writers.

Then there were all these second-tier and next-gen poets who I'd never heard of before, like **Jack Micheline** and

Andy Clausen, who impressed the hell out of me. The going phrase for these guys seemed to be "street poets," but whatever they were called, I called them the conscience of the conference: shit-kicking poets — what punk was to classic rock — a new generation of loud in-your-face passionate practitioners using the same medium as their predecessors but with the fresh verve and brio that the founding fathers originally had.

These two, and a few others I never got to really know, were quite prevalent in every setting from the classrooms to the readings to the bar hangs. Micheline was a big tall guy with a striking head of spiky white hair and a booming baritone. He was a brash New Yorker, filled with spirits both distilled and natural, and as an extreme extrovert he was comfortable holding court and being the center of attention. I never saw him with less than a half-dozen people around him as he was riffing some blend of stand-up comedy and a sermon. I think it was Mel Brooks who coined "the stand-up philosopher" ... and that's what Micheline and some of these guys were. Comedic preachers. Poetic comics. Alan Watts meets Richard Pryor ... just a few doors down from Lenny Bruce and Lord Buckley.

And Micheline and Kerouac were truly a pair of Jacks — chumming around in the late fifties & early sixties, when the more famous half wrote a highly praising introduction to his junior's first poetry collection, *River of Red Wine*, in 1958, so Jack The Younger was definitely in with the ins.

And if you put him on a stage — watch out! He had

an uncommonly competitive drive for a poet and would make it a point to be the best damn reader / performer on any bill he shared. And he usually won that battle. He could have been a great union organizer or football coach in another life — but in this one he was a poet's mix of Jack's working class mindset and appearance with Gregory's gregariousness and anti-authoritarianism and Allen's sense of rebel poetry.

Andy Clausen, who made it here from Cherry Valley, New York, reminded me of Ralph Steadman's drawings of Hunter Thompson. He was always sort of bent over and darting about frantically on some urgent mission. They were both kinda football physical poets, and if Micheline was the coach, Clausen was the rookie running back. He'd just made the team and had all the confidence in the world and was really eager to get the ball and run with it. Very much in the Beat spirit, these guys were challenging the status quo. In amongst the Mount Rushmore legends of the game, were wild hungry energetic players who weren't yet resting on the dais in the Hall of Fame but rather forcing the veterans to keep on their pencil tips cuz the next rotation were playing their way onto the team right before our eyes.

And then there were all these scholars like **John Tytell** — it was this whole crazy gathering of writers writing about writers who wrote about each other. And now I'm writing about it — and you're reading it — because it's *still* a driving force. And everyone here got that in their own weird way. It was a crazy improbable collective of laughing Edies and reserved Ferlinghettis, of Prankster Keseys and thoughtful McClures, of composing poets and note-jotting students.

At one of the pre-show brunchy affairs I ended up talking to Tytell who had this cool wife, **Mellon**, who was always running around taking pictures of everyone. He had one of the only Kerouac biographies published, *Naked Angels*, and was super-crazy-smart, and a fellow New Yorker to boot! So we start jammin and he goes into this whole thing about Kerouac's enthusiasm, and how that word "enthusiasm" comes from "of God" or "possessed by God" and I'm thinkin' —

"Yeah! —

Enthusiasm!!"

And then he starts talkin' about the whole process of writing and how it's a lifelong journey and how some writers don't hit their stride until their 40s or 50s, and for the first time I'm seeing the long strange trip ahead. I'm the age Jack was when he was just a Columbia dropout shackin' up with Edie Parker and before he ever met Allen or Bill or anybody. There was a whole *life* ahead. And here was this bearded college prof prophesying where the long and winding road could go. It was about *time* — and how you use it, manipulate it, morph it, grow with it, go with it, dream with it, push it, this is it — your One Life, there's only one beam pointing forward, and the whole point is to follow the light.

It was starting to make sense.

5

Opening Night — Allen, Gurus and Daisies

Opening night, Friday July 23rd, Allen gave the keynote address. Whenever he spoke in public, he became this poetic improvising human thesaurus, creating elaborate word-pictures on the spot. "Welcome fellow beatniks, fellow hippies, fellow Americans, fellow dharma heirs, fellow poets, fellow lovers, fellow banner bearers, fellow open minded folk, fellow lovers of Jack Kerouac. Welcome Jack Kerouac fans in the mass communications industry, in the silver diamond eyes of the cameras, in the diamond pens of all poets and journalists and prose writers, all psychedelic kings, old friends, and welcome most of all — *tender hearts*."

And on and on like this he'd riff. It wasn't annoying, but mesmerizing and really colorful, and you couldn't believe how quickly he was composing off the tongue. When reading a good line on the page, a reader can ponder and conjure many fully formed pictures and harmonics — but listeners don't have the advantage of pausing a conversation or lecture at the end of each line — so Allen fills in all these colors and alternate meanings and poetic resonance within his flowing speech so that what he's painting isn't a dashed-off verbal sketch but rather a dense, many-coated canvas.

"Art, Heart, Tenderness — is the basic theme," he summarized. "As a gathering we can assay what's happened in the 25 years of mindfulness and delicacy of pen since *On The Road* came out. We can explore where we are now, where we've come from — including indulging in great orgies of delicious nostalgia — and where we can go from here — make some new kind of vision for America and the world in the next quarter century.

"And we will make new art during these ten days. There'll be lots of poetry readings and film screenings, but new films will also be made, including by Robert Frank who'll make new art out of our meeting of history. There will be creation on the spot; lots of people writing poems, as well as scholarly papers, and rock 'n' roll songs — so **it's a festival of making it up on the spot** as well as checking out what happened in the past and making an agenda for the future, a prophesy, some kind of oracle.

"The main prophesy for myself will be 'vulnerable tender cheerful heart,' and sensitivity in America. That was the one major tone you find throughout Kerouac's work, an awareness of our mortality and the transitoriness of our schemes, and the fact that we are all living phantoms grasping in the emptiness of this room."

Well benedicted, boss.

Another thing I noticed opening night — and every other night for that matter — was Allen (and others) kept suggesting that everybody go sit in one of the Meditation Rooms they had here at the U of C or across town at the Buddhist center on Spruce Street. God bless 'em for stressing this stress-reduction program every chance they got, and I did look in once and saw all these people sitting there cross-legged in total silence, but I was 21 years old and sitting still was just not an option. If I ever stopped moving for a half a minute, I immediately thought of about a hundred thousand other things I could be doing, and to be honest I couldn't picture Neal or Jack or Kesey or Burroughs or Gregory or Holmes or Abbie or anybody like that ever sitting there on the floor for hours making their mind go blank, so, good intentioned though it may have been, I sadly missed out on the meditation mantra miracle.

Then this completely crazy thing happened.

Since I'd gotten there, Allen and Anne and others had been speaking in reverential tones about this **Trungpa Rinpoche** guy, the Tibetan Buddhist master who founded the Naropa Institute in Boulder in 1974. Whenever his name came up among the staff, everybody got all serious and deferential. And speaking of his name ... the way they all said it, I thought for years "Trungpa Rinpoche" was his name-o. Turns out "Rinpoche" is a title in Tibetan Buddhism. And his first name's Chögyam — but I never heard that word pronounced the whole time I was there.

Anyway, I'm a pretty spiritual person myself, and strictly follow the teachings of my guru, Mark Twain, who preaches, "I cannot see how a man of any large degree of humorous perception can ever be religious." But I was open, and if Allen was taking it so seriously, I figured there must be something to it.

So, it was this big deal that The Master was going to speak to us opening night. And this is how we're all introduced to him: There's some commotion in the wings, and in a scene right out of *Monty Python's Life of Brian*, which this whole thing really was, from behind Oz's curtain came four young strongmen struggling to carry this heavy dude on a chair doin' his best Jack on the Buckley show. And with straining red faces the servants lowered the big prophet down front n center, and in this roomful of journalists & scholars from around the world you could see eyes bulging and nervously scanning sideways, silently asking, "Are you seeing this too?!" About two minutes into it you could hear Carolyn Cassady getting up and saying, "Well, I've had enough of this. I'm going out for a ciggie."

The guru began to talk about very deep and spiritual matters. Or, I'm assuming he did — but no one in the room could really understand anything but the odd phrase. And boy, some of them were really odd. There was something about "the nuclear age is not going to happen because we don't want it to," and "we can kill ourselves on the spot," and of course, "milk is the only way to solve problems."

Who knew?!

But the good news was — we were all totally off the hook for any more guru classes. Not that he ever showed up again after this — but if there's anything that unites us Beats, it's that we don't cotton to being told who's boss.

Since he became a subject of conversation for the rest of the conference because of this bizarre appearance, I learned about The Great Naropa Poetry Wars, which was actually the title of a book that had just come out by Beat scholar and poet Tom Clark about some crazy scandal that happened here a few years earlier where this Rinpoche had a visiting couple stripped naked in front of everyone at some retreat in the mountains ... and that his guards broke down their door to get at them and the girl was screaming for help but nobody would do anything and it all sounded super creepy and like someone my mother would want me to avoid at all costs. So I did.

A much more successful endeavor on opening night were the two screenings. This was before any documentary had ever been made on Jack — but Allen told us with a glint in his eye that he'd dug up a special treat for us — and without another word the theater lights went dark and there — suddenly flickering on the giant movie screen in front of us came ... this unknown unseen unheard of historic footage of Kerouac himself actually reading aloud! And *to musical accompaniment* no less!! Suddenly before our eyes was full-color live talking moving Jack! — on ... *The Steve Allen Show!!*

Yep! Believe it or not! And the whole theater broke into spontaneous applause at the end.

'Course, not too many years later Jack fans would have this whole clip memorized because it's included in every documentary ever made on him — but back when this went down nobody in the room had ever laid eyes on it before! There was even a rumor they'd made an album together! Could you imagine?!

And THEN they screened **the single greatest Beat creation ever made — the film *Pull My Daisy*.** This 28-minute short from 1959 is the earliest prime footage of both Allen and Gregory that exists. It's made by a master American filmmaker, photographer, and Beat cousin, **Robert Frank**, who's actually Swiss-born and lives in Canada, but it's often the outsiders who see the inside the clearest. The movie is a scene from Kerouac's *Beat Generation* play/screenplay that's based on the night a local Unitarian bishop came over to visit the Cassadys in Los Gatos when Jack was there, and the entire dialog of the movie is the author voicing all the characters' parts in **the best single audio track he ever laid down.**

Allen and Peter were also there at Neal & Carolyn's that night and play themselves in the improvised recreation, with Gregory Corso in the role of Kerouac and the painter Larry Rivers playing Neal who was in San Quentin serving his two years for two joints when it was filmed in 1959. Since the real people were reenacting real events, many details are exactly as they happened that memorable night in 1955, as later corroborated by Carolyn's own sober memories in her great book *Off The Road* and to me in person — Allen and the boys being at the house early and enjoying some "tea" before the company arrived; the two old ladies (the bishop's mother and aunt) unexpectedly showing up with the guest of honor; Allen awkwardly squeezing in between the two of them on the couch; Jack sitting cross-legged at the bishop's feet sluggin' a jug and asking him questions; the bishop gamely and seriously engaging the boys even as they were asking him about sex; the two ladies never speaking except when indicating it was time to go; Neal leaving into the night with his friends at the end of it.

There are so many reasons why this film is so glorious and invaluable and cherished by all Beat fans and why I consider it the greatest single Beat creation: that it's a nearly 30 minute Jack rap set to music (by David Amram); that Jack actually speaks in the voices of the various characters he immortalized in his novels; that Jack's humor and playfulness are boldly out front and center; that it's seen through the lens eye of someone who saw America and the world very similar to Jack — Robert Frank — shortly after the pair had taken an epic road trip together to Florida and back to pick up Mémère and so they were as locked in as they'd ever be on their visual visionary simpatico; the raw footage of wild Allen & Gregory in their natural environment getting high and goofing; that it's based on a real event in the Duluoz legend; that it dramatizes the conflict of Jack's two spiritual worlds — Catholicism meeting the new Buddhist challenges — heaven in the afterlife vs. heaven on earth; the whole merging of Jack's second artform, painting, into his writing — it's set in a painter's home (as Carolyn's was) and stars a painter in the role of Neal — which all harmonizes with Jack actually *being* a painter at different points in his life ... and was all the time painting portraits of his friends with words, inspired by Denver buddy Ed White's suggestion of *sketching*; and that in the main it's the Beats captured in action on film in their prime drinking, smoking tea, and goofing in their universe of the 1950s.

Only two prints were ever made from the original negative, and up until '82 (and beyond) the only way *Daisy* could be seen is if one of the two filmmakers was there to screen it. It'd been tied up in some legal squabble between Robert and co-director Alfred Leslie ever since it was made, which has never been resolved to this day. So, seeing it on the big screen was mind-blowing — and alone worth the price of the pilgrimage. Most everyone's seen it by now, but then it was like finding The Holy Grail — like hearing an unreleased *Sgt. Pepper . . . with The Beatles in the room!* There was Allen, there was Gregory, there was Peter, there was Robert — who I happened to have been lucky enough to spend an afternoon with the year before when I was living at *Rebel Without A Cause* director Nicholas Ray's loft in SoHo with his widow Susan — who was very young and hot may I add.

Robert came over to visit one day, and she introduced us knowing I was interested in Kerouac — and basically he ended up interviewing *me*. Shoulda been the other way around, but he had this really gentle curious inquisitive way about him and wanted to know everything about why I liked Jack. He was almost like a Buddha in the way he sat and the way he looked, bald and vaguely pear-shaped, exuding this utter calmness and centeredness. And here tonight, thanks to him and his movie, Jack's voice was singin' to us in the voices of his characters over Robert's motion pictures — Jack very much alive and in the house at his own Conference. The whole thing could've been over that night and it would have been the most amazing Beat experience of my life. But this was only the beginning of a ten-day hike into the diamond mine of the golden eternity.

It was also opening night of this **cat-and-mouse game with the university security**. There were all these beatnik hobos in town, and as is our wont, we sorta take over places and make 'em home. And y'see the thing of it is, ol' Cliffy lived back Denver way, which was a bit of a hassle having no car and such. And well, they had these nice big couches in the student lounge that I'd spotted earlier. And ... apparently I wasn't the only one. I went there to cop some zzzs in order to wake up right on-site tomorrow you understand, and apparently a couple other Roadsters were thinkin' the same thing, and one of them was brushing his teeth in the water fountain, which seemed perfectly normal, so I just stretched out full length on one of those cushy couches and was out like a light.

Until suddenly the light came back on! And there were two uniforms standing there going, "What the hell are you people doing?! This isn't some gawdamn hotel! GET UP!" And I opened my eyes to see about a dozen other Napoleons in rags who musta come in through the night and were covering every couch, chair and open carpet, and the whole woebegone tribe of us got roused from our happy sleep and tossed out into the cool Colorado range.

No idea where I went after that — somehow I survived it. But the local screws were onto us. And since sleep was a resource in short supply, for the whole rest of the conference I'd go catch a power nap between shifts anywhere I could on campus, knowing I could count on some Hassler McUniform waking me before my next show.

6

Why The Sixties Followed The Fifties

There were *three* major '60s icons at "Camp Kerouac," as people started calling it right from the git-go — **Ken Kesey, Abbie Hoffman and Timothy Leary**. To this day, two of these are heroes, and the other not so much — and ya gotta wonder how much is a result of how each came across in Boulder. Kesey's the Chief, and Abbie was a loud 'n' proud practicing Groucho Marxist — whereas Leary just came across as a joke.

Although Abbie and Leary both spent time in the '70s on the lam or in jail on drug charges incurred during Nixon's "war on drugs™," that's probably where their similarities end. Abbie grew up the small Massachusetts town of Wooster just 40 miles from Jack's hometown of Lowell, and shared his working class background and sensibility. He went underground and continued to work as an environmental activist in upstate New York under the name Barry Freed, and had only just turned himself in and finished a brief jail term the year before the conference. Leary had been out, or some say outed, since 1976, and by the time of this summit was in bed with G. Gordon Liddy of all people doing an embarrassing "debate" tour that sadly cemented his reputation as a schmaltzy show-biz sell-out.

He walked around the conference in this white sort-of gauze outfit like an old tennis instructor on the make, or maybe a TV maharishi, or some California EST guru guy with this perpetual ridiculous exaggerated grin on his face like you see on insane inmates or old salesmen or just really insecure people. Which was in such stark contrast to Abbie showing up in fighting shape, muscular like a boxer in training wearing a tight "HOWL FOREVER" t-shirt that was busting at the biceps — and he positively *killed* when on stage — passionate and optimistic but also well grounded in the nuts-&-bolts of functioning reality.

To me, Abbie was doing the work for millions too scared or too shy, putting his life on the line and his thick neck in the noose so that others could be free. And how he did it all with a sense of humor — like throwing money on the floor of the stock exchange and watching the suits reveal themselves — and I'm sure it was that rebel prankster's approach that led John Lennon to seek him out when John first moved to New York City. Neither one of those guys would or ever did hurt a fly, but both of them would stand up to any fight and use the media in ways only the straight world had manipulated it before to raise awareness of truths that otherwise went unspoken. He was a nonviolent warrior, fearless truth-teller, volunteer foot soldier in the war of awareness, and a clear voice of the new consciousness that was replacing the old — all character traits I loved in the Beats.

And speaking of John, that little leprechaun from Liverpool had picked up on the Beat aesthetic even before he named his band after them. Right around the time the San Francisco obscenity police did deviants everywhere a huge favor by making *Howl* world famous, John began writing his own newspaper at Quarry Bank High School called *"The Daily Howl,"* with detailed but completely imaginary news reports — oddly reminiscent of the detailed imaginary news reports Kerouac himself wrote about his own fantasy baseball league, which was complete with player gossip, field conditions and sensational headlines.

It was when John's band The Beetles backed up British Beat poet Royston Ellis in 1960 that they were prompted to change the spelling of the band's name to reflect their mutual interest. As Royston remembers, "Since they liked the 'Beat' way of life, were 'beat' musicians, and would be backing me as a 'Beat' poet, I suggested to him why not spell the name with an 'A'?"

And it was Beat confidant and journalist Al Aronowitz who brought Bob Dylan to The Beatles' Delmonico Hotel suite in New York in the summer of '64 specifically to get them high on marijuana for the first time. And you might say that had some effect on their music. I'm tellin' ya — these Beats are nuthin' but trouble!

As everyone knows, marijuana is a gateway drug ... and before you know it you're reading poetry! So the band decided to start a spoken-word record label as part of Apple, called Zapple, and although it was short lived and didn't release much, some of the first people they signed up were Allen Ginsberg, Lawrence Ferlinghetti, Michael McClure, Richard Brautigan and Ken Kesey.

McCartney would later famously and wonderfully perform and record with Allen on his 1995 poem *"The Ballad Of The Skeletons."* "I wrote *Skeletons* because of all that inflated bull about family values," Ginzy told the *L.A. Times.* "The 'contract with America,' Newt Gingrich and all the loudmouth stuff on talk radio. It seemed obnoxious and stupid and kind of sub-contradictory, so I figured I'd write a poem to knock it out of the ring." The Beat and The Beatle would get together in England later that year when Allen was there to do a Royal Albert Hall show. Macca liked the poem so much, he showed up to accompany Allen on it at the reading (also attended by Carolyn Cassady), then contributed guitar, drums, organ and maracas to the recorded version the following year.

And that same sacred majestic Royal Albert Hall was also packed to its very high rafters for one of history's pivotal (and largest) poetry "happenings" —

The International Poetry Incarnation, in June 1965 — staged with good old Allen organizing and headlining the night, and including a restrained Gregory, a playfully political Ferlinghetti, and Burroughs on tape, joining all sorts of British Beat Bohemians like Michael Horowitz and Beatle bud Adrian Mitchell in a moment of group enlightenment for Londoners that the Human Be-In would be for San Franciscans 18 months later (as seen in chapter 13) in the way it brought out of the basements and into the light thousands of underground artists of varying disciplines (including a young Jimmy Page) who suddenly realized they weren't alone in their pursuit of the unknown. As The Clash's Joe Strummer laid it down — "... you can mark the beginning of the British underground scene of the 1960s to that particular night."

And it only happened because of a perfectly timed confluence of a freshly blooming loosely networked London underground coming in contact with typically wild American grandiosity. The operators of the small Better Books store, the only all-paperback bookstore in London at the time, who hosted a reading with Allen a couple weeks prior, and were part of the loose Poets' Cooperative that put on the event, admitted they would never have *dreamed* of renting the biggest venue in town for a poetry reading. According to Allen, it was catalytic New York underground multimedia artist, Barbara Rubin (who introduced Warhol to the Velvet Underground among other things), and was in Allen's traveling troupe at the time, who came up with the idea. And with a mere 10 days between booking the venue and the gig, using only street posters, word of mouth, and a typically successful Allen press conference that the BBC reported on held at the Albert Memorial in Hyde Park directly across the street from the Hall, they not only sold all 7,000+ seats and standing room promenade but reportedly had upwards of 1,000 more people filling the courtyard outside. If you're into it, you can see 35 minutes of this historic chaotic event in Peter Whitehead's award-winning cinéma vérité film of the night – *Wholly Communion.*

And then there's William Burroughs on the cover of *Sgt. Pepper.* He was probably on their mind since at the time they were letting him use the rehearsal studio they'd built into Ringo's unused London apartment on Montague Street in the spring of '66 — when there was music in the cafés at night and revolution in the air. Bill was there experimenting with backward tapes, recording things at different speeds, and dropping in random radio broadcasts or reading newspaper reports into the recordings. And yes, all of that should sound familiar to Beatles fans. Over the next year the band would run all those same studio experiments as they recorded *Revolver,* *Yellow Submarine, Strawberry Fields Forever,* and *Sgt. Pepper,* then *The White Album* the year after that.

"William did some cut-ups and we did some crazy tape recordings in the basement," McCartney remembers. "We used to sit around talking about all these amazing inventions that people were making, like the Dream Machine that Ian [Sommerville] and Brion Gysin had made. It was all very new and very exciting."

And not fer nuthin, but after that rehearsal studio experiment ran its course, Ringo let a new guitar player on the scene named Jimi stay there for a spell. After he moved out, John & Yoko moved in, and it would turn out to be the place they got busted for pot that the Nixon / Edgar Hoover administration would later use to try to kick John out of the so-called land of the free.

And ol' John, he carried that Beat spirit with him across the pond when he famously emigrated to New York in 1971, making sure to meet up with Allen Ginsberg when he landed, including inviting Allen to John's 31st birthday party at a hotel in Syracuse, New York, where they were for a Yoko art exhibit opening, and a camera was rolling and there's actually footage of them all partying together. John also asked Allen to be a part of the only full concert the former Beatle ever staged after he left his band, the One To One benefit at Madison Square Garden where Ginzy joined John on stage for the climactic *"Give Peace A Chance,"* just as John had him join in on the original live recording of the song in Montreal in 1969.

The other most influential musician of the decade, Bob Dylan, was even more overt about his debt to Jack and the Beats. In interviews he's often talked about how he personally identified with Kerouac as "a young man from a small industrial town who had come to New York as a cultural outsider. ... I came out of the wilderness and just naturally fell in with the Beat scene, the bohemian Bebop crowd, it was all pretty much connected. It was Jack Kerouac, Ginsberg, Corso ... I got in at the tail end of that and it was magic ... **it had just as big an impact on me as Elvis Presley**."

In his epic song of a memoir *Chronicles, Vol. One,* Dylan describes loving Jack's "breathless, dynamic bop poetry phrases," and how *On The Road* "had been like a bible for me," and that "It changed my life like it changed everyone else's." About leaving home for the first time he writes, "What I was looking for was what I read about in *On The Road*."

Or as he told the great Kerouac and presidential scholar Doug Brinkley, "*On the Road* speeds by like a freight train. It's all movement and words and lusty instincts that come alive like you're riding on a train. Kerouac moves so fast with his words. No ambiguity. You grabbed a hold of the train, hopped on and went along with him, hanging on for dear life. I think that's what affected me more than whatever he was writing about. It was his style of writing that affected us in such a virile way."

Dylan even made a de facto "*Road*" album — "*Highway 61*" — where he put Kerouac phrases directly into his own lyrics. The album's climactic song "*Desolation Row*" lifts lines (and perhaps the title) directly from Kerouac's *Desolation Angels,* such as "the perfect image of a priest" and "her sin is her lifelessness," and "*Just Like Tom Thumb's Blues*" incorporates Jack's "Housing Project Hill." And he even put him in his videos, like the joyously surreal and Jack-heavy "*Series of Dreams,*" like he put Allen in what many consider the first music video, "*Subterranean Homesick Blues*."

Besides the obvious lyrical "borrowing" and

imitation of style and content, he went ahead and put a picture of a top-hat-wearing Ginsberg on his landmark 1964 *"Bringing It All Back Home"* album, and wrote in the liner notes, "why allen ginsberg was not chosen t read poetry at the inauguration boggles my mind," just in case anybody missed the cultural lineage.

The two maintained a friendship until the Beat bard's death, and Allen could be seen everywhere from the D.A. Pennebaker Dylan documentary *A Portrait of The Artist As A Young Man* called *Don't Look Back,* to backstage whenever their two schedules coincided. I can still see him beaming away sitting next to JFK Jr. on the sidestage at Roseland in New York in '94 when Sheryl Crow was opening and Neil and Bruce came out and joined the Bobster for the smokin' *"Rainy Day Women"* and *"Highway 61"* encore.

Allen included Bob in his epic *"Wichita Vortex Sutra"* poem just as Bob included Allen in his *"Subterranean"* video, whose title is at minimum an echo of Jack's *The Subterraneans.* By the 1970s they'd end up recording together, and Bob had Ginzy write the liner notes to his mid-decade masterpiece *Desire* just as Allen was founding The Jack Kerouac School For Disembodied Poetics, which is credited on the album sleeve, and is where this whole book is taking place.

Then on Bob's Rolling Thunder tour in '75, the live album and concert TV special of which were recorded right here in nearby Fort Collins, Colorado, Bob made sure to include Allen as part of his traveling roadshow of American arts, and the two of them would famously make a pilgrimage to Jack's gravesite in Lowell, just like thousands of fans would do in the decades to follow. Part of this visit can be seen in the ultra-weird film of the tour, *Renaldo and Clara*. While sitting next to Jack, they played guitar and harmonium and read from "*Mexico City Blues*," Bob telling his Beat elder it was the first poetry that spoke to him in his language — "It blew my mind." Bob even dropped the book's title into "*Something's Burning, Baby*" on *Empire Burlesque*.

And it wasn't just the world's most famous band and songwriter who drew their inspiration from the Beats, but many of their influential contemporaries as well. Van Morrison wrote about reading "*The Dharma Bums* by Jack Kerouac over and over again" "*On Hyndford Street*," as well as in his 1982 masterpiece "*Cleaning Windows*." Jimmy Page called Burroughs "an all-time hero," and Frank Zappa and John Cage would back Bill on his recording of *The Nova Express* (the book where "heavy metal" was first coined). Laurie Anderson would have Burroughs read as part of her perky '80s hit "*Sharkey's Night*," as well as appear in her concert movie *Home Of The Brave*. When he recorded his *Dead City Radio* spoken word album a few years later, members of Steely Dan (who were of course named for the sex toy in *Naked Lunch*), Blondie and Sonic Youth would all back him up, much as members of Aerosmith, R.E.M., The Clash and Sonic Youth (again) did a few years later on the posthumous Kerouac disc *Kicks Joy Darkness*.

Paul Simon namechecked Kerouac in the first line of "*A Simple Desultory Philippic*" on his debut *Paul Simon*

Songbook. Britain's progressive rock band Soft Machine took their name directly from a Burroughs' title. Fellow Brit Donovan would eventually release an entire album called *Beat Cafe.* The Band would feature two major Beat poets, Lawrence Ferlinghetti and Michael McClure, in their filmed farewell concert *The Last Waltz,* as well as Diane di Prima, Lenore Kandel, Emmett Grogan and Robert Duncan who also read but didn't make the final cut. Jim Morrison of The Doors was close friends with McClure, and the band's arranger and keyboardist Ray Manzarek summed it up bluntly — "If Jack Kerouac had never written *On The Road* The Doors never would have existed." Manzarek would then later team up with McClure for years of poetry and music performances, and Haight neighbor Janis Joplin would make a hit out of Michael's "*Mercedes Benz*" song-poem.

In Animals lead singer Eric Burdon's autobiography, *Don't Let Me Be Misunderstood*, he clarified for us, "We also embraced Beat writers and poets. I avidly read people like Jack Kerouac, Lawrence Ferlinghetti, William Burroughs, anything I could get my hands on. The wonderful thing was to find there was a connection between these writers, these books, and this music."

In fact, even David Bowie! As journalist Al Aronowitz remembers it, "The night before Bowie's Carnegie Hall debut in New York, I'm sitting with him over a room service dinner in his Plaza Hotel suite while he amazes me with the story of how, when he was a teenager, reading *On The Road* had been his turning point. It opened up all possibilities for him. It uplifted his spirit. It freed him to dye his hair different colors."

And speaking of colorful types, it also had a big effect on the legendary underground comic artist R. Crumb: "When I was 17, I read *On The Road,* and it sickened me, because my reaction was, 'Oh God, these guys are out there having so much fun. I'm not having any fun at all. I'm just sitting here in my parents house. But them — the girls, the adventures — they're just having a fuckin' lark *On The Road.*'"

Not long after Jack's Beat bible became a national bestseller, CBS television would unabashedly rip it off by having a smart college kid and a streetwise rebel drive around the country together having road adventures in one of the most popular shows of the early sixties, *"Route 66."* Then putting two buddies on motorcycles and driving around the country together having road adventures — *Easy Rider* — became the iconic movie of the end of the decade, written by Beat cousin Terry Southern.

And that's not even getting into the whole Greenwich Village music scene which grew directly out of the fertile Beat coffeehouses, spawning the whole genre of folk singer-songwriters that was one of the dominant sounds of the decade, with Beat-centric New Yorkers like Simon & Garfunkel, Peter Paul & Mary, John Sebastian and others dominating the airwaves. Which was shortly followed by the next wave of vocal New York area Beat aficionados Lou Reed, Patti Smith, Bruce Springsteen, David Byrne, Laurie Anderson ... and even Billy Joel who namechecks Kerouac in his *"We Didn't Start The Fire."*

And it wasn't just a New York state of mind — Jack

was changing tunes way down in the Louisiana gris-gris grounds of Dr. John's musical stew: "To me, Kerouac was like a tree planted by the water," he told me in an interview once. "His roots moved through the rivers and all the bayous of life, but he still had the strong silent thing, playing it all with deep, deep roots. He told it all. He told the good, the bad, the ugly, but he mainly just told the freakin' *truth*."

And it stretched up to Canada and into Leonard Cohen's notebook, for instance, inspiring him to come to New York in 1957 in search of the bohemian roundtable, ultimately catching Kerouac at his famous Village Vanguard shows, actually meeting Jack once at Ginsberg's apartment, and later describing him as a "certain kind of genius who was able to spin it out like some great glistening spider ... the great tale of America."

Tom Waits was another one. In one of the first stories on him in *Rolling Stone* (in Jan. '75) he told them, "Kerouac liked to consider himself a jazz poet, using words the same way Miles uses his horn. And it's a beautiful instrument. He had melody, a good sense of rhythm, structure, color, mood and intensity. I couldn't put *On The Road* down. And I got a subscription to *DownBeat* magazine right afterwards." He dropped Jack's name in innumerable songs, most obviously *Jack & Neal*, and later took some lyrics Jack wrote in *On The Road* and riffed them up into a song with his friends Primus, and also collaborated with Burroughs on the musical *The Black Rider*.

And as The Great Rock n Roll Movie continued to

unspool —> there's Iggy Pop working part of *Howl* into his *Little Miss Emperor,* and *The Ticket That Exploded* into his *Lust For Life*; The Eagles' Glenn Frey forming his first band "and we named it The Subterraneans, after the Jack Kerouac book;" The Doobie Brothers' rockin' *Neal's Fandango*; Mott The Hoople copping Jack's poem *The Wheel Of The Quivering Meat Conception*; Blue Oyster Cult setting his *"Home"* poem from *On The Road* to music in *Burnin' For You*; as did Kurt Cobain to Burroughs reading his *"The 'Priest' They Called Him;"* 10,000 Maniacs having their name-check hit with *Hey Jack Kerouac*; Rage Against The Machine riffing Allen's *"Hadda Been Playin' On The Jukebox;"* U2 putting Burroughs in one of their videos; The Beastie Boys scratching Jack into their *3-Minute Rule*; Fatboy Slim doing *Neal Cassady Starts Here*; The Smashing Pumpkins writing *Tristessa* inspired by Jack's novella, and on and on and on like the endless Road of life.

Then there was the proliferation of the "underground" press that connected the fringes through a thread of small printings, which started because the straight world just didn't get it. Tiny 1950s publications with 3-digit print runs like Jay Landesman's *Neurotica* (first published in 1948), Hettie and LeRoi Jones' *Yugen* (pronounced like "You-Gen"eration), Robert Creeley's *Black Mountain Review,* Diane di Prima's *Floating Bear,* Irving Rosenthal's *Big Table* out of Chicago, Paul Krassner's satirical *The Realist* a billion years before *The Onion* or *SNL,* Bob Kaufman's *Beatitude,* or on a slightly larger scale Barney Rosset's

Evergreen Review or the original *Village Voice* which started in 1955, were the precursors of the publications that would both define and unite the counterculture of the 1960s like the *San Francisco Oracle* and *Berkeley Barb*, *Ramparts*, the *East Village Other*, the *Georgia Straight* in Vancouver, the *International Times* out of London, and scores of others, but ultimately and most famously *Rolling Stone*.

And then there were the less tangible extensions of Beat visions in American life like the whole back-to-the-land environmental awareness that Jack had famously championed in his bestseller *The Dharma Bums* spawning what became known as "the rucksack revolution." Or the widespread use and acceptance of marijuana that the Beats first popularized beyond the secret world of jazz musicians.

Their color blindness and embrace of negro culture during a time when racism was an accepted part of everyday life in America presaged both the civil rights movement and the adoption of black styles and music and fashions that took place in the white middle class in the decades that followed.

Their embrace of Buddhism and Eastern philosophies broke down the thick old stone walls of what was acceptable as religious thought. And speaking of Stonewalls, it was Allen famously "putting his queer shoulder to the wheel" as well as the laissez faire approach to a person's sexual orientation that ran through all Beat writing and consciousness that was a crack in the door of letting everyone into the room that is America.

Much of what we picture as the revolutionary full-color psychedelic spectrum of the rock 'n' roll free-love '60s and all the subsequent supposedly groundbreaking generations that followed can be traced directly back to the poetic openness of expression and candor of heart of the Beats who first shook the American cultural and artistic foundations in their tenderhearted way.

7

On-Stage Dynamics

The first night following Allen's opening benediction, the big Saturday event was a panel on **"The Political Fallout of The Beat Generation,"** moderated by quick-witted razor-sharp Prankster comic Paul Krassner, who was a recurring blessing of laughter all conference, and featuring Allen, Burroughs, Abbie Hoffman and Timothy Leary — a wild one-time combo if there ever was one!

Among other things, Abbie and Leary hadn't much liked each other for decades, and that reared its bickering head a few times, with Leary trying to compare Abbie to G. Gordon Liddy, and Abbie snapping back, "I think you took one too many acid trips, Tim." While in the other corner Allen and Bill were going at it over who thought Jack was more apolitical.

Abbie was in rockin' shape and delivered a knockout opening statement that brought a roaring sustained rock star ovation from the packed Glenn Miller Ballroom audience as he was boppin' up and down in his seat and beaming and laughing and bonding with brother Krassner beside him. In fact, almost every one of his riffs or answers to questions during the colloquy brought crazy loud applause and cheers. This guy was a born rabble-rouser.

Meanwhile, on the other side of the stage, Leary was seen squirming uncomfortably, slouching down like he was trying to disappear into his chair, and then was the only speaker to nervously jump up and start pacing around the stage like a lounge lizard working the room with badly delivered pre-fab jokes that fell on silence. And the whole time there's old Burroughs making about a thousand uncomfortable grimacing faces, and Krassner's in the middle crackin' wise in between the improv theater. "This is Ginzo Marx, the missing Marx Brother," he riffed on Allen.

And a wondrous feature of all these panel discussions all week — there were microphones set up in the audience aisles for questions, and quite often it would be Ferlinghetti or Holmes or di Prima or somebody else who knew Jack telling some personal poetic remembrance or perspective to supplement the on-stage discussion. It was like a super-cool family gathering ... with a P.A. system. And there was this one question the first night that I've never forgotten. A random attendee voiced a thought that was probably floating unarticulated in most people's minds: "How come it's you guys up there, and not Jack and Neal?"

There was an awkward, stumbling mumbling long-form pause from all five of them on stage, then Allen finally stepped up with eight words that laid it down: "Neal too much amphetamine. Jack too much alcohol." Silence. No need to say another word. It was the shortest answer of the week, and the longest lasting.

But talking about Jack and politics is sorta like talking about Reagan and culture — they just didn't mix. And neither did the panelists. And that's what was so funny about it. The two guys from the '50s were arguing over what didn't happen back then — and the two guys from the '60s were arguing over what did.

And that's one thing to know if you ever get into this line of work — every single Beat person has a *completely* different opinion about *every single thing* that ever happened.

And speaking of that, a couple days later there was **a classic moment, or should I say "Gregory moment,"** during Abbie's headlining turn on the third night — the only person to get the 1,200-seat ballroom stage to himself for a featured evening show all conference. Meanwhile, Gregory had some real animated contempt for these next-generation interlopers, and just that afternoon had lit into Abbie during the press conference, with the world's most famous yippie trying to make really positive statements about the importance of the Beats, and Gregory would find something wrong with everything he said and it became this alternatingly funny Beat heckling and a sad display of insecurity and bitterness on Gregory's part as this fellow warrior and person who respected his cultural elders sat there taking Gregory's shit in front of a roomful of reporters. It was brutal.

Among so many other things old owl Allen wisely planned for, he put both Abbie and Leary early in the conference. By the time Tim was finished his commitments the first weekend, he knew enough to get the hell outta Dodge. But Abbie was Monday night and this was Gregory's last shot at either of them. So what does Wise Old Om do? He asks Gregory, as a personal favor, if he'd introduce his rebel son. Despite Gregory's antagonism, these two were so similar — both authority-hating East Coast big-city plain-talkin' speak-truth-to-power shit-kicking multi-term convict writers. And surprisingly Gregory goes along with Allen's request and is quite nice about it. At least for his brief intro.

Later on, as Abbie was on stage delivering his

inspiring, upBeat, funny, well thought out speech to an enthusiastic standing-room-only "Question Authority" button wearing crowd, I happened to be out in the adjacent press lounge when Gregory wandered in surrounded by his usual coterie of characters and criminals and he was talkin' loud and had worked his way into a fighting stew. After warming up a little by running some of his beefs by us outside the room, he burst through the closed double doors at the back (with me on his heels cuz I wasn't gonna miss this!) and he immediately starts yelling at Abbie. And poor old Abbie was right in the middle of his fantastic performance, had the room in the palm of his fist, and all of a sudden he was getting heckled (again) by one of the Founding Fathers of Heckling. "Aaa, you don't know what you're talkin' about! Whaddya you know about anything? You weren't there."

And of course a thousand necks all crane around at once and start facing the back of the room, and then spin back to the stage as Abbie responds, then back to Gregory as hurls some more. "Go back into hiding, you phony!"

And Abbie, God bless 'im, was respectful and it was probably the only time in his life he ever backed down from a fight, but he did it in this really clever way, at one point calling Gregory "Mr. Corso" like he was old and somebody's dad. And he never took Gregory's bait, but rather said, "If you'd like to come up, if you have anything to say, please, the microphone is all yours," as he stepped back from the podium and motioned to it.

But of course Gregory just wanted to yell and make a scene — as he quite prides himself in doing — and Abbie brilliantly let him yell himself out, and without anybody to fight with, pretty soon he just gave him a dismissive wave of his hand, "Aaa, you don't belong here, you don't know nuthin' about nuthin'," and turned and sort of waddled like The Penguin back out the door. God, it was crazy.

And then Abbie said something like, "And THAT, ladies and gentlemen, is the Beat spirit alive and well," and the whole place exploded, applauding the spontaneous theater, and he went right back into his wild Abbie's History of The World speech. What a moment.

Holmes is Where The Heart Is

I had a pretty loosey-goosey schedule with this loosey-goosey crew, and with the little official all-access staff button I was able to walk into any event. At the time I was very novel-centric, and the biggest I-can't-believe-I-can-be-in-his-presence of the early arrivals was **John Clellon Holmes**. I loved his novel *Go* — the barely fictionalized account of having adventures in New York with his buddies Jack Kerouac, Allen Ginsberg, Neal

Cassady, Bill Burroughs, Herbert Huncke and all the rest on Manhattan's Isle.

In fact — he riffed vivid character studies of Neal and Allen to rival Jack's, but importantly also captured Kerouac in ways ol' Duluoz couldn't himself while they were both covering the exact same events. He painted rich literary portraits of poor literary artists in the earliest days of the Beat Generation, whose term was coined in his living room by Jack, and it was John who jumped up and said, "That's it! That's it!!" and then was tapped to explain it to the world in his historic *New York Times* article, "This Is The Beat Generation," in 1952.

But he was also the most normal of this kooky crew. Holmes was the first to leave Manhattan and settle in the suburbs, and he looked like any middle-class Joe you'd meet at the corner store on a Wednesday afternoon — a freshly ironed button-down shirt with a pack of smokes in his breast pocket, dorky big-framed glasses, with short, neatly combed hair. But still somehow he was the coolest.

I never did have a one-on-one with him cuz he just seemed so beyond this 21 year old. But even in 1982, I guessed he was Jack's closest writing brother — long before all the biographies and letters and notebooks and such were ever published revealing him to be — I just sensed that this was *the guy*, the only other real novelist in Jack's circle — I mean, they were even born on the same day — and both had the same first name!

Something else that wasn't revealed at the time of the conference was that John had cancer of the mouth and jaw. He didn't tell anyone, and had postponed the first of several "overdue operations" in order to gather with his friends once more, and after he went under the knife he confessed he "would never be quite the same man again." In fact, he later referred to this gathering, sadly accurately, as his "last appearance as a charter member of the Beat Generation," as he would go on to join Jack & Neal at that great endless New Year's Eve party in the sky about five years later.

So I went to his writer's workshop and was hanging on his every word.

And there he was! John Clellon Holmes in a tiny U of C classroom, maybe 25 people, with a wall of windows behind him filling the room with high noon sunlight, and damned if the guy wasn't chain smoking through the whole class!

The workshop group was pretty evenly split between women and men, and people of all ages, ethnicities, and reasons for being there. There were scholars like Ann Charters quietly in the corner, boisterous Jack-heads, reserved Holmes-heads, beginning writers, midstream writers, read-only non-writers — all engaged in a wide-open free-flowing group conversation. And the teacher was *super* nice and polite and friendly and helpful. He even said at the beginning, "Ask me anything you want." And people did. Including about Jack.

One little side note here — besides all the other cool stuff I brilliantly and bizarrely brought with me in that backpack on this unexpected trip and which you'll hear more about later, I also packed this little pocket-sized cassette tape recorder I used to capture everything from people who picked me up hitchhiking to conversations with my Beat heroes who didn't seem to mind at all when I'd click it on as we were talking. So I used it constantly. Including when John talked about being the first human being to ever read the scroll of *On The Road*.

"I've got the facts about how *On The Road* was written, and I've corrected Allen and now he's got them, too. He didn't have them before. There is still this notion afoot that the version of *On The Road* that's published is the third version he wrote. That is not true. He *tried* to begin the book three times. But he never got any of the characters out of New York. And some of these sections were sixty pages long. Almost *none* of that material, which he took over a year doing, those three false starts, almost none of that is in the book as published. And the book as published *is* what he wrote in 20 days — plus the changes he made in it when he typed it up two weeks later. He did nothing with pencil, he did it with his head; he was correcting sentences, he was adding things that seemed proper, cutting other things out. But the version as published is substantially the version I read as the first human being to ever read it. It was two days after he finished it. He brought the scroll over. He couldn't bear to look at it because he was so exhausted and I think he wanted to get it out of his house so he wouldn't be tempted till he was recovered from this feat.

"The scroll as I read it was considerably longer than the book as published. *He* made the cuts, at the suggestion of his editors, but also I told him I thought the stuff at the terminal points — he had lots of stuff about New York that was not connected with the other material at all — I had suggested why didn't he thin that at least. He didn't follow my suggestion until his editor at Viking agreed, and then he did it willingly. Their feeling was that the book was too long and lopsided and that it should concentrate more on Neal, and Jack didn't rewrite any of that stuff, he simply cut away the dross to reveal it as being the true subject of the book.

"There are many misconceptions about how the book was written but this is how it was written — I know, I was right there. *Right* there. I read all those three false starts, or he read them to me, and they were *terrific*. But he didn't like them, it wasn't what he wanted to do. And often the artist *doesn't* know what he wants to do, or can't succumb to it until after he's gone through false start after false start after false start."

So, there was that.

And then there was the part where he went on about . . .

"I think *Visions of Cody* is Jack's best writing; not his best novel. There's a difference. Jack was not a novelist in the conventional sense after *The Town And The City*. The bridge into the mature work is *On The Road* which is still a linear narrative with characters, with events that happen in sequence, with some kind of shape. The shape is an erratic shape, it's a zig-zag shape, but the book does start somewhere and it ends somewhere. Now, *Cody* on the other hand is a collection of materials that should have gone into *On The Road*. Jack's intention in writing it was to tell the truth. He felt that *On The Road* was not the truth — that it was the method by which *On The Road* had been written that was false. So, to give full shape to his remembrance of experience, *Visions of Cody* is this great sort of potpourri of stuff — what redeems it is the writing, is the range of feeling, is the range of material over which this single consciousness is playing. Because it's all happening in the consciousness of Duluoz, it's not happening in the world, it's not meant to be a transcription of the world. None of Jack's books are. He thought, 'What do I know about the world? All I know is what my senses tell me.' So he tried to be as accurate to what he knew and felt as he possibly could be, and yet limited to his own subjectivity."

And, y'know, this is just coming from Jack's closest prose-writing pal. Who I'm sitting a few feet from. As he's casually but emphatically imparting all these learned laws of literature . . .

Like — the hardest thing for a writer is to find their own voice; that you can't just wish it into being, you have to earn it by continually writing, and it may not come for many years and many books. ... like Miles Davis's line — "You have to play a long time before you can sound like yourself."

And about how writers have to be able to look at themselves objectively, but then write *subj*ectively — that only you have your unique view of the world and you have to practice accurately transcribing your visions and impressions into sentences.

And that an effective trick for beating a temporary writer's block is to read something you've recently written to remind yourself you can do it — but that every author winces when reading something they've written many years earlier. "I'll read a passage from years ago that I didn't know how to make work then, but now I can fix in ten seconds."

And how writers read all the time, and how you've got to continue to self-educate, that if you're a committed writer it's an ongoing never-ending process until you die, and that reading books + experience = an education.

And that the Beats formed their own school-without-walls, with living rooms and bar booths as their classrooms, and anybody could add a new book to the syllabus. That you don't have to be accepted into a university or pay somebody tuition in order to follow a reading list and learn.

And the importance of journal writing — how he's kept them his entire adult life, and so did Jack, and how you can be completely honest and straightforward there. You don't have to worry about sentence construction or paragraphs or linear flow — it's just a sketchpad, a confessional, a best friend, a hard currency memory bank, a place where you can find your own truths.

And how Mark Twain was a great writer but a bad novelist. How Yeats was born physically tone deaf but was the most musical of all poets. How Hemingway read a lot of poetry to keep up his prose chops. How Jack and John considered Henry Miller a kindred spirit and a direct father of what they were doing. How they both loved D.H. Lawrence. How younger readers want action and a fast moving plot, but as you get older you see how Henry James is just as exciting as any shoot-'em-up novel. And how Holmes was in the nightclub the last night Charlie Parker played, and he actually talked to him that night, and how that became the basis for the last two chapters of *The Horn*.

He riffed repeatedly on the importance of writing every day; and to make the reader feel what you do; and that every person's life is interesting — it's all in how you expose it, reveal it, present it. And to write the Beat you hear. And the only character you can and must have control over is the narrator — once you've given life to another you must allow it to do what it will. You should *feel* the shape of the story, and keep it in view through the months or years of creation. Don't tinker, just flow. Write always. Listen always.

If you don't *want* to write all the time, you're not a writer.

If you want to write — don't do anything else.

Yeah. I was in the right place.

9

The Professor in The Park with The Knife

After the Holmesian mind blowing, I had to go for a walk and find some place to write for the rest of my life.

Not far from where the classes were held was this little park area with trees and benches and space and quiet and greenery and birds and I found my sacred spot, as I always search for, and began scribbling secret scatological thoughts — getting everything out about my plans and dreams and doubts and hesitations and why I wasn't "going for it" more — when in fact I'd pretty much gone for it over here.

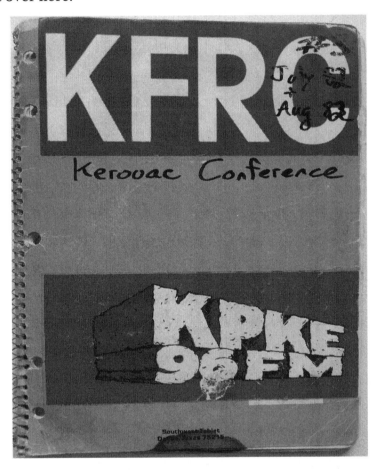

I began using my word sketchbook like a coach talking back to me, expelling my scared deer fears — at times it was my encouraging mother, at others the writerly spirit of Jack admonishing my procrastinations, at still others my confidence-building girlfriend Sue shooting down my insecurities ... but I followed John Holmes' advice that if you just sit and tune in the mental radio ... some days it'll come through clear and loud, and other times it may be staticy, but if you really listen you can eventually catch the words. And on this day in this park I didn't need my Walkman to hear the music play!

After a while, as I was in one of those look up and around moments in between historic revelations, this old guy who was in the Holmes workshop came amblin' up the walkway. We were both sorta lookin' at each other as he grew larger along the path, and by the time he got to where I was sitting we both laughed at the long staring goof of it, and maybe it was the voice of coach Cassady that spoke up from my notebook and said, "Hey!" which was enough to slow him to a stop.

"What did you think of that Holmes class?" he asked.

"Well," I said, looking around the park for words. "He cut through the bullshit. ... Like, writing isn't some theoretical concept for him. It's cool to meet somebody who writes every day. 'Oh. So *that's* how you do it!'" and he laughed.

I asked how he came to be here, and he's an English prof from some school in Virginia, and teaches Beat Lit courses "whenever I can get away with it," he said. "It's a constant battle. Most of my colleagues think Kerouac is a joke. They conflate him with Hunter Thompson and Ken Kesey covered in day-glo paint throwing acid around like confetti. And it's even worse if I bring up Ginsberg or Burroughs who they think should be locked up," and I laughed even though it was horrible. "I'm hoping to gather some more rebuttal ammunition."

"Ya getting any?" I asked.

"Well, that footage of Kerouac on *The Steve Allen Show* would be helpful," he said. "They wouldn't believe that was him if Steve didn't introduce him. And talking to some biographers last night, there's a couple major books coming out next year. One's a memoir by his girlfriend in New York when *On The Road* came out. There's only four biographies of Fitzgerald. If I can put a foot-high stack of books on the table in front of them, that's going to help."

"So ... you teach a class on Jack?"

He nodded yes, "But there should be an entire Beat Studies program like they have here. The students want it, but I can't get the department to okay the courses," he said, pointing to the bench and taking off his little daypack to sit down. I grabbed the cassette deck out of mine and found a blank side of a tape and popped it in. And him being a college professor, was right alright with me recording the lecture.

"Kerouac clearly fits in the continuum of American literature," he said. "*Huck Finn, Leaves of Grass*, Thoreau, Jack London, Thomas Wolfe — my *students* can see that for gawdsakes. They're ahead of the faculty on this. I can get them to read Thomas Wolfe because they like Kerouac's version of it. If they don't first have a contemporary voice that speaks to them in their language, they have trouble with the older material. And that's the bridge Kerouac's been, for my students anyway, going back ten years now.

"He's a gateway author," the prof kept riffing. "With most writers, if you're really interested in them, there's only that one writer's work and life to read about. But with the Beats ... there are all the core '50s writers, then that can branch off into Robert Frank and his films, which connects to Jonas Mekas and the whole avant-garde film world. Then there's the next level of writers, like Berrigan and di Prima .... Then there's the whole Ken Kesey direction, which branches into Tom Wolfe, Hunter Thompson, Bukowski. Or there's the musical angle — and that alone could be a degree program.

"Kerouac loved jazz so much, you can hear the music in his prose. When I was younger," he went off parenthetically, "I loved the stories. Now it's not so much the story, I relish the *language*, it's his *voice*, his command of his instrument. I know the books so well now I just pick up one and flip to any page and start listening to his music. . . . But what about you? Why are you here?" and I gave him the nickel sketch backstory. Then he goes, "But why did you come half-way across the country to go to school on your summer vacation?"

"Okay ... let's see ... I love Kerouac's writing, like you said," I began, holding out the first finger to start counting the ways. "He's writes about cool stuff. He was so influential to so many major people ... y'know, from Lester Bangs to Jerry Garcia. And ... he was writing about real things that happened. Like, it's not just some fictional story set in some imaginary town. For one thing, it's usually either in New York or San Francisco, so right there, that's cool. Or they're on the road — and that's a place I always wanna be. But ... it's that he was there when everything was happening in New York — Abstract Expressionism, Method acting, Bebop — and he was the writer. That whole era is fascinating to me — I think it's the coolest time in American history, other than maybe San Francisco in the sixties. But New York in the forties and fifties, man, that's when it was happening.

"I live with Phyllis Condon," I soloed on. "The widow of Eddie Condon, the jazz bandleader — and she's still totally with it. She knows more about what's going on in New York on a Saturday night than I do! And she talks about this cross-pollination a lot — how everybody hung out together in the Village — the musicians and actors and writers and comedians and painters. And they all drank like fish. But that was this magical time. And Jack was there for all of that. *Rebel Without A Cause, The Wild One* ... he was the writer's wing of the party ... *and it was a helluva party!*" and he laughed.

"That's what I was saying about Kerouac being an entry to a whole other world, or series of worlds," he said.

"Yeah, and there's the whole music thing, and how that goes both ways," he kinda got me goin'. "On one hand he's turned me onto Charlie Parker and Monk and all this stuff I don't know when I would have gotten around to. Then — you can see how Springsteen or Dylan or Tom Waits or something are telling Jack stories about the same types of people. Like, Springsteen's *The River* that just came out. That's Jack. So — he isn't just turning me on to *his* music, he's turning me on to *my* music."

"That's great," the professor said. "The door opens both ways."

"Yeah. .... And also Jack is so *confessional* — maybe it's his Catholic thing," I said. "But he's so honest and ... it's like he's a friend writing you a long letter. You get sort of adopted into his whole family — Mémère and Gerard and Nin and all that — but more Neal and Carolyn and Allen and Burroughs .... Like — I can't go read books by Holden Caulfield's friends, or Vonnegut's characters, but with Jack, just about every character has his own book out, or a bunch of them."

"Right. That's great," he said.

And just then this couple came walking along. I'd seen them around — she was a real chatterbox, but always had this quiet serious guy with her. She was wearing one of the conference t-shirts — basically the poster with Jack's face and all the names — which had already become sort of the "colors" for our crew. I never did get one. And they never gave me one, and they were like 25 bucks or something, which ... I was kinda broke. But then, it would be way too small for me now anyway.

I said "Hi!" and they came right over. It was this cool thing that was already happening where we were all at this kind of crazy summer camp together with all these wayward spirits who were drawn like sprinkled iron shavings from across the continent by the magnetic pull of Jack. And since there weren't that many other students around this abandoned campus in the middle of the summer, it was really easy to talk to people. Nobody here but us freaks. Ha!

Bob the professional inquirer asked why they made the trip, and right away she was jibber-jabber jamber jooling — "You know, I read a lot of writers, I'm a big reader, and Jack Kerouac, well, his road books, they have something I haven't found anywhere else. I love it. An openness ... to people. Yeah . . . people. We're always supposed to care for the least among us — but nobody really does that. Not even in fiction. But Kerouac, even when he got famous he didn't start hanging out with Dick Cavett and all them but would stay in flophouses and spend time with street people. Real people. Not phonies and poseurs. He was more like Jesus than all your *Godspells* and *Jesus Christ Superstars* put together."

"He *listened* to people," the professor harmonized.

"Yeah, that's what I get, too," I said. "You know they're real people, not some fictional Hemingway lion hunter or something. I'm taking ear training at NYU for music, but Kerouac is like ear training for voices. Whenever I'm reading him I get way more aware of people around me. Like, every person is a character. Everyone is interesting in their own weird way. He makes your whole day like a novel or a movie — like everything's part of some grand story, and everybody you meet is in it."

"Yeah, that's it — he was open to everyone," Chatterbox enthused. "He's always meeting new people. He seems like he'd be fun to go out with," and right away caught herself. "I mean, just to hang with, honey," as she squeezed her mute boyfriend.

"Did she drag you along on this?" the professor queried Quietman.

"I'm getting my Masters at Boston College in American Lit," and he paused hoping somebody would say something else so he wouldn't have to talk, but no one did. "I gave her *On The Road* right after we met — to see if we'd get along or not," he said, smiling to her.

"So *you're* the problem," the professor ribbed. "What was it that got you into Monsieur Kerouac?" he asked, surgically cutting the surface with his quizzical knife.

And just like that Quietman opened right up. "Okay ... there's all kinds of escapism — romance novels, Heinlein, Harlan Ellison, Stephen King — but Kerouac was writing about *actually* escaping ... the same mundane existence that leads people to science fiction or pulp fiction or television, but Kerouac was writing about very real ways out — like *50 Ways To Leave Your Lover* — 'Slip out the back, Jack ...'" and we all caught the kismet namecheck and laughed. "No, but I think this is why he reaches so many people — and for so long. It wasn't just one book or one way out. He had the road, ..."

"This is his whole thesis," Chatterbox let us know.

" ... which is one very valid way out — out of town, a lousy relationship, a bad job, it's a direction, right? But then there's *The Dharma Bums* that points to the mountains, getting back to nature. Go for a hike. Get away. And then there's the whole escape through drinking and bar-hopping — *The Subterraneans.* Or there's the everyman fantasy of jumping on a ship out to the open sea — *Vanity of Duluoz.* Or there's staying at home and escaping through your imagination and childhood memories — *Doctor Sax.* Or everybody wants to sneak away to a cabin in the woods with their friends like *Big Sur.* He offered all these different routes that if a reader was at all prone to his style, there was something that would speak to it."

"That's good," the professor said, quite seriously,

academic to academic.

"He's so often portrayed as this one-trick-pony, this *On The Road* guy ..."

"Tell me about it!" the professor burst.

"Right?! But how can you lump *Visions of Gerard* or *Scripture of the Golden Eternity* in with *The Subterraneans* or *Visions of Cody*? Or *Old Angel Midnight* with *The Town And The City*? If his name wasn't on the cover you'd never believe those were written by the same person. So, yeah, this guy's worth traveling across the country to get to know a little better. And to actually meet the people he wrote about!"

"That escape thing is totally right on," I jumped in. "I live in Manhattan, and even there the road is an option. Like, you hear people say 'the road' isn't really there anymore, but I live in the densest populated part of the country, and about a minute after you cross the G.W. Bridge you can hang a right and be on the Palisades Parkway, this beautiful tree-covered road through the forest alongside these cliffs. I mean, from Greenwich Village you can be on the open road in a matter of minutes and pulling into some roadside diner listening to total strangers from another world and order yourself some apple pie with ice cream."

And just as they were laughing at my reference to Jack's favorite road food, the cassette in my deck came to the end and loudly clicked off and we all laughed some more at the synchronistic timing and knew class was over and each returned to our regularly scheduled adventures.

10

The Boulderado Bash

That night there was a reception party at the Boulderado
— this super-cool ancient hotel — well, early 1900s anyway
— which is about as old as yer gonna find by paleface's
hand in these hills.

It's big and ornate and made out of blazing orange
sandstone that makes it stand out in Downtown-anywhere
let alone Boulder. As soon as you walk in the lobby your
eyes are blown open by the hand of God reaching down

from a lit-up stained-glass canopy ceiling. And everything's dark natural wood and regally appointed from bygone times with plush Victorian chairs and shiny brass gaslights coming out of the walls.

The Boulder Beat boogie was already raging in the upstairs rent-a-ballroom with loads of the usual troublemakers ... Allen, Anne, Holmes, Burroughs, Ferling, the Charters, the Knights, Diane di Prima, that Nanda Pivano translator woman from Italy who everyone seemed to be making a big fuss over, and a bunch of the Naropa staff I'd seen around.

I got there just as twilight twinkled the mountains, in time to see the blue hue of the setting city out the big windows before they slowly turned into a house of mirrors reflecting the Beats at a literary cocktail hour. Actually, for a lot of them, it was almost always cocktail hour, but this was the perfect excuse to be official about it.

Burroughs was in a big easy chair in the corner, twiddling the handle of his cane, with Allen on one side and a handful of others encamped around them. But most guests were standing, animated in full party mode — and I'll tell ya who stood out among the standing — **Anne Waldman**! What a goddess! A hip Cleopatra — composed and poised in colorful flowing robes, surrounded by men, and jangling her jewelry in dramatic gestures like a born theater actor. She sure knew how to make herself into a blooming centerpiece bouquet and arrange it for all the angles!

And from the stolen glances of the male eyes in the room, you had a feeling every dude in town had a crush on her, including Allen Ginsberg, or so went the rumor. There was something about her confidence and directness, her cut-through-it and go-for-it-ness ... sort of Janis-like — one of the boys, but very much a girl. And man, could she sing! Her performance poetry was like that Maxell ad in every *Rolling Stone* with the whole room being blown back like a hurricane. THAT's what Beat poetry readings were in my imagination, and here she was in the present tense rippin' the yin to Allen and Gregory's yang.

And speaking of Gregory! He makes a boisterous booming entrance like a whole other party moving in! He's got this almost football huddle of guys surrounding him, and Corso's got the ball, breaking through the unsuspecting defense of cocktail-holding bookworms charging for the goal line of his pals Ginzy and Burroughs in the far corner.

He's carrying on a rum 'n' commentary, I don't know about what, as Jack's "mad ones" flashed through my head. This whole *scene* was mad. People as old as my parents were exploding like the fabulous Roman candles of my buddies. And I was dancing with them as I'd done all my life, now in the unchartered territories of the American Rockies with the unqualified crazies of the American Bop night.

I naturally gravitated to the all-star corner, as Gregory was doing to Allen & Bill what Bob did to Newport in '65 — blasting their quiet comfortable acoustic world with a raging electric assault of poetic imagery and caustic slices ripping the room and world apart. He ain't gonna work on Maggie's Farm no more! Allen laughed and spoke quietly back in hopes Gregory would get the hint and turn down the volume. Didn't work. As Bill sat there all mute and motionless as usual, darting his eyes back and forth seemingly uncomfortably. And I made sure I stayed the hell outta Gregory's visual line of fire lest I catch some improvised "*Positively 4th Street.*"

In the center of the party ring, were the polar opposites of scene-stealing Gregory — the positively unfazed Beat aristocracy of Ferlinghetti and Holmes and all the others unslouched in Bethlehem and unbroken in their professional conversational cocktail flow — veterans of the midlife schmooze, standing straight as smiling arrows, focused on their moment's target, following the moment's tangent, riffing on the magic transcripts and rallying the miscreant transients.

Ferlinghetti was talking about painting, John was riffing on Melville, Anne was talking about some new poem-song she'd just recorded, "*Uh-Oh Plutonium!*" and Sam Charters was telling a story about recording Dizzy Gillespie — an' the whole thing was spinning me dizzy, Miss Lizzie.

And not just me, but good ol' King Arthur Knight was spotted blindly stumbling for the doors, and a pretty girl was sitting on a gorgeous couch in a million dollar room crying over some emotional overload, as three wisemen were arguing poetry over a hookah, and somebody spoke and I went into a dream.

The next thing I knew, a couple'a joculars are tellin' me about this secret bar in the basement — the oldest in Boulder — and I'm freakin out, being a history nut. Before ya know it we're smuggling drinks through the lobby and down some mysterious dark wooden staircase into this labyrinthian maze of narrow hallways and little rooms somewhere between a subterranean New York nightclub and a Wild West brothel.

There's couples and groups clustered in comfortable cubbyholes, and *The Shining's* bartender is wiping glasses behind some little bar the size people have in their basements, and suddenly from one of the sacred little grottos we pass, I hear "Broyan!" in a thick British accent — and there's this lighting guy I knew from the Stones tour!

"Jimmy!" [I'll call him in print] "how ya bin, mate?!" as I hadn't seen him in forever and a year.

"Just got off Simon & Garfunkel — Europe and Japan — same old — Paul Simon, Mick Jagger ... 'new boss, same as the old boss,'" and we laughed.

He an' 'is bird were on vacation and wanted to experience "the Barcelonas of America," as he put it. He had no idea the Beats were in town, and didn't seem terribly transformed to learn so, but was happy to see a familiar face in an unexpected place. So happy in fact, and assuming these guys were "me mates," he broke out massive lines just for old times' sake on the worn shipping trunk table.

And as the high was rising, through our jibber-jabbering he suddenly sparked, "Hang on — this bloke you're on about — Crimson's new album's about 'im — it's called '*Beat*' ... I thought they meant the music."

"Wait ... *what?!*"

"The new King Crimson album, mate ... the first song is '*Neal and Jack and Me*' ... how 'bout that?! I just found out what's that's about! Thanks, mate!"

"King Crimson just did an album about _what_?!"

And he kept riffing on about what turned out to be true but I could hardly believe at the time — this alien reporting alien doings from foreign lands about the very thing we were gathering in secret hideaways in the Rockies to celebrate. How is this possible?! His book's not even in bookstores but it's on an album?! By *King Crimson* ... who aren't even *American*? Why ... ... what? How is this messenger from afar the one breaking the news that Jack & Neal are being feted *In The Court of the Crimson King*?!

And the melody line jammed into a Caribbean groove of smuggler's tales and island sails and ways to Beat the heat. Above me's Gregory Corso, and beside me's Jimmy Moreso, and I'm remembering my mommy's primary commandment: *Whatever you do — don't get arrested!*

And as the twist spins 'round, some longhaired sweeties pass by with a giggle and a leader bold enough to say High, and don't we though, into a bigger jam of flowered hair as the boys perk up and the girls flush cheeks, and all segueing into *"Whatever Gets You Thru the Night"* — singers behind sunglasses, goofing, seducing, dancing Goldie Hawn bikinis, warm embraces and summer faces, seeing the light in the strangest of places as I looked at it right.

Buzzy Pickupsville was the motivating director around all these method actors at the Grande Boulder

Theater — as this Canadian innocent sat wide-open in awe while gawd nose what was going on in front of him. Jazz cigarettes and *Shining* bars may have been involved. Bawdy schnapps and dreamy trips, funny lines and razor quips.

At some point we split, and about a half block of boisterous sidewalk carousing later we stumbled across the historic and brightly colorful Boulder Theater. "Holy shit!" . . . "Elvin Bishop tonight!" the marquee blared. And in the magic of it all ... it was late in the evening and the doors seemed lax so we just slipped right on in there like the pros we were, workin' the gig.

The floor was about three-quarters full and everybody was up and dancing, and it was the last I saw of my crew as I beelined straight down the theater aisle at magnetized speed to the lip of the low old-world movie theater stage — and there was the cat in the cowboy hat who jammed with the Dead and just about everybody else in the extended family, thrashin' his country cowboy blues like he was Neil Young ridin' the Horse. Musta been near the end of the set — everybody was goin' bananas ... and it was *so* America ... so just-a-cat-on-a-stage in the middle of nowhere, right outta nowhere, beyond the silent midnight streets, bashing the raging all-night beats, blazing the night into a blazing sunrise with a thousand dancing friends.

There's images of an old car full of people and a couch in the rest of the night's memory footage, but they're only fragments.

11

Then Along Comes Kesey

I was well into Jack — and this whole conference kicked *that* up a few dozen notches — like it did everybody else — but The Chief and The Boys (the Grateful Dead) — those were the magic beans I wanted to come home with handfuls of.

Kesey (pronounced Key-Zee) had this operating philosophy of having his rural home address and phone number publicly listed because he didn't want to "pull a Pynchon," as he put it, but rather remain accessible to readers and the rest of humanity. Somehow through the grapevine I'd learned this inside trick before the conference and had written him a letter telling him I was coming. What a nut. But I was ballsy, and I've found these happening dudes are way-hip to straight-up energy. And this was one happening guy I had to meet. (see, also: *Kool-Aid, Electric.*)

Kesey and Kerouac had a lot more in common than just synchronistically sharing the same fiction shelf in every bookstore in the world. In fact, it's almost eerie how similar their lives were.

- ☒ They both grew up in low-income working-class households in small towns just outside a major city, not far from the ocean — Kesey in Springfield, Oregon, Jack in Lowell, Massachusetts.
- ☒ Both were strong of build and star athletes in their youth — Kesey a champion wrestler and Jack a star running back in football.
- ☒ Both got their big break by getting a scholarship or fellowship to the large liberal intellectual city on their respective coasts, San Francisco and New York, and both suddenly found themselves in a small but intense bohemian enclave with other writers who were so good they would become internationally known in their own right — Kesey in the Perry Lane crowd at Stanford with Larry McMurtry, Wendell Berry, Ed McClanahan, Robert Stone and others, and Kerouac in the extended Columbia scene

that soon included Ginsberg, Holmes, Burroughs, Lucien Carr and others.

☒ Both wrote an unsuccessful first novel about roughly the same subject — small-town boy goes to big bohemian city — Kesey's *End of Autumn* and Kerouac's *The Town and The City* — and with that out of their system both exploded creatively, struck gold, and were forever defined by their second novel — Kesey's *One Flew Over The Cuckoo's Nest* and Kerouac's *On The Road*.

☒ And in another cosmic karmic twist, just as their surnames appear next to each other on bookshelves, those two defining works are often sequential in alphabetical lists of major 20th century novels.

☒ Both books had the exact same champion in the publishing world, and ultimately their editor — Malcolm Cowley — and both were published by Viking Press.

☒ Both had the same editor years later at Viking-Penguin, David Stanford.

☒ Both were represented by the same literary agent, Sterling Lord.

☒ Both ended up writing famous tributes to the other — Viking asked Kerouac to write the blurb for Kesey's *Cuckoo's Nest* ("A great new American novelist.") and Esquire asked Kesey to write the tribute to Kerouac for their landmark "50 Who Made The Difference" Golden Anniversary.

☒ Both were into sparking the sparkling highs of marijuana long before it became popular, and

- ☒ Both were involved in a community of artists seeking out mind-expanding drugs before the drugs entered the national consciousness — Kesey & company famously with LSD, and the Beat crew pioneering the search for and experiential reportage on yage, aka ayahuasca.

- ☒ And for Men of Letters, both had an unusually strong connection to the cutting-edge music of their time — Kesey with the Grateful Dead, and Kerouac with his passion for Bebop jazz, which saw him produce some of the most vivid descriptions ever written about the small-club birth of that idiom.

And . . .

- ☒ Both were driven by Neal Cassady on the pivotal road trip of their life.

But one thing Kerouac didn't do was organize large scale acid parties, and have somebody write a really colorful book about them, and have his house band evolve into The Grateful Dead and light shows and spontaneous street theater and psychedelic art. As somebody on the magic bus trip I took across the country myself in 1978 put it, "The whole counterculture of America spilled out of a house party at Ken Kesey's."

So, you can see why I was attracted to this particular conference participant, and why I immediately parlayed myself into being Kesey's handler — the guy who was supposed to make sure he was where he was supposed to be.

Good luck with that!

The only time my trusty Kodak X-15 camera ever malfunctioned and shot psychedelic multiple exposures was Kesey arriving and getting out of his convertible

His first event was a big press conference with Allen and Burroughs.

Actually, Allen was at all of them. Every day we'd have one with a different headliner or two as the focus — Gregory, Burroughs, McClure, Abbie, Leary, etc. — so, over the arc of the conference, whatever day some press person might be covering it, there'd be at least one press availability, with Allen as the omnipresent moderating moderator.

And of course Kesey's late. Way late. I'd called him at the house where he was staying, and he promised they were just leaving. Like — an hour ago. And while I was pacing back and forth out front, there was one of the comical incongruities of the festival — Allen's limo! Here's this guy promoting scribbled "first thought, best thought" poetry — which for your average practitioner doesn't produce enough lifetime income to fill one tank of gas — being driven around like a captain of industry!

O Captain! my Captain! our fancy trip awaits,

The ship has weather'd every course, poverty abates.

The Beatnik in the Batmobile — the bats inside the belfries;

The inmate's in the driver's seat, and Hell's about to freeze.

Obviously this wasn't his state of regular affairs. Allen wouldn't be Allen if he was some limo guy, and I wouldn't have hitchhiked a thousand miles to hang out with a phony, but in The Grand Synch of it all, an old student of his had unexpectedly shown up and had just become the proud owner of his own one-car limo service! He volunteered to be Allen's wheels for the whole Road show — joyously acting out that priceless passage in *On The Road* with Sal & Dean and the Cadillac.

After much pacing and looking back and forth from my watch to the furthest cars driving anywhere near —

you'd think I would have taken up smoking right then and there — Kesey finally just "appeared," all alone, blissfully walking up the sidewalk ... a half-hour late. I was quickly learning what was known as "Buddhist time" in Boulder: Things were supposed to happen at a certain time. Unless they didn't.

You're immediately struck by his size and stature, and I don't just mean literary reputation. This was a big man — a wrestler with a tree-trunk neck, a barrel chest, and Popeye forearms; a mountainman with ruddy cheeks and glowing skin; but more impactful than anything was his ever-present smile, his big, easy and infectious laugh, and the Prankster twinkle perpetually flashing in his leprechaun eyes.

"How was the trip here?" I asked.

"Great. We drove 40 hours non-stop," and he turned and smiled a wide one in pride at their Cassady-like achievement. In fact, I'd hear him tell people this for the next week. "All the way from Eu-gene," he'd say, emphasizing the first syllable and not the second, like he always did.

This all sounded well and good and very On The Road and In The Spirit and all that, so I never broke it to the old guy that I got here from Portland, which is *furthur*, in 42 hours — *and I didn't even have a car!* Smoke that in your pipe and hold it.

As we speed-walked the sidewalk to the gig, he also shared, "It was a return trip." I looked at him. "My pa packed up the family and moved us from right near here to where we live now. I was born not far from here. Smack in the middle of the war he up and moved us all to Oregon, been there ever since. But this was my first home."

And then, oh man! **That press conference was sumpthin!** I'll just say straight out — there are very few people I've been around who change a room just by walking into it, but Kesey's one of them. This was just the first of many times I would experience it. It has to do with energy, there's no other way to explain it. People radiate energy, and I saw the effects of Kesey's many times. He'd enter a room, and the whole space would change, even for people who didn't know he was there or who he was. It would get louder and more animated. He was this huge splash in the energy pool, and ripples would roll across the room, hit the far wall, and come rolling back again. Mind you, he was also partnered with his Lieut. Babbs, the former Vietnam helicopter pilot and Senior Prankster who's got a bellowing baritone to match his big Oregon frame. So . . . things change when they walk in a room. As they did to the nines in the Glenn Miller Lounge at this press conference. (And if you hadn't guessed yet — yep, Glenn Miller went to the U of C in Boulder.)

Lined up next to each other were Babbs, Ginzy, Anne Waldman, Burroughs and Kesey in front of the microphones and cameras and tape decks and standing-room-only reporters. The first question was to Kesey, and he was off, galloping with words and thoughts and obscure references, and leaning forward into the questions — not sitting back in his chair — and playing the room, merging the artists and audience like the best musician magicians can do.

Allen Ginsberg, Anne Waldman,
William Burroughs, Ken Kesey

He and Burroughs and Allen and Babbs all chimed in on Jack being cutting edge *now*. And then as now, these assembled minds knew before the rest of us that we were at a turning point, that the decades-old disdain for Jack in bookstores and college curriculums and editorial pages was just beginning to change. Not long after this conference you would never again walk into a bookstore and *not* find *On The Road* — and often a whole shelf of others. Not long after this, Kerouac's words would be carved in marble monoliths in downtown Lowell. Not long after this, there would be whole stacks of biographies and lovers' memoirs and documentaries and dramatic movies.

It had taken two decades of the old-world establishment critics and professors to die off, but by the turn of the '80s, the smart people who came of age in Jack's published time were writing books and running publishing houses and heads of English departments from high schools to grad schools. This was the beginning of the wave that has grown larger with each passing year, and just like the first time, Allen saw it and drove it. And God bless 'im — as he riffed on ... "reminding everyone of Jack's tender heart, vulnerable heart, American heart, right heart, crazy heart, ACTIVE heart, talented heart, genius heart, angel heart."

And in this just-dawning light after a long dark night for His Jackness, Kesey waxed prophetic — "After I read *On The Road*, I thought I'd done it, and I knew this man. But then I checked and found this whole much bigger body of work there. As we move away from this period into the future, this man's life's work will stand, and I don't know that about any of the rest of us."

And Allen did something I'd hear him do a few times over the course of the conference — correcting people on how to pronounce "Duluoz" — the surname pseudonym Kerouac came up with as his nom de plume in the roman a clef series of novels he dubbed "The Duluoz Legend." As Allen would stress, "It's Du-lu-oz, like Ker-o-ac. The three syllable beat. Jack often named his characters with the same syllabic pattern as the real name. Raph-a-el Ur-so / Greg-or-y Cor-so; El-mer Has-sel / Her-bert Hun-cke," he said, his two hands in front of him chopping out the syllables into visual pieces so everybody could see it as well as hear it.

And Anne, Allen and Kesey did some wonderful three-part harmony on the power of friendship, each jumping in with different lines — "We're getting a community together here that existed then. A continuity of friendship, and that's important. Keeping the beat alive. It was Walt Whitman who asked for great friendships in America. That's what America needs is great friendships. And what we have here is old tender buddies, comrades, boyfriends, girlfriends, together, fellow artists that have known each other for decades and are *still* friends and exchanging new information."

And there was a series of questions about Jack the man, and who was he really, and is his character being whitewashed here, and finally Kesey put an end to it — "You judge a poet by his poetry, not how his shit smelled. Look at this interest here. That's what it always comes down to — (whispering) *What did he do when the doors were closed?* What the hell do we care what he did when the doors were closed when he's serving up such a dish. Let's get back to the dish."

And the ever-gorgeous, colorful and confident Anne Waldman chimed in, "You know, all of his faults and foibles are in his books. It's not like he was hiding anything about himself. And to these sexism charges, we've got whole panels of women here who knew him and were personally involved with him, and they're not critical of him that way, and in fact they all liked him and loved him very much."

And Kesey went to the big stuff: "There was a change that took place in the continuum of literature that the Beat writers had a tremendous influence on. It made me realize I had to move fast, or I'd be just a reflection left behind in a mirror. I had to act before I thought about it. Suddenly we began to deal with literature not in the way it ordinarily goes along that tells a story and works out a moral on that kind of template, but something in which there was a helping hand guiding us across the page and we were creating little things that would go off in people's head and complete a ritual of human endeavours that was going on, and Kerouac was the only one who was able to do it in extended fiction. There were a lot of burning poetic types, but to do it over such a long period that encompasses the whole vision, he was the only one who's done it."

And Allen talked about the purpose of the gathering: "I was always interested in Kerouac as a standard of mind, as a teacher. I was interested in the miracle of a writer so much put down as Kerouac to have a school of writing named after him. The Jack Kerouac School of Poetics."

I noticed Allen often dropped the "Disembodied" from the title when speaking to the press. It was funny — he'd go back and forth all conference, almost *alternating* that word in the title or not. I later learned he was never sure if he liked it. Sometimes he'd claim it was intended as a joke and he was just being playful; sometimes he'd say it was because they didn't have a physical school when it was founded; sometimes he'd say it was attention-getting and good marketing. But the part I liked best was that Allen Ginsberg would go back and forth agonizing over a word choice. *It wasn't just me!*

"I was interested in seeing the permanent transmission of his insights and his method of writing," he went on. "I was interested in this conference as a large scale exposition of that — transmitting Kerouac's particular spark to a large number of people and be able to change minds, and giving an opportunity for elders to teach a younger generation directly, with direct transmission, and transmitting that message out through their writing and the electronic media. And to give a chance for a lot of people who knew each other for many years and were very intelligent to get together and exchange information, and create new works of art on the spot. Robert Frank and other filmmakers are here capturing this process. So it is a recollection of the past, but also a chance to dig each other in the present, and to create works that will be usable in the future.

"The main message is — spontaneous mind. Or frankness. Public frankness as distinct from public manipulativeness, which you will find coming from other kinds of poets in the White House [Ronald Rayguns at the time] who are making up other kinds of words and other kinds of scripts that are calculated to manipulate people's minds rather than uncover people's minds. What we're trying to do is lay out once and for all in public what we think in private, so that we may end some of the hypocrisy that has led us to this Juggernaut Armageddon 200-billion-dollar-a-year military budget that could destroy us all. So, it's about the light of frankness, and the means for that is spontaneous mind, in art as in public."

And the always observant Anne added — "Kerouac presented an incredible range of possibilities. For instance he said look at your dreams, your dreams could be interesting, don't let them slip away, grasp them. And he'll give you some idea of how to record them. And to work with tape recording to capture the world and your characters. He did this long before anyone else ever did it. Look at *Visions of Cody* with actual recorded conversations. And some of his references and allusions will send you back to Shakespeare. There's very pure beautiful rhythmic passages that make language come alive in this very vital way and should be interesting to any writer who should be able to learn from that. There's a playfulness of language that follows the sound of the mind, trying to get close to how the mind works, how the thoughts come one on top of another, and the syntax and grammar of thinking, which you can actually display in a very beautiful way if you are mindful to the art. It's important for this work to not be in a closet but to be out in front of students and presented in a way that's alive."

I loved how Anne mentioned the practice of making audio recordings as one of Kerouac's legacies, and that Kesey and Hunter Thompson were doing it shortly thereafter, and the Grateful Dead and their fans after that — as I was looking at my cassette tape spinning in the deck on the coffee table right in front of her.

And ol' Allen was right there taking it furthur as always — "Jack's work was enthusiastic and expansive. But not without grounds. And the ground was: Fresh Mind. And that already sets a limit to the bullshit. Because you have to be clear in expressing the Fresh Mind and the Natural Mind. When you have that you don't have to worry about limiting yourself formally. And it's a source of optimism today — the tremendous spread of Fresh Mind poetry going out through electronic media, rock 'n' roll, from Dylan and The Beatles through The Clash and New Wave so that all the younger generations are sensitive to language."

And if you're wondering why I haven't quoted Burroughs it's only because he spoke in such an inaudible low volume mumble neither myself nor my tape deck a few feet from his horn could pick up a damn note he blew all day. Or all week. But I did stage manage a reading the next day with him, Holmes and Huncke, and the one vivid memory I have is being backstage on the stairs to the stage, and just behind his chair Bill had laid down his cane and hat, and I remember crouching there staring at this historic still-life. Wherever Grauerholz (his life partner and excellent estate executor) is going to build The Burroughs Museum, that hat and cane have to be the first thing behind glass when you walk through the door.

After the presser, **I captured Kesey saying something that changed my life in an important way**. Someone in the crowd who obviously looked up to him as almost a person who could do no wrong, said to him, "No regrets, eh Ken?" And Kesey's voice changed right away as he responded very earnestly and somberly. "Oh yeah, I've got a lot of regrets. A lot of things I'd have done *much* differently. For instance, my dad died of Lou Gehrig's disease, and I was in England messing around with the Druids for the solstice instead of being there for him when he died. But there's nothing you can do about it afterwards. Its just a bad guilty feeling. And I don't regret feeling regrets at all — it's how you learn and grow."

For me, hearing The Great Man, The Chief, The Supreme Prankster have his voice change and his cadence slowed by this lifelong regret, I vowed then and honored it to the end to be there for my parents when their time came, and I was. And I still thank Ken for that.

Another thing Kesey said that afternoon that always stayed with me — "The world is not run by us. We were never meant to be student body presidents. We're never going to be the most popular kid in class. We're never going to be part of the majority. We will always be a part of the minority. And there have always been hard working enlightened people like Ginsberg who will bust their butt for thousands of other people. Yet he's never going to be student body president. Real power is truth and mercy and the old verities, as Faulkner says. And every time we stray away from that we've got to wrench it back.

"Kerouac's power was that you could feel him sopping up the badness in all his books. All through his work, Kerouac never puts anybody down. You can only judge a writer by what they reveal in their writing. If there's going to be somebody who's the villain or is to be criticized it's always him. It's always — *he's* the dumb one.

He's the one who fucks up. *He's* the one who makes the mistake with the woman. You never find him blaming the woman or blaming the government or anything. What an effort of the will and the heart to do that for 30 years. No wonder he died of it. This is hard damn work.

"This is a yoga so o'er leaping any old fashioned Oriental yoga. This is the new world yoga of saying, **'I'm going to do the best I can and I'm gonna sop up the bad stuff and I'm going to make everything around me as good as I can all the time, and I don't care.' And the guy did it**. And there's nobody else I know of who's been able to perform that kind of thing. Everybody else wants to find somebody to blame. But Kerouac was a sponge who soaked up poisons. And they hurt when you do that, and you gotta do something for the pain.

"Fame is not the most comfortable thing in the world. *These* are not the most comfortable things," he said, waving his hand around the press conference room. "It's a very uncomfortable thing and you gotta drink or take dope to get through it. It's why the bane of American writing is alcohol. Look at Faulkner — he drank not to achieve enlightenment but because it's a way to make it through the poison you absorb.

"I think Kerouac qualifies as a Catholic saint. These Buddhists are after him with every hook you could imagine. But this is straight Catholic business: I'm going to soak up the poison and die of it. And that's what he did. And when some real pious students 200 years from now look over his effect and his literature, somebody will say, 'This man deserves to be sainted.'

"I was talking to John Barlow who writes lyrics for the Dead, and he's a big Kerouac fan, and he was comin' on about this and saying he was a saint. Barlow was raised by Jesuits, and he said, yeah, he qualifies as a saint, because he soaked up the poison and died of it. And somebody said you ought to be able to soak up the poison and transmute it, which is what I believe too, but Barlow says — 'Not if you're a saint. You soak it up and you can't transmute it, you die of it.' And you really feel that about Kerouac as you read his work. At the very end of *Vanity of Duluoz* you feel this tremendous *siiiigh* comes out of him. To be able to do this — what a wonderful thing. This is a hero. This is a thing above us, and he's there to help us, just like any angel. And we've got to trust our angels."

Photo by Allen

12

The Chautauqua Porch Scene

After this heavy hang, the Kesey Krewe and I retired to **the unofficial conference clubhouse** — the Lodge at the Chautauqua compound on the edge of town where most of the featured speakers were staying. It's a huge old tree-filled 40-acre encampment right at the foot of the face-slamming Flatirons, this steep cliffridge millions of years old rising up to form the backdrop of the city. This Chautauqua retreat started way back in the 1890s as an educational enclave with a spiritual/nature bent — so we fit right in.

There were a couple of old rambling two-story lodges with about 20 rooms each, then a whole meandering hamlet of funky little bungalow cabins that housed a few others, and a big central park that we used for the farewell picnic on the final day. Although the Kens were crashing back in town, this was the homebase on Baseline for Holmes, Corso, Huncke, McClure, Ferlinghetti, Creeley, Edie, Abbie, Amram, di Prima, Micheline, McNally, Carl Solomon, Ted Berrigan, Ray Bremser, Ann & Sam Charters, Tytell & Mellon and lots of others, but maybe most importantly Robert Frank, who filmed his *This Song For Jack* documentary almost entirely on the lodge's front porch.

It was actually two porches: the second directly above the ground floor one, accessible from a narrow hallway between the small spartan guest rooms upstairs. I remember looking out the second floor windows and thinking, "Man, I could hit those mountains with a Frisbee from here!"

The porches were only big enough for about four or five mismatching chairs that looked like they'd been dragged in off the street. On the downstairs porch there was also this wide balustrade you could sit on along the two L-shaped sides that weren't the stairs or the building. There were always about a half-dozen people out there at any given time in freewheeling shifts of improvised inspiration from dawn till dawn. As John Clellon Holmes described the scene later in his essay, *"Tender Hearts In Boulder,"* "We were improvising like after-hours musicians, without topics or agenda, taking our choruses, building towards a heart-lifting ensemble riff."

Allen had arranged for there to be tea and coffee and croissants and such — but I mostly remember cans of Coors. This was the off-site dressing room where the costumes came off and the players could play just for themselves. And play they did!

You couldn't see exactly who was on the porch from the street as you approached, and as our eyes crested the top of the stairs, there was Huncke, Jack Micheline and some girl I never saw before or since.

And Kesey, of course, being the ball of fire that ignites whatever sages he brushes up against, the moment his storm rolled in everything went Whoosh!

Big greetings and loud laughter. "Meet The Porch People!" Micheline announced with a waving gesture to the seated crew. These guys didn't really know each other ... but they did. There was this whole family vibe that was happening everywhere. Even if we didn't run in the same circles, we were all part of the same tribe. Jack's tribe. Spread out around the world, but united at the heart. And I was a young stray cub they were accepting into their wild pack. Here I was suddenly surrounded by Masters of The Art of Life who jammed the light fandango like exploding spiders across the stars and I was in awe!

Right away Babbs booms out, "Well, alright! We're *home* now!" and laughs and claps his loud hands together then pulls out a finger-sized joint. And we all get stoned. Or at least I sure did. Fresh sweet Western buds, yum-yum zoom-zoom.

It was funny — in this rustic campground setting, if you didn't know these guys, this whole crew coulda passed as just some animated buncha middle-aged fishing buddies. Huncke and Micheline wore regular button-down shirts, and the Kens were in their standard Oregon casual farmwear. Even Abbie Hoffman was just walkin around in a t-shirt and short hair. Between the bunch of them, these guys instigated an awful lot of lawlessness over the last 20 or 30 years, yet looked so totally passably *normal* compared to the abnormal lives they live, lived and inspired. Compared to the Boulder hippies that peopled this town, these guys looked like the cops!

I'd run out of blank tapes recording the press conference and post-yak, so I don't know exactly what happened next, but at some point I ended up next to Huncke, who was so tiny in his big wooden rickety Adirondack chair, he could almost turn in it sideways like a couch. He asked me why I was here and what I was doing in life, and I told him my whole vision of show production that grew out of the Acid Tests and then Bill Graham, and about the book I was writing based on my real adventures — and he was right into it.

And the whole time he has this jet-black hair and these dark deep-set eyes and this ... skull head — even in the middle of the day he looked like it was late at night

— but with these beaming watery puppy-dog eyes staring right into you with real genuine interest. I never got anything but a passionate curiosity and love of humanity, of human stories, from Herbert. And that must have been part of the common bond he had with Jack — an internal, innate desire to hear and empathize with other's stories, other's lives. He certainly did with mine.

And meanwhile on the other side of the porch Kesey and Babbs are loudly finishing each other's sentences while jamming and laughing with Micheline and the girl. Those two guys had perfected a telepathy like identical twins, or like a comedy duo who've been on the road for decades, constantly playing off each other, and you got the feeling they did it even if there was no one else there to hear it. And everybody was just so jazzed to be here they were talkin' a mile-a-minute and jamming with new players they hadn't played with before — or hadn't in years but fell right back into the wild groove they used to swing.

Then at some point Huncke excused himself, most formally — almost like a parody but it was absolutely earnest and heart-felt and "him." "Well, gentleman, I must apologize, but I have some matters I must attend to. If you will excuse me, I shall see you back here ... or somewhere else, I'm sure," he said, followed by his short but jovial smoker's hack of a laugh. He had such a funny way of talking and such a gentle regal royal manner — it was just the same as rich refined people I've spent time with. Polite in the extreme. And yet it's *this* guy who's always been broke and a hustler in more ways than one. In fact, he actually hustled up participants for Alfred Kinsey and his earthquaking reports on *Sexual Behavior* in the 1940s and '50s. The guy had a rap sheet as long as the pedigree lineage of royals he behaved exactly like, and yet they all could have blended graciously and famously, I'm sure.

And no sooner did he go inside than we heard voices in the dark foyer beyond, and before long out popped . . . John Clellon Holmes!

"Ken!!" he boomed!

Kesey leapt from his chair in a revelry of reverence I don't think I ever saw him show for anyone else before or since. I mean, Ken was the guy *Neal Cassady* called the "Chief." The guy *The Grateful Dead* looked to as *their* psychedelic leader. The only guy in attendance who had a movie made from not just one but *two* of his books — and the most recent *won Best Picture!* ... and Director & Screenplay & Actor & Actress .... The guy who has one book that's probably sold more copies than any writer at this summit's work *combined* ...

And who does *he* look up to?

"John! Good to see you!" exclaimed our beaming hero!

"You made it!" Holmes bounced right back, both of them glowing in joy at seeing the other in the flesh.

"Yeah — just drove here from Eu-gene, 40 hours straight. ... Well, not straight, but we made it," as the old teaheads of time laughed loudly — but then they would have laughed at just about anything in this first-meeting flush of giddy.

"Have you checked in with Allen yet?" John asked.

"Yeah, we just saw him over at the press conference and Buddhist conversion seminar," and everybody laughed again.

I never did ask how they knew each other, but they sure were old brother souls of the road.

You couldn't swing a peasant skirt in this town without hitting a poet — but long-form web-spinning novelists were a rarity in this multi-disciplined collective of crazy creatives. These two were born ten years apart, and had their first novels published ten years apart — *Go* in 1952 and *Cuckoo's Nest* in '62. Both had a love of characters (both real and imagined) who didn't fit into the straitjacket of society. And both were happily long married and had carved out a nice life for themselves in stable homes far from the city, but still enjoyed the occasional wild adventure in wilderness hideaways with like-minded spirits.

Oh, and speaking of spirits — drinks and herbs — they had that in common, too.

Babbs offered to fire one up, but Holmes begged off. "I've got to go do one of these bloody film interviews. Watch out for these guys — there's crews swarming all over this place," he warned Kesey. "You could end up answering questions every damn minute of the day."

"Oh, *we'll be invisible,* don't worry about us!" Kesey said, and the whole porch laughed!

And I suddenly starting thinking, "Oh geez, I bet he *does* make himself invisible when he wants to," as I remembered my ostensible job in this whole racket.

The Pranksterhood was kicking in. And who *knows*

where it's gonna go from here!

Especially since tonight The Grateful Dead were opening at Red Rocks Amphitheater!

13

Jack Manifested As Music

This was the Super Bowl of the Beats — and The Grateful Dead were playing the half-time show.

The Boys were doing three nights at the most gorgeous outdoor amphitheater in North America, and over the course of this succulent psychedelic triptych played every Jack-&-Neal road song in their repertoire. It was a beautiful thing.

I began to live this long before I fully understood it, but **The Grateful Dead were Jack manifested as music**.

It wasn't simply that City Lights had been the band's bookstore and North Beach their campus, or that they were working improvisational music the way Jack did spontaneous prose, or that they broke every rule of showbiz just as Jack did of publishing, or that they both celebrated the road and risk-taking and adventure in their song-stories, or that Neal Cassady fell in with the band and slept over at their house, or that they backed him up while he rapped on stage . . . it was that The Dead took the torch and kept *The Road* trip going and growing organically for some 30 years after Jack went and took that long backseat nap in the sky.

On hanging with Neal, Jerry Garcia said, "Cassady was such an overwhelming ... *trip!* He was <u>so</u> singular. For one thing, he was *the* best sight-gag / physical comedy person. He had an incredible mind. He would do this thing, he did it to everybody — where you might not see him for months, and he would pick up *exactly* where he left off the last time he saw you. Like, *in the middle of a sentence!* First of all, you'd go, 'What the hell?' And then you'd realize, 'Oh yeah, this is that story he was telling me last time!' It was so mind-boggling, you couldn't believe he was doing it.

"He was also the first person I met who he himself was the art. He was an artist, and he was also the art. And he was doing it consciously. He worked with the world. His face could go through millions of expressions and contortions, and his body language was *so* communicative. It was *amazing*. He was like a musician in a way. ... It was an art form that hasn't been discovered yet ... something between philosophy and art.

"Off and on he stayed in our attic when we were at 710 [Ashbury St.]. He had a little camp up there with a mattress and his old chinos, and he'd come in and live there for a week or so, every month or couple of months." And it wasn't just Neal Cassady they housed. Furthur on down The Road the band began to cover original Beat Herbert Huncke's rent at the Chelsea Hotel until the day he died.

And if sharing their home wasn't enough, and by golly it should be, they also shared their stage at one time or another with virtually every Beat figure — starting at one of their very first gigs, The Trips Festival, in January 1966, with Neal Cassady, Allen Ginsberg and Michael McClure — but perhaps most famously a year later at the January '67 **Human Be-In** at the Polo Field in Golden Gate Park where 20–30,000 people appeared out of the zeitgeist to hear Gary Snyder open the day with a conch shell blow, Allen close it with a chant, as well as read parts of an early version of *"Kansas City to Saint Louis,"* and McClure debut his *"The God I Worship Is A Lion"* while playing the autoharp Bob Dylan gave him.

In fact, it was in McClure's apartment in the Haight that he, Allen and Gary planned the poetry of the day — and it was another Haight heart Michael, Bowen, who was the Michael Lang of this proto-Woodstock.

The date (Saturday, January 14th) was chosen by the San Francisco spiritualist and astrologer Gavin Arthur ... who became friends with Neal Cassady in 1959 when he was teaching classes at San Quentin, and remained close with both Neal and Carolyn for the rest of their lives. He picked the date because it was the time on Earth when all the living were equal to all the dead. And it turned out to be a rare perfect warm sunny January day in San Francisco ... that was pretty transformative thanks to both the living and The Dead. ;-)

Lawrence Ferlinghetti was on the bill, and Lenore Kandel (Romana Swartz in Jack's *Big Sur*) read from her banned but popular *Love Book* as the Dead set up behind her and 20,000 people sang her *Happy Birthday*. Some sources say Lenore's boyfriend Lew Welch read as well; 23-year-old just-blooming Beat poet Andy Clausen came in from San Jose for it (and heard the just-released Buffalo Springfield anthem *For What It's Worth* for the first time on the way in); Owsley was there handing out acid — and as luck would have it, Timothy Leary was on stage telling everybody to tune in and turn on (an expression he'd just picked up from Marshall McLuhan). Quicksilver and the Airplane played, and then the Dead laid down a positively prototype psychedelic-rock performance as the main and final band (and were in fact joined by jazz great Charles Lloyd on flute and improvised vocals. And double in-fact — damned if they didn't go play *another show* that night at the Fillmore with another Jack-influenced band, The Doors!)

Legendary music critic and Dead appreciator Ralph J. Gleason was in the Polo Field that afternoon, and happened to bring Dizzy Gillespie with him. During the Dead's set, Dizz turned to Gleason and said, "Who *are* these guys?! They sure can swing!"

And it was when McClure was in that same apartment around the corner from 710 that he got together with Garcia and worked on turning one of his poems, "*Love Lion*," into a song.

As Jerry told Al Aronowitz: "After I read *On The Road*, I began to hear rumors that it was about real people. When I heard that," and Jerry broke into a grin, "I *had* to meet them." After first meeting a few North Beach imposters who were scamming their dinner off being "the real Dean Moriarty" he finally encountered the genuine article. Jerry went on: "It was Neal who taught Kerouac how to write. Jack was trying in very orthodox ways until Neal got him off of it. Jack learned from Neal's manuscripts. I've read them. He wrote like he talked. He could keep me spellbound for hours. Nobody could tell a story like Neal. He had the best timing. Someday his manuscripts'll all be published and recognized."

In fact, it was going "on the road" with the real Moriarty a few years later that caused Garcia to make the commitment to the band instead of painting. As he told Babbs the year before our Boulder Bash for he & Kesey's *Spit In The Ocean* special Neal issue, "Cassady did something that changed my life. It was after the Acid Test in Watts. I hit him up for a ride back to our house, and it was just me and him for some reason. He was mellow Neal, just a guy, just like us. But there was a mysterious thing there. I had a feeling that I was involved in a lesson.

"I was flashing on Neal as he was driving that he is one of these guys that has a solitary kind of existence, like the guy who built the Watts Towers, one person fulfilling a work. And I made a decision that night to be involved in something that wasn't a solitary pursuit. I was oscillating at the time. I'd originally been an art student and was wavering between one-man / one-work, or being involved in something that was dynamic and ongoing, and something in which you weren't the only contributing factor. That night I decided to go with what was dynamic and more than one mind was involved with. **The decision I came to in the car with Neal was to be involved in a group thing — and I'm still involved in it.**"

In fact, the very last question in the very last interview Garcia ever gave on camera (to the Silicon Valley Historical Association), was about Neal Cassady. "I got to be good friends with him. He was one of those guys that truly was a very *special* person. In my life, **psychedelics and Neal Cassady are almost equal in terms of influence on me**.

"Neal *was* his own art. He wasn't a *musician*, he was a 'Neal Cassady.' He was a set of one. And he was it. He was the whole thing — top, bottom, beginning, end, everything. And people knew it. And people would be drawn to it. He was an unbelievable human being— the energy that he had, and the vocabulary he had of gestures and expressions — oh boy he was funny. Phew! I really loved him." ... were the last words Jerry Garcia ever spoke on camera.

The Dead's main lyricist, **Robert Hunter**, who actually met Cassady before Kesey did at a communal house nicknamed "The Chateau" near Perry Lane, said of Cassady to *Relix* magazine, "He was flying circles above me. He used to visit me a lot. He paid me the compliment of saying that when he goes to New York, he visits Bill Burroughs and when he comes here, he hangs at my house.

"He was Mr. Natural for us. He would say things and, if you had him on tape and could listen back, you could hear replies you hadn't heard before — multifaceted replies. The man was phenomenal, a phenomenal brain. Yeah, he was a *wonderful* guy.

"It was hard *not* to be Neal after he was around. He was such a master of any social situation that you'd learn it yourself, and when he was away it would take weeks before you'd stop being Neal. This was true of all of us. He was such ... an original. He had such a dynamic life and it was just *packed*. He just enjoyed the *hell* out of it."

Of the music in Jack's writing, Hunter said — "That's bop!" And he later put his voice where his heart was and read Jack as part of both the *Kicks Joy Darkness* CD, and was the voice of Dr. Sax on the audio recording of Jack's play *Doctor Sax and The Great World Snake.*

John Barlow, the Dead's other lyricist, who wrote the words to *Cassidy* among many others and was hanging in the wings at the conference, called Neal "The Most Amazing Man I Ever Met" (capitalization his). Bassist Phil Lesh phrased it, "Neal was the closest thing to poetry in motion I've ever seen." Garcia called him "the 100% communicator" and "the powerhouse of the Acid Tests." And those were gatherings with a lot of power! Imagine an evening with Cassady, Ginsberg, Kesey, the Merry Pranksters, the Grateful Dead and a barrelful of Owsley's freshest!

In fact, at one of those early Tests, rhythm guitarist and band youngster Bob Weir discovered that Ginsberg "was pretty damn amazing, the stuff he would say and do. So I figured, okay, I'm gonna sit next to this guy, which was okay with him."

To *Garcia* biographer Blair Jackson, Weir said, "When I fell in with Ken Kesey and Neal Cassady, it seemed like home sweet home to me, to be tossed in with a bunch of crazies. There was some real serious crazy stuff going on . . . For one thing I had to abandon all my previous conceptions of space and time. ... I thought I was pretty well indoctrinated into the 'anything goes' way of life, but I found much more than anything goes with the Pranksters. There was a world of limitless possibilities. It was ... God, it's hard to say anything that doesn't sound clichéd, but it was really a whole new reality for this boy. We were dealing with stuff like telepathy on a daily basis.

"We picked up a lot from those guys. Particularly from Cassady. He was able to drive 50 miles-an-hour through downtown rush-hour traffic, **he could see around corners** — I don't know how to better describe it. And that's useful if you're playing improvisational music; you can build those skills to see around corners, 'cause there are plenty of corners that come up. We gleaned that kind of approach from Cassady. He was one of our teachers, as well as a playmate."

Another time Weir went even furthur — "We're all siblings, we're all underlings to this guy Neal Cassady. He had the guiding hand." Describing hanging with Neal, he said, "It was pretty free-form, but it was also — I hate to use the word cosmic, but I don't know how else to describe it. We were together in this big mind meld, and he would be having a conversation with what was going on in your head."

At their first show after hearing the news that Neal had died — Valentine's Day at the Carousel Ballroom in S.F. — Garcia made a special announcement, something he *never* did, and dedicated their set to Neal.

As Phil put it in his Grate book *Searching For The Sound*, "I truly believe we were channeling Neal that night. The music was such a living thing: growing and changing from bar to bar, with his turn-on-a-dime responsiveness to context and novelty. When we listened back to the show, it was spectacular — vivid, protean, and relentless." In fact, right away they realized the Neal-channeled series of songs that flowed out that night should be the sequence for their upcoming studio/live amalgam album "*Anthem Of The Sun*" released later that year. And that's what they did, and it included live tracks from this Neal show as part of it.

Phil devoted much ink in his memoir to this milestone moment in his life, including, "It hardly seemed credible that a life force like his, so generously endowed with the *rhythm* of motion through time, could be smothered and shut down at such an early age. ... Neal's death had hit me harder than I knew; I'd been obsessing on the loss of one of the most inspiring people I'd ever known personally. . . . **I vowed to myself that in the future I would live up to Neal's inspirational example**."

"His life is nowhere near over," Weir told *On The*

Road director Walter Salles decades after Neal's passing. "He lives in me and through me, especially when I'm on stage. He was more present than any human I've ever met. What I didn't learn I just osmoted from him. Living purely and completely in The Moment. What he saw in the present was an accumulation of all things past and future. 'Now' is all he was really involved with. That's what I've always drawn from when I'm playing — forget everything and just be there."

Kesey's and later Garcia's famous girlfriend, Mountain Girl, met Neal before she met any of the others and described him as someone who "ripped people out of their suburban homes" and "changed their minds totally, and from that day on they'd be different people. He had fantastic power over people, and it was all benign."

Phil Lesh wrote a score setting Allen Ginsberg's *"Howl"* to music. Diane di Prima wrote a poem when the band's founding member died — *"For Pigpen."* The Garcia interview book, *A Signpost to New Space* became a practical new-world how-to-live update on Jack's *Dharma Bums,* both books birthing out of Marin County. Their song *"Truckin'"* was a musical version of *On The Road.* And if ya wanna go furthur ... *"Wharf Rat"* was *Big Sur,* and

>"*Box of Rain*" was *Visions of Gerard.*
>"*Attics of My Life*" is of course Jack's *Book of Dreams,*
>"*Bird Song*" is clearly about *Tristessa,*
>"*Mexicali Blues*" is obviously *Mexico City Blues,*
>"*Dark Star*" was of course originally titled "*Doctor*

Star" and based on the very weird *Doctor Sax,*
"*Goin' Down The Road Feelin' Bad*" is the Dead's interpretation of *Satori In Paris,*
"*One More Saturday Night*" is nuthin but *The Subterraneans* non-stop party,
"*Standing On The Moon*" is clearly the pining ballad of *Maggie Cassidy,*
"*China Cat Sunflower*" is of course *Old Angel Midnight* set to music,
"*Big Railroad Blues*" is lifted right from *Book of Blues,*
"*So Many Roads*" was how *Visions of Cody* came to be written,
"*I Need A Miracle*" was Jack's plea by the time of *Pic,*
"*When Push Comes To Shove*" was where he was at by *Desolation Angels*
and of course "*And We Bid You Goodnight*" was Jack's show-ending *Vanity of Duluoz.*

And what would you say if I told you the most important poetry reading in Beat history was brought to you by the most important teacher in young Garcia's life?

It's true!

Wally Hedrick was the connecting rod. He was one of the six artists & poets who opened the Six Gallery on Fillmore Street in San Francisco in 1954. By the following summer, Hedrick had emerged as their event director, staging what years later would be known as "happenings" — poetry and music performances in the middle of an art gallery with a rainbow of participating creative people and altered consciousness. By the summer of '55 he asked a young on-the-scenester Allen Ginsberg if he wanted to put on a reading there. According to Wally — Allen said no. Then he finished "*Howl.*" Then he said yes.

On October 7th, 1955, with young Ginzy as the catalyst and publicist — hey, wait, is there a pattern here?! — Wally and The Six put on a "charming event" (as Allen called it) — "**Six Poets at Six Gallery**" which turned out to be the coming out party for the Beats. What the Human Be-In and London's International Poetry Incarnation were for the generation a decade later, this was the moment the participants all first realized there was a larger community of like-minded souls. These were The Big Three public events ... followed by Monterey Pop ... then Woodstock, the US Festival, Live Aid and so on ... but these were the first Magic Three mass moments that spawned a cultural / consciousness revolution.

M.C.ed by the unofficial poet laureate of San Francisco at the time, Kenneth Rexroth, it featured a 23-year-old Michael McClure in his very first poetry reading (who also writes about the evening extensively in his *Scratching The Beat Surface*); a couple of Philips, Whalen and Lamantia; a young nature lover named Gary Snyder raving on about "*A Berry Feast;*" and one Allen Ginsberg reading "*Howl*" in public for the first time. "It drew a line in the sand," as McClure put it, for confessional, honest, candid, sexual, rebellious Beat poetry, and which prompted attendee Lawrence Ferlinghetti to send Allen a telegram the next day — "I greet you at the beginning of a great career. When do I get the manuscript?" refraining Ralph Waldo Emerson's famous letter to Walt Whitman upon experiencing *Leaves Of Grass*.

Allen Ginsberg's postcard announcement

Kerouac himself was also present, but in the capacity of a "Go" yelling cheerleader and Go-for-wine running ringleader, gathering up change from "the rather stiff audience" and nipping out to score "three huge gallon jugs of California Burgundy and getting them all piffed," as he vividly described the evening in his great Northern California Adventure novel, *The Dharma Bums,* where he also mentions how a reserved Neal Cassady and his girlfriend-of-the-moment Natalie Jackson (one month before her death) were also present at this historic evening that's widely and rightly regarded as the public Birth of the Beat Generation.

And wouldn't you know it, but Doctor Wally who delivered this baby became an art teacher at the California School of Fine Arts where a couple years later a wayward young artist named Jerry Garcia would enroll in what he described as the only school he was proud of attending. Hedrick became not only his teacher but a guiding force in Garcia's discovery of the Bohemian arts, at one point telling the young rebel who was still without applause that he and his friends were the real Beat Generation.

The mighty Dennis McNally, who was speaking at the conference, wrote such a Grate biography of Jack and the world around him, *Desolate Angel*, that Jerry anointed him to write the official history of The Grateful Dead, which he eventually did, called *A Long Strange Trip*. In it he shares the detail of how Hedrick "sent Garcia over to City Lights Bookstore to pick up Jack Kerouac's *On The Road*, a book that changed his life forever. Kerouac's hymn to the world as an explorational odyssey, an adventure outside conventional boundaries, would serve as the blueprint for the rest of Garcia's life."

And it wasn't just City Lights, but the original first-of-its-kind flag-planting Psychedelic Shop (and unofficial community center) opened on Haight Street in January '66 (back when LSD was still legal), by a guy, Ron Thelin, who *On The Road* had directly inspired to go on the road and more, and he made it a point of not only selling the magazines, posters and pipes of the new generation of consciousness, but also an ample selection of books by the Beats and their extended psychic family to give the early explorers in the new frontier neighborhood a roadmap to inner space.

Then there was Jack's "'secret' skid row hotel" as he described S.F.'s Mars Hotel in *Big Sur* that the Dead would later immortalize as the title and cover of their 1974 studio album, and is seen (sadly) being demolished in *The Grateful Dead Movie*.

The way Garcia himself remembered his transformation — as captured in the liner notes for the 1990 Rhino re-release of Jack's three records put together by James Austin — "I recall in 1959 hanging out with a friend who had a Kerouac record, and I remember being impressed — I'd read his stuff, but I hadn't *heard* it, the cadences, the flow, the kind of endlessness of the prose, the way it just poured off the page. It was really stunning to me. His way of perceiving music — the way he wrote about music and America — and the road, the romance of the American highway, it struck me. It struck a primal chord. It felt familiar, something I wanted to join in. It wasn't a club, **it was a way of seeing. It became so much a part of me that it's hard to measure; I can't separate who I am now from what I got from Kerouac. I don't know if I would ever have had the courage or the vision to do something outside with my life — or even suspected the possibilities existed — if it weren't for Kerouac opening those doors.**"

Or there was the time later in life when Jerry was looking back and said, "I read *On The Road* and fell in love with it, the adventure, the romance of it, everything.

I owe a lot of who I am and what I've been and what I've done to the Beats from the fifties. I feel like I'm part of a continuous line of a certain thing in American culture, of a root ... I can't imagine myself without that — it's what's been great about the human race and gives you a sense of how great you might get, how far you can reach. And I think the rest of the guys in this band all share stuff like that. We all have those things, those pillars of greatness to lean on. If you're lucky, you find out about them, and if you're not lucky, you don't. And in this day and age in America, a lot of people aren't lucky, and they don't find out about these things."

Or there were the liner notes Robert Hunter wrote for the *One Fast Move Or I'm Gone* DVD where he said, "We have the scriptures of a butterfly dreaming he is a man dreaming himself a butterfly.

"Jack captured the guts of his own soul, if not the soul of our times, in torrential cloudbursts of exalted prose, egotistical letters, improbably immature journals — both drunken and sober — for all to see. And he did want us to see. Why? God knows ... but he did, and we have, and there you go. Maybe so that, despite all, we would love him. And we do. Case closed."

Another uncanny brotherly commonality between Jack & Jerry (besides both losing their fathers at a relatively young age) was how they both meticulously archived and preserved their own work. Whether due to an awareness of their own legacy or simply for practical creative purposes, you're hard pressed to find a writer who maintained better records or a band who recorded more performances. Jack regularly drew on his filing cabinets full of letters and notebooks to produce his next book, and the Dead would listen to how their alchemy sounded out in the room beyond the circle of players. And both these archives would also turn out to be invaluable both historically and financially as there were vaults of material that could be drawn on in the years after their passing.

Starting even before Jack died and continuing for decades afterwards, no single creative entity in America caused more people to go "on the road" than did The Grateful Dead. I called them "**The World's Largest Travel Agency**" because of how they got so many people to go so many places they'd never been before — physically as well as psychically. Where Cassady expanded the Road trip from a Hudson to a school bus — the Dead turned the bus into a *Space*-ship.

And speaking of traveling, their legendary tour manager, Sam Cutler, who guided the Good Ship Grateful Dead on all their road trips during their formative traveling years in the early '70s, was a huge Jack fan long before he met the band. As he attests in his book *You Can't Always Get What You Want* and in person, "A friend of mine named Brian [of course!] had this book called *On The Road*, and he just banged on and on about this bloody book until finally I took it home, smoked a joint, and read it, and it was an absolute revelation and had a fundamental effect on me. It's the only book in my life that I read once, then went back to the beginning and read again, then read it a third time. After that I knew I was a 'Beat,' or I set out to become a Beat, guided by the book.

"It made me realize I wasn't particularly 'sinning' here — that other people had the same experience with jazz, sex, dope, and hope. I loved it with an unbridled enthusiasm. It touched a bone, if you will. I was 15 in 1958 when it had first come out in England, and it made me want to not just leave England, it made me want to drive into Mexico City, walk in the Pacific Ocean, travel all over America and find people like the magical Dean Moriarty. And it made me an incurable romantic, which I've been ever since."

Or their drummer Bill Kreutzmann described in his book *Deal* how he'd read *On The Road* even before he'd met the rest of the band, and how "It became influential to me in the same way that certain music was influential. It was jazz, on the page. ... it was a boarding pass out of Palo Alto and into destinations unknown — my life's great adventure. ... that there was something greater out there, and even if it didn't appear within my reach, I could grab ahold of it anyway, just by believing it was possible. That's really important. Because after that, I started reaching for it. And sure enough, I was able to grab ahold."

Or as their first co-manager Rock Scully sketched the band's North Beach birth in his memoir *Living with The Dead*: "The hungry i, Vesuvio's, and City Lights were our shrines. Kerouac, Kesey, Corso, Burroughs and Ginsberg were our holy madmen. We idolized the Beats ... Jerry was 15 when *On The Road* came out, and it became his bible ...." Or as Weir revealed their roots in a 1966 interview, one of the band names they were considering before they landed on Grateful Dead was Reality Sandwich (!) — the title of Allen's popular City Lights book that had been circulating in the Haight during those years.

In fact, one of the band's earliest partners in Prankstering, Hugh Romney, had been a practicing Beat poet and M.C. at The Gaslight next door to the Kettle of Fish in Greenwich Village, before he formed the Hog Farm and changed his name to Wavy Gravy.

In his epic remembrance of Cassady, *"The Day After Superman Died,"* Kesey described the Fastestmanalive as "Lenny Bruce, Jonathan Winters and Lord Buckley all together for starters." And funnily enough, Garcia also became an apostle of the official unofficial Beat comedian, Lord Buckley, that hip-semantic finger-poppin' language slinger from Flip City, Daddyo. As Jerry told the world's leading Buckley authority Oliver Trager for his definitive biography *Dig Infinity!*, "His work was part of the whole bopster deal — the whole Beat thing. It was the other side of the Neal Cassady/Jack Kerouac reality.

"Lord Buckley and Grateful Dead philosophy merge in a certain irony of viewpoint. It's not literal, it's indirect. The other guys in the band knew about him. Pigpen used to do whole Lord Buckley routines. Phil was really into him as well. I saw him perform someplace in North Beach when I was about 16 or 17. It was hilariously funny. He used language like a musician uses notes. It's all part of the same thing. At that time, I was starting to discover the richness and whole experience of American music: black music, white music, country music, city music. So, for me, seeing Lord Buckley was just throwing another set of doors open. I wish I could make music with him. Oh God, I'd leap at it."

Like Jerry heard the music in Lord Buckley, to these ears the Dead were the music of Jack's writing. There could be lulls and less-than-polished passages, but they were always leading explosions of unequalled color and light and joy and life. And like Jack's books, the Dead's performances were not formulaic, conventional, predictable or repetitious, and their songs celebrated the lives and aspirations of the American Everyman, the workingman — like one of their definitive albums, *Workingman's Dead*. They both painted American Beauty, lived on the American Road, sang songs of The Road like Whitman before them, and spawned a trip that more adventurers jumped on than any other in history. Jack may have written the book, but the Dead extended his vision into a functioning Road lifestyle that is still thriving to this day.

Every member of the band were proud flag-waving Beats who were keeping the beat in a whole new way. Just as Jack took a novel approach to novel construction, the band did the same with song structure. Just as Jack wanted "to be considered a jazz poet blowing a long blues in an afternoon jam session on Sunday," the Dead were stretching their lines into Spaces unheard in music save for the best of Jack's beloved Be-Bop.

And to that end, to that proof, *they* were the ones funding this Jack Kerouac Conference, not his publishers (who certainly knew what year it was cuz they just put out a

25th Anniversary Edition of *On The Road*!), not his widow, not Bob Dylan, City Lights, or Columbia University, but it was this rock 'n' roll band that had so internalized, so valued Jack's contribution that they put their money where their heart was and funded it and scheduled their shows at Red Rocks to coincide with it. In fact, they'd also given a bunch of tickets to the conference for people involved to go to the shows, and of course I was the first one on it and snagged a pair so I could take brother Cliff who I was staying with to his first show.

14

Hiding Out In A Rock 'n' Roll Band

And so it is I'm holding two tickets to The Promised Land in my hand as my Canadian connection drives up in his long black Rat Pack Cadillac — and we head to the show early, cuz that's whacha do. This easygoing friend from early childhood and I were having our first bona fide

American Adventure after years of training in the wilds of Western Canada. We'd pulled off many a cottage caper, house shaker, boiler maker and were now Certified Risk Takers — fearless and unstoppable at getting into or out of anything we wanted.

About two miles from the venue we came to a backup of cars — they weren't letting anyone near the site without tickets, all stemming from the infamous Red Rocks Riot at Jethro Tull in 1971 when hordes of ticketless bunglers in the jungle showed up and stormed the gates. The cops used tear gas to disperse them, but the wind blew the smoke into the audience bowl then onto the stage and it was an historic hacking eye-watering disaster. So they never had rock concerts there again for years. And they're *still* nervous about it.

So, we're waiting in this slow-moving ticket-check line out on the mid-mountain highway, flashing the secret-handshake 3½ fingered salute to passers by, when this happy hippie comes dancing along and says, "Hey-Now!

(head bop, head bop) It looks like you guys got a big trunk. Mind if I hide in it to get through this line?"

"No, sure man, go ahead," says good natured Cowboy Cliff at the wheel. Of course he's got his crazy tailgate party bar-b-que and gawdknows whatall in the giant black boot, but the hippie's just happy to hop in. (What was that about a one-legged hitchhiker?)

And we doo-dah through the ticket-check, and slowly weave in the snail trail up the winding mountain road to Shangri-Jerry and find the parking lot and get our first glimpse of the traveling circus in action and Cliffy's eyes are Christmas morning saucers!

Eventually we crawl through the ragged clowns and sounds to a good spot under the Rocky skies. We pack up our pockets with whatever we're gonna need and leave the rest and roll up the windows and batten down the nest and make sure the doors are locked and head off into the colorful noisy endless party. And then, "Oh yeah, shit, whatsisnoodle's in the trunk!" as we break out laughing, and head back and open it up and the guy's just *covered* from bandana to sandals in the grey ashes of the tipped over bar-b-que!

"Alright!!" he beams at the first trunk-opening light! "Thanks for the ride!!"

"Hey man, you got, like, *bar-b-que dust* all over you."

"Oh, that's okay, man. I'm cool. (head bop, head bop) Thanks for the lift!" And he hops out and dance-walks away like Pigpen from *Peanuts* leaving swirls of scuffling smoky dust.

And man — what a scene! A Grateful Dead party on top of a gorgeous red rock mountain with a natural amphitheater carved right into it! And the colors immediately start kicking in — 10,000 tie-dyes, maybe more, tripping through nature's brilliant rock masterpiece to nature's brilliant rock band under a brilliant multi-hued sky at a giant family reunion. *Everyone's* infectiously smiling, and hugs are free n flowing.

There's girls in short shorts and bikini tops, and guys in short shorts and no tops. There's colorful clown costumes complete with jester bell caps, and straight looking doctors and lawyers and such with close-cropped hair, ironed alligator shirts and expensive watches ... coming to their 100th show. There's people walking around with giant backpacks like they just came down from the Himalayas, and unencumbered wide-eyed Coloradans at their first show, meandering in mouth-opened silence.

Moveable feasts surround every car, van, customized truck and psychedelic school bus — every one with a different state's license plate — and you can just walk right up and start talking to anyone who looks interesting. "Strangers stopping strangers just to shake their hand..."

Veterans could talk to veterans — but someone at their first show was absolutely golden and had an All Access Pass to everything. Deadheads really make a fuss over show virgins — anyone who has the interest and the courage to make the trip is immediately embraced. It can appear to the uninitiated as a most intimidating world that's functioning on a very evolved party level — and if you haven't been through the arc of a night even once, well, help's on the way.

Which reminds me of a beautiful moment from the Dead's Rainforest Benefit at Madison Square Garden — the ninth of a nine show run when they broke the Garden record for most sell-outs at the world's most famous arena by anything other than a sports team. All sorts of special guests joined them that night — Mick Taylor, Baba Olatunji, Jack Casady, Bruce Hornsby (who later became a member of the band for about a year and a half!), Hall & Oates (?!), and ... The Muppets via satellite!! And at one point Suzanne Vega came out, this petite fragile sensitive singer who I was hanging with on the bar stools at Folk City in the early '80s daze when we were all regulars there and before she became famous. So this now well-known tiny delicate flower walks out onto this giant dark and Deadly stage in this roaring arena full of the only unbroken chain of raging concert goers since the sixties, thinking, "We aren't in Folk City anymore!" But the beautiful part was — with this petrified little bird at center stage and all the spotlights on her, Jerry walks from his normal spot in the shadows by his amps to the front and center line and stands right beside her and looks to her and plays to her and smiles to her ... and carries the whole room with him. He gave her his 100% attention, and by so doing, he brought this whole crazy rock 'n' roll audience along — and graciously handed them to her. It was the most touching generous beautiful thing.

And that's the spirit we show everyone, especially the most fragile among us.

And then on a whole other level — there's countless tourheads strolling the scene holding up gorgeous hand-dyed / hand-lived t-shirts for sale, who quickly flipped them around so you can see the back as well. Asking 15, but they'll take 10. Some are printed with classic all-purpose Dead lines — "The bus came by and I got on" — and others are customized just for these shows with "Dead on the Rocks" or "Mountain Dew" along with the dates.

In between unicyclists and bike riders and girls twirling hula hoops are people hawking bumper-stickers like "𝕲𝖗𝖆𝖙𝖊 𝖙𝖍𝖎𝖓𝖌𝖘 𝖍𝖆𝖕𝖕𝖊𝖓 𝖙𝖔 𝕲𝖔𝖔𝖉 𝖕𝖊𝖔𝖕𝖑𝖊" and "Who are The Grateful Dead and why do they keep following me?" or buttons with the original family motto "The Good ol' Grateful Dead" which was first winked between the knowing as early as 1966, or carrying bags of gooey-gum-balls (basically, round pot brownies), or there's a long-haired girl in a long-flowing summer dress with tinkling ankle bracelets passively carrying a small rack of homemade jewelry as she silently and blissfully wanders the rows of cars in the spiritual belief someone will just walk up and buy one. And someone does.

And there's the didgeridoo guys blowing their long horns like strange animals in the wild. And every parking lot row has at least one impromptu band of acoustic guitars with maybe a harmonica and a couple drummers on different size djembes, and if they're hittin' the groove there's a loose crowd around them dancing or swaying or singing or talking or all all at once. And at the end of a row some guys are spread out in a circle kicking a small beanbag in the air that they tell me is this new thing called a "hacky sack."

And then there's all the little storefronts, usually in front of an open-doored van, with music playing and people swaying and dancing in the street and others in chairs out front selling anything and everything — a full line of tie-dyed clothing including kidswear and socks and underwear, or a million different kinds of pipes, or bracelets, or fruit cups, or Jäger shots, or Jello shots, or Gregory shots, or any kind of stir-fry or veggie burritos for a dollar or two from fully functioning kitchens, or cold beer from a rainbow of coolers in rainbows of colors wherever you look — the clothes, the cars, the tents, the flags, the spinning wheel prisms twirling like a kaleidoscope you can walk in . . .

Breaking News !! We interrupt this reverie with an important parenthetical here —

I'd gone to my first Dead show only two summers earlier — a whole other long adventure story — but the following morning, my 19th birthday in fact, when my girlfriend Sue & I and our extended Canadian crew came-to in an inexpensive motel near the Seattle venue and went to breakfast at the next-door Denny's — the place was *full* of Deadheads! We knew nothing of the huge family and traveling scene that goes On The Road with this band, and it blew our minds — that all these people seemed to be *friends* and at a party that never ended and was still going on. And on. And on.

As fate would have it, when we were hanging in the parking lot after breakfast, this jolly older bushy-haired bearded bear came up and started talking to me, his face giggling and his belly jiggling to see our "Friendly Manitoba" license plate and the innocent good vibes we were putting off. After some joyous mutual morning beaming, the guy says, "Is this your van?" And I says, "Yeah," and he says, "Let's step inside for a minute," and as he says this, jolly-jiggling away, he pulls from the left breast pocket of his jacket a huge *baggie ... full* of cocaine, and shakes it in front of my face like a sacred Tibetan bell as his eyebrows pop up and he giggles some more.

While my friends were off playin' in the Frisbee band, me and this guy and his petite and pretty "old lady" step into my Dodge '67 window van named Bessie and he breaks out lines the size of your finger. And of course we get to talking, and he takes a real shine to me, and tells me he's an acid distributor. Not an acid *dealer*. He's the sole connection to the chemist where it all comes from. And he wonders if I'd wanna be his Canadian franchise!

Next thing ya know we're outside his luxury sedan exchanging addresses, and he's so jazzed it's my first show, and knowing the importance of that more than I ever could at the time, he fishes around inside the car and pulls out his own Master Recording of the first set of last night's show ... and gives it to me!!

Still treasure it to this day, of course.

Then he reaches back through the open window and pulls out a fat paperback book and starts flipping the pages until ... all of them turn into little patterned squares ... and I realize this is a whole *book* of acid! He tears off a strip and hands it to me as a sample.

When he finally drives off to the next show after strongly suggesting multiple times that we all, "Come to *Spo-kaaane, maaaan!*"

I'm thinking, "How good is this acid gonna be that some guy's just giving away in a parking lot?!" So we all gobble it thinking nothing's gonna happen, and Holy Bazanga! 24 rainbow hours later we're flippin out over the sunrise from the balcony of some mansion in Seattle with eyes flying like saucers!

'Course, I didn't end up opening an acid outlet, but I did move to Manhattan a couple months later, where this golden connection known as Brother Tom and I soulfully rebonded and became Roadsters For Life.

The Mighty Brother Tom

So — as Cliffy and I are walking through the Red Rock garden of delights, I'm keepin' an eye out for ol' B.T. — and firing up that clear instinctual internal telepathic magic radar of Deadland — and of course Ping! We naturally appear right in front of each other! HA! "I didn't know *youuuuu* were gonna be heeeere!!" he giggles like Buddha — and weir all blotto blotter set.

Then Cliff and I walk into the venue for the first

time and — POW! You GET IT right away, right in the face! This is *God's* amphitheater! — not by the hand of man was this carved into a mountaintop.

On either side of a wide perfectly-graded audience bowl are giant wind-carved red rock monoliths that form a natural audience and acoustic frame, with the back wide open so the sound just goes forever. Everyone from The Beatles and Jimi Hendrix to symphonies and operas have played here, and everyone from Indian tribes to Easter parishioners have prayed in this sacred place first known as "The Garden of The Angels." It's awe-inspiring in the most literal sense — whenever you first walk into it, you're humbled that something like this exists on the same planet as you. Giant natural sandstone sculptures surround you and are moving in waves even without psychedelics! Spirits of the ages overwhelm you — a remindful wave washes over you that there's forces bigger than us. The Colorado Rocky Mountain sky is the stained glass, and the stage is the altar in this Cathedral of Music. And the choir was fixin' to sing!

And sing the psalms of Jack they did — this entire show dedicated to our Spirit Father without directly saying so — pulling out every road song and stringing them together like an adventure novel. They opened with a blasting *"Jack Straw"* ... "keep on rollin' just a mile to go ..." train-hoppin' across the country. "Catch the Detroit Lightning out of Santa Fe; The Great Northern out of Cheyenne from sea to shining sea ..." we "Gotta go to Tulsa, first train we can ride ..." and everyone chanting the grown-up mantra, "We used to play for silver, now we play for life ..."

After years of the band living this — in fact, ever since the Acid Tests in '65 — right away the audience and the band synch up and become a single performance ensemble — the collective connection locks in and everybody in the space knows it and works it. The veteran musicians can feel it on that big stage just as they could in a small California ballroom. The audience is following and reflecting every solo every crescendo every diminuendo. And the music is new. No one including themselves knew what they were gonna play. Every version of every song is one time only. You can't step in the same river twice.

And before you know it weir *"On The Road Again"* something they only ever played electric a handful of times, and the uber rarity spark ricochets off the Rocks and the hootenanny dancing kicks up a step.

Then Bobby drops a *"Me & My Uncle* went ridin' down, South *Colorado*, West Texas bound," being on the road with hustlers and rustlers before there were cars, and that apropos Cassadyan "I'm as honest as a Denver man can be," as the audience roars and yes yes yes everything's comin' around. Directly into Johnny Jack's *"Big Sur"* — I mean Johnny Cash's *"Big River"* — yet another road song, but this one on America's first interstate, the mythical mystical mighty Mississippi.

And they close the first set with a freakin' sparkling ... *"China – Rider"!* — Yeah. First set. And from the opening notes every ear on the mountain knows this whole suite's building to Jerry's mighty, belting, hoarsed-voice refrain:

> "I wish I was a headlight
> on a northbound train,
> I'd shine my light through
> *the cool Colorado rain.*"

But first the *"China Cat Sunflower"* blooms the room away ... the high-range dancing riff winding through a playful open forest of glistening discovery — a funk-crazy bass thrumming below the Alice-in-Wonderland dancing above. And the tempo escalating — the punch, the highs, the breathlessness, the loss of self, everyone dancing in unrehearsed choreography in a troupe of thousands as the peaks lift everyone off the ground in unison — musicians and audience alike, all Howling in collective joy as the rapids splash the rim and we almost tip, but holding on and riding it, everyone paddling frantically, crazily, for life-and-death, as the rocks roll away the dew and the whitewater breaks into diamond-eyed Jacks at a double-E waterfall all over our back.

And of course ol' Cliffy's noodle's exploding — this bein' his first show n all! — and the fresh acid's taken him off like a soaring balloon, copping some altitude while losing some attitude, surrounded by calliopes of rainbows, as The Boys are on their best behavior cuz Uncle Ken and all his beatnik buddies are in the house, in fact including Carolyn Cassady as I later learned, and we're already half-way up the mountain to heaven playing to Cowboy Neal as he's parking cars lickety-split just inside the Pearly Gates, pointing proudly to his embroidered nametag —

Neal Cassady - Heaven's Valet

After the first set we somehow stagger lee back to poncho-wearing Brother Tom who's giggling away like a joyous little kid in his perpetual utopia due I imagine in no small part to knowing he's supplied the majority of the psychedelics that the audience is tripping on. And he still can't believe he's seeing me in the middle of the continent in the middle of the tour. "You gotta come back to the hotel, *maaaaan!*" he says in his happy extended California drawl and pops his big fuzzy eyebrows in the promise of more adventure ahead.

A wonderful thing about summer outdoor shows is the first set is played during the last hours of daylight, and the second set opens to a setting sun like it's a whole other venue, with a slowly growing dome of darkness as stage lights gradually get noticed and the weirdness of the night takes over. And this place is weirder than anywhere with the orange setting sunlight illuminating the already red rocks and making them blaze like fire. And then these soft atmosphere lights come on them so you're never unaware of the towering monoliths, like dancing at the foot of the pyramids, another sacred stony place the Dead traveled to to make magic with the spirits of eternity.

And sure enough, Jack and Neal are Playin' In The Band tonight, and they've brought their jazz with them, as Bobby starts inexplicably scat singing to Garcia's guitar lines, the only time he ever did this in 30 years of gigs, as the jam into "*Space*" takes on a distinct Bebop feel, into a "*Drums*" that had the whole mountainside playing along — and, "Holy shit! There's that guy from the conference!" As some cat I'd seen around the scene was invited to take over Mickey's kit and was calling out a vocal beat while he drove the beast.

> Out of drums and into space,
> they take The Wheel and steal your face.
>
> "Small wheel turn by the fire and rod,
> Big wheel turn by the grace of God,
> Every time that wheel turn round —
> *Bound to cover just a little more ground!*"
>
> BOOM! and the place explodes!

Suddenly the conference and the show are melting together as Ginzy and Kesey are channeling The Road, and Anne Waldman's twirling in front of me, and Abbie Hoffman is *everywhere!*

And of course this being the historic Jack & The Roadstock, The Big One, or at least The Other One, before you know it, Bobby's singing,

> "Coming, coming, coming around,
> Coming around, in a circle."

Yaaassss, of course it is!

> "Escapin' through the lily fields, I came across an empty space,
> It trembled and exploded, left a bus stop in its place,
> **The bus came by and I got on, that's when it all began,**
> ***There was Cowboy Neal at the wheel*** **of the bus to never-ever land."**

I don't know what percentage of the audience knew about the conference, but at that moment it felt like everybody — the mountaintop earthquaking and the audience rumbling as loud as the stage. With a bunch of the conference heavyweights standing in the wings who knew Neal before the Dead did, The Boys were doin' it right for their elders. They had to, and did, lay down the ultimate musical Jack & Neal tribute to the assembled writers who'd already painted the most famous portraits of their fallen catalyst Cassady. And the whole show was just cracklin' snappy and popped!

And like Jack and his love of America, they encored

with a patriotic flag-wavin' dance number,

"I'm Uncle Sam, that's who I am,
Been hidin' out in a rock 'n' roll band ...

Wave that flaaaaaag,
wave it wiiiide and high,"

... as this Canadian was doing in the Land of Free, *on the road*, climbing that mountain, looking for God to show me his face. And I think I saw Him there at Red Rocks for a minute! But I was definitely seeing Jack's, as he carefully folded the flag the last time he and Neal were together — and it was Kesey the catalyst on the stage tonight who united them for that one final summit. Every time that wheel turn round ...

And by the time Garcia brought down the final guitar neck cue to his crew, ol' Cliffy's just a wide-eyed beaming puddle of joy! And of course, little does he know, **the night's nowhere near over.**

Thusly, we commence to wobble a wander among the glowing apostles of ecstasy long before there was a pill named for it, and naturally find big bear Brother Tom, and scoop directions to the hotel but know we're gonna take our time cuz first-timer Cliff absolutely must fully experience the post-show hug-n-whoop, to which he's most blissfully obliging. In fact, by the time ol' Jerry finally joined Jack in the big city lights in the sky, I'd taken 36 different people (that I know of) to their first Dead show. And there was nary a one who didn't come back for more.

Linger inside for as long as possible, then it's off to the parking lot scene where tapes of the show just ended or from last night or last week are blaring from crystallized customized sound-systems through giant speakers on a car roof or propped in a trunk. Like waiters in a bar, industrious roadsters are working the crowd with coolers on wheels, "Cold beers, two bucks," as smoke's sizzling off grills making every kind of post-show food you could desire in the real city that never sleeps.

A cluster of wild twirling peasant skirts are circling a crisp *Scarlet Begonias*, then a few spongy paces up the road some drumming comes across the sonar, hmmm, yes, as we weave toward the sound, and there's the bouncing dreadlocks and shirtless backs of drummers in a Beat circle, Mickey and the Hart Beats, the Rhythm Devils in flickering *Apocalypse* candlelight joyously pounding out the jungle rumble in the darkness, keeping the demons at bay by dancing the blues away.

Evocative of everything, take your trip, all the world's a stage, surrounded by players, if you're here you're in on it, you're On The Bus, everyone goofing, everyone curious, everyone open and grooving on the Beat and rhyming in the poetry, surrounded by sounds of a party that's never stopped swinging since The Beatles played shows, passing the pipe to each year's new crop, people coming and going, searching and knowing, in a self-made, self-played, self-sustaining world of peace, love and music.

And after a long carousal around the large carousel, we remember there's still a hotel party waiting for us, so we gradually begin to weave our way back to the Rat Pack Cadillac, and suddenly have to — micro-focus on the melting blue ink handwritten directions . . . and dancing light dials on the dashboard . . . collectively knowing this was gonna take two to drive to make it alive. "Easy Does It" as the bumper-sticker on my first hitchhiked car instructed.

The trick to these acid driving tests is — you've gotta *both* be focused on the job at hand at all times, *talking* about the drive, how it's going, what we're seeing on the road in front of us. Silence is Deadly. Can't drift off into acid dreams. Stay on it. Stay engaged, stay focused, lock in on the wheels rolling through space, call out the real world unfolding in front of you, talk your way through every moment and motion . . .

And wop-bop-a-loo-bop before you know it we've beaten the mountain mists and unexpected twists and are at the very electric lights of the schmancy Granada Royale, with one of those palm-tree-filled glass-topped atriums going all the way up to the sky. And as we pull in, suddenly ol' Cliffy's like, "You know what? I have to work tomorrow. I gotta go." The poor bastard — he thought he was just going to a concert tonight. Oh well, he learned. And of course he's been a dancing bear ever since.

So, there I was, with no direction home, stepping into the eye of the late night atrium on a Tuesday in July with said acid ears hearing everything in echoing loops and whoops of laughter and Jerry's guitar singing from a dozen rooms, the sounds bouncing around on a most molecular level, all weaving in and out with the waves. And as far as I could see — there was no staff at all. Just sounds. Special, swirling, sacred, psychedelic *sounds*.

Up to Brother Tom's sweet suite, and it's *a scene*. In fact, the whole mad hotel is a *scene*. Turns out of course the band is staying there as well, and it's all the high rollers and trustafarians in Deadsville circa 1982. There's mounds of blow on the table, multiple rolled up bills, cigar size joints of fresh Humboldt County floating around constantly, roaches stubbed out with more pot in them than I roll in a joint, Tom's crystal clear tape of tonight's second set playing on this kick-ass little system he travels with, and all these people from all over, and everybody's talking, and everybody's tripping and seeing right into each other, and it's a beautiful thing.

Howloween — after the Grateful Dead's closing night
at Radio City Music Hall.
Photo by Brother Tom in his Gramercy Park Hotel
suite ... proudly wearing my Phil Lesh button.
And the crazy thing is —
the whole reason I asked Tom to take the picture
was not because the historic Dead shows had just
concluded — but because I'd just found my first
bottle of Canadian beer in a deli since moving to
New York!
See, also: that same (steal your) face at 1:29 during
the Not Fade Away in their movie of this night
Dead Ahead.

And I'm talking to these gorgeous flowing glowing flower-bedecked girls, and then some diamond-sharp dudes who didn't even have long hair, and at some point I turn around and ... there's Phil Lesh! I dunno what my face did but he made a funny face back, and I was just whoa way too high to talk to him. He hung for a while then at some point was gone, and I'm thinking, *man*, there must be parties *all over* this place! So I go out to the railing overlooking the giant atrium and wave to other people across the space doing the same thing up and down twenty floors, and I'm not even gonna tell you what happened next, cuz frankly ... who knows!?! But I woke up on Tom's oh so cushy couch sometime the next day.

And the first thing ya know old Tom's a millionaire. I mean, everything's taken care of, and weir all going to the show again that night! I checked in with Camp Buddha back in Boulder and told them I was hiding out in a rock 'n' roll band — which didn't go over so well seein' as I was scheduled to stage manage a show that afternoon! But I assured them I'd be back tomorrow to work the "Kesey & Babbs Present Cassady" show. Doing field research, you understand.

The next thing I remember we're in Tom's big fancy car which he'd already trashed like Neal's new Hudson, and we were in that line on the highway where they're checking for tickets, and there were the same ticketless Deadhead Roadsters working the line for a miracle extra, and Brother Tom, and why he *is* Brother Tom, always bought extra tickets. And he's always talkin' and carrying on a funny monologue that we can jump in on or not, but the whole time he's eyeing the Deadheads on the side of the road, and whenever he'd see one he recognized or liked the vibes of he'd call him or her over to the slow moving car and just miracle them. He musta given away a half-dozen on this one roadway, giving back to the family, as he constantly talked about "the magic of The Boys," and in fact, at the end of the conference, Kesey signed my *Cuckoo's Nest*, "The boys can produce the spirit!"

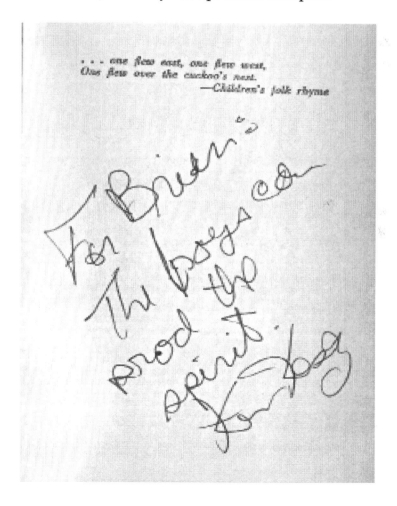

And then it was on to the show and the usual circus of fireworks, calliopes and clowns, and everybody's dancing from the *Shakedown* opener to the *Sugar Mag* closer, come rain or shine, it don't change. And even though this night was not as overtly Deadicated to the Writer of The Road — there was a *He's Gone* into *Truckin'* — their hymn to a missing member into their musical *On The Road* — and suddenly it hit me — **it was The Grateful Dead that led me to that book and Jack in the first place!**

Reading articles about or interviews with them, I kept seeing references to this book by some weird-named guy I'd never heard of. Coming across it once or twice, it might not have stuck, but after seeing it three or four times, including his face in the back of every issue of *Rolling Stone* during those years that ran a classified ad for t-shirts with Jack's classic picture that was also used for the conference posters — and it became — *"I've got to find this book!"*

The first time I ever held a copy was the same summer I first saw the Dead — 1980. A friend's older sister in Vancouver had it, and I had *Fear and Loathing in Las Vegas,* and she'd never read that — so we traded — the one and only time I ever let go one sacred text for another in my life. And it became just the first of many copies. Still have her original of course. But from that sequence of synchronicity, I was forever on this most wondrous Road.

Classified A

The Beats and The Pranksters —
Carolyn Cassady and Ken Babbs
Partying in Boulder

15

Cassady Comes Alive

After the duet of days in a daze of debauchery I somehow made it to **Base-Camp Kerouac** — back from the Dead, but just barely — lookin' like old bar-b-que-ash Pigpen in a cloud of smoke and debris falling off me like an old car rattling out of a bomb blast, and suddenly everyone there looked so *straight* and put together — shirts with buttons on, guys with short combed hair, girls wearing bras ... what a weird scene!

It was clearly up to me to keep the smoke machine filling the stage — and thank Jack I had some allies! Back in the day, our fearless heroes used a little of the magic muggles to soothe the savage beast, with Neal & Jack being some of the only white weed smokers west of Mezz Mezzrow. And although Gregory and Burroughs and others may have employed a different kind of high to cure their blues, it was really the sacred herbs that kept our playboys playful.

Field General Babbs in action

And gawd bless 'em, the Kens were traveling with a garbage bag fulla the stuff in their trunk. A fistful here, a fistful there, and everybody was just alright. We got together for a little pre-production meeting and I could see how Babbs was the Field General in Kesey's Army — the guy dispatching marching orders and putting the troops in motion with his big drill sergeant Oregon drawl and bass drum laugh.

This was the very first time they ever staged their **"Kesey & Babbs Presents Cassady"** show. They'd been jamming for a while on how to best present their old pal Cassady, as they knew him, to the world. Jack did it with words, but they wanted to go "beyond the novel" as Kesey described the bus trip and his life post *Sometimes A Great Notion*. They had film, still images, audio tapes, transcribed raps and a variety of personal Prankster memories that they blended into one giant frenetic collage of the Fastestmanalive. And I was running the projector.

The year before, Babbs had put together "The Cassady Issue" as part of Kesey's small press series *Spit In The Ocean*. He read from that as part of the show, telling how he stumbled across Cassady's famous juggling hammer on Kesey's farm and how that prompted him to reflect on their missing troupe member. They gathered reminiscences from everyone they could think of who knew Cassady, and Babbs read from them as a way of evoking his spirit, including a tribute by John Clellon Holmes who was sitting in the front row.

They also worked in the idea of Cassady's soul going on trial, judged in some cosmic court with different people testifying for and against him, which actually ended up being released some years later as a book called *The Further Inquiry*. For the trial part of the show fellow founding Prankster George Walker came out and laid down his truth, and Babbs read a piece by Prankster Jane Burton who was also in attendance making it fully 1/3 of the original dozen who actually rode the psychedelic bus into history in 1964 with Cowboy Neal at the wheel.

Kesey read his tribute "The Day After Superman Died" in the middle of the show, but the real Neal deal was the opening and closing segments when they (well, I) ran the film footage of him with different audio tapes accompanying, and Kesey & Babbs riffing an improvised conversation along with the talking Cassady as though we were all at a wild noisy party together.

And what a party it was! — the ballroom was literally Standing Room Only with not only all 1,200 seats filled but people lined two and three deep along every inch of wall space and all hooting and laughing and clapping all night. During the staging downtime as Kesey was solo reading "Superman," I looked around the room and it suddenly hit me — *"I'm running the projector at 'Kesey & Babbs Present Cassady'!"* . . . after reading *Electric Kool-Aid Acid Test* a million miles ago in my bedroom in Winnipeg and thinking these were just about the coolest guys ever — "Man, I wish I was there" — and it seemed so far away and never possible. But it wasn't and it was.

Not only was I seeing moving images of Neal Cassady for the first time — *I was the one making them move!* And ... Kesey & Babbs know who I am! And they

seem to like me! I mean ... *was I really here at all?*
Somehow I'd managed to escape that small prairie town a
hundred miles from the nearest gas station, north of North
Dakota, and was now not only orbiting but *functioning* in
Kesey & the Pranksters' world. It *was* possible.

And the show went off without a hitch, planned
chaos and all. For one wild night in this Festival of Jack,
Neal was most definitely present and accounted for.

Paul Krassner, who was sort of becoming the
unofficial guest moderator of the conference, came out to
guide the post-show Q&A, and the very first question was
to Kesey who cleared up something I'd always wondered
— who was the Lars Dolf character in "Superman" based
on? He's the guy in the story who has a showdown with
Cassady ... and beats him! The leading rumors were always
Alan Watts or Philip Whalen. Turns out it was neither, but
rather some guy I've never heard of – Phil Wilson. But at
least we had that cleared up.

There were also questions about The Three Stooges
(Kesey: "I see their influence everywhere I look."), Tom
Wolfe's book ("It was the best thing he ever wrote. It's
hard to make brass out of gold."), meeting Kerouac in New
York on the bus trip ("Jack was in the background most all
the time, and chose to be there, so he really chose to not
make much of an impression. By the time we got there
we were cranking at such a rate and talking a hundred
miles an hour that Kerouac just didn't want to play."), and
people coming to his farm to see The Bus ("Oh yeah, a lot
of people come to see it. After Lennon's death we had a
real rush of people. 'Oh, okay, it's still there.'")

You'd think I'd'a done the afterparty to the max, but I was so bagged after two all-nighters skippin' the light fandango, I only did the pre-afterparty post-show breakdown hang.

And Kesey and them rural Oregonians are so funny. They drink G&Ts, with limes of course — but out of clear vacuum-sealable preserve jars! They can have 'em anywhere, and toss 'em in a bag when they're on the move. And in stark contrast to most of the other speakers and participants, with the possible exception of Gregory, these guys were a raucous party wherever they went. As the Intrepid Traveler would remind us at just the right moments: "Confucius say, 'Man who drinks too much thinks too little.' Babbs say, 'Man who thinks too much drinks too little.'"

Original Prankster Jane Burton was hanging out after the show. Her Prankster name was Generally Famished, but she must have gotten over that because she was Definitely Skinny and looked like a yoga instructor or something. She was quiet back then and quiet now, but she'd done the whole '64 trip from Kesey's place in La Honda through Texas and New Orleans and up to New York for the World's Fair, where she took a break from Prankstering for a while, but here she was now, still *on the bus*, still coming out of the woods and into the mountains to rejoin her eternally bonded family.

After drinking in the liquid scene, I had to hit the sea for Cliff Island. It had been many days On The Road and I was gonna make it home tonight.

It's late on a Thursday night and **I'm hitchhiking on the side of the road** leaving the college town and heading for the big city. Cars are screaming past — "Can they even *see* me?"

Some drunks lean out a window and swear at me, and I can see headlights swerving all over three lines of the road in a free-for-all dash to Denver. I actually write in the dark desolation of my notebook, "I wonder if the papers tomorrow will read 'Hit & run victim found near Baseline entrance.'"

The next car comin' up the ramp is a taxi, but I stick out my thumb anyway and give him my best shot even though taxis never stop. But it kinda slows down as it passed me, then it slows down some more and stopps! Then the back door swings open! I run up quick like a scared rabbit on the side of the road — and gawdamn if it isn't a New York Checker! Suddenly I leapt from the pitch-black mountain night of sure death by the roadside into this huge lit-up backseat of a Checker cab with a pretty woman holding a freshly lit joint between her long-nailed fingers!

Turns out she and the driver are friends, and they're both from New York! The guy's got a whole cabbie's routine down, with a Brooklyn accent and a working class cap and New York wisecracks and cursing at the other drivers. And she was a workin girl heading to town for a job, happy and upBeat as her get-up. And suddenly we were three New Yorkers smoking a joint and giggling down the highway at great speeds in a sea of green in our yellow submarine.

Every one of us was all we need.

16

The Beat of The Rolling Stones

A couple things happened the next day that caused quite a buzz around Camp Kerouac. The first was **the New York Times article came out**. There'd been a guy there covering it all week, and a big point of having the conference was to get favorable press for Jack and start to turn around the public perception that he was a passé irrelevant juvenile drunk. Like anyone emotionally involved in putting on any show, everybody on staff was really on edge about the newspaper reviews — and there were decidedly mixed reviews about this decidedly mixed review.

On the one hand, it got huge play in the Friday *Times*, probably the biggest article on Jack that paper ran since he died, but it also mentioned him being a drunk and quoted that crotchety old woman Capote again and didn't focus enough on Jack's writings. There were a bunch of people freaking out about it — like a little mini tornado blowing through town — but being a New Yorker I thought it was a pretty normal story from my hometown paper and certainly didn't see it as something to get all upset about. But people did.

One press thing that was going unabashedly well was the interviews most of the headliners were doing with Len Barron for the local hugely popular public radio station KGNU. This guy was sort of the Bob Fass of Boulder and basically turned his entire daily show over to the conference for about two weeks, interviewing Allen, Carolyn, Holmes, Ferlinghetti, Diane di Prima, Krassner, Ray Bremser, a whole whack of 'em. And unlike a lot of the straight-world press, this guy was spending every non-working hour over at Camp Crazy soaking up the sounds and souls — so he knew of what he asked. We may not have had all the press in the world on our side, but we certainly had some. And it was a start.

And one other parenthetical that was going on the whole time was this renegade street poets alternative programing.

There were people who could somehow make it to Boulder but not have the final $5 to get into an event who created their own art outside the venues and in the streets all during the conference, including Kush, and the Denver Union of Street Poets. It was a whole second de facto street conference going on in parallel with the official one. They'd set up right outside the doors of featured events in this passionate poetry reading protest and counterpoint scene that seeded the fields for crops to come. And both the Naropa producers and the paying customers didn't seem to mind the whole rebel sideshow addition one bit.

The second big thing that day was **Robert Frank screening *Cocksucker Blues***, which again, like *Pull My Daisy*, could only happen because the filmmaker was present to screen it. Of course the movie was legend in the rock 'n' roll world — the backstage footage of the bacchanalia of the Rolling Stones' '72 tour. In the '70s, about the coolest thing a rock fan could own was a vinyl bootleg of something not officially released. *Nobody* could claim having even <u>seen</u> *Cocksucker Blues*.

After Frank completed the film and showed it to the band, they knew it could never be seen by anyone ever or they'd all go to jail or at least be banned for life from the U.S. and just about everywhere else. A court injunction was ultimately reached that mandated the film could only be screened a limited number of times, and only at art / film festivals, and only with the filmmaker present. So, this being 1982, ya gotta figure, with the years of post-production and legal tie-ups, this was one of the very first times it was ever projected on a screen in public.

As if I hadn't already collected enough Adventure Cards on this trip! – I could now sashay into my future being able to describe seeing the holy grail jelly roll of banned rock 'n' roll films.

And boy, you could see why! Roadies having sex with groupies on the plane; various people scoring, cooking and shooting heroin; the unhinged violence committed by their security while on the first tour since Altamont. It was disturbing even to a 21 year old who'd been in the rock world for years and lived in Manhattan during some of its lawless heyday. It was certainly a cinéma vérité of the Stones on tour, as they gave this filmmaker unrestricted access, allowing him to make this movie and also shoot the photos for their then current album *Exile On Main Street* — after having seen *Pull My Daisy* and Robert's book *The Americans* with Jack's passionate introduction. It's not a big leap to figure Kerouac's lensman would never have been offered the gig in Junkieland if he didn't already have the cred of being a first-generation eye.

The sad/crazy thing is — you could easily cut the sex n drug scenes, keep all the candid behind-the-scenes rehearsals and pre-show, show, and post-show footage and have a great almost G-rated documentary of the tour.

Wonderfully, there's this one particularly priceless scene that's right out of *On The Road* —

The bandmembers decide to drive to the next scheduled city in the South just to get a feel for the road and the land and the people rather than more airports and airplanes — so they go *On The Road.*

And it's a testament to their regard for Robert that he's riding in the car with just Mick, Bianca and Mick Taylor. And somehow he's running his old-world rat-a-tat camera in this cramped space, capturing, just like Jack, the adventure of the road, the laughs about things just past, and the plans and hopes for what lies ahead. And they stop at some roadside negro dive with a pool room in the back, and besides this being a Kerouacian capture of unscripted authentic backroads America, it's also a classic Prankster maneuver in that the biggest rock 'n' roll band in the world is hidin' out and shootin' pool and the breeze with these small town local black guys who don't seem to know or care who they are. The whole thing sure makes you wish Robert had been in the Hudson with Jack & Neal & LuAnne & Al!

17

Lifelessons From McClure

After the screening ended, it was still early and light and nice out and I bumped into **Michael McClure and we went for a walk**. And I just happened to have my trusty cassette deck with me. He and I had bonded earlier over Marshall McLuhan and nature and music and a passion for action. He seemed like the poet-activist wing of the Beat Party — that poetry was more than composing and reading, but *living*, and this jibed with my affinity for Abbie and Cassady and Kesey and Lennon and such.

Right away we started jamming on the difference between poetry as performance versus reading at home alone from a book.

"When a person reads poetry quietly on the page it's essentially received with one part of the brain," he tells me. "When it's experienced aurally, it also registers in the pitch region of the brain, like music, so it's a more complex experience. The listener becomes more engaged and understands more, feels more, takes more away. The more parts of your brain and body you use, the more you become engaged. Consequently, poems that might seem esoteric or difficult to understand become luminous when read aloud. Like Shakespeare. Hearing it is a vastly different experience. That's not to diminish reading on the page, which for me is a very beautiful experience — I believe in the page as much as I do in performing. But hearing a poem is a more complex and richer experience ... if it's a fine poem."

So I asked him about poems versus songs, and he said, "I don't really think in those distinctions. That's something that's difficult for people to grasp today. We go back to the mid-'50s or mid-'60s before rock 'n' roll had been commercialized to sell beer and t-shirts, when the serious artists were all part of the same community, whether they were musicians or poets or dancers or painters, we all knew each other, we were exchanging ideas, and mediums, and learning from one another.

"One of the great learning experiences was the

dances at the Fillmore and the Avalon, where you're dancing to great bands with light shows. And there were drugs deepening your consciousness. But you didn't even need drugs when that many things were happening to your consciousness at once — you're taking it to an extreme level, yet it's not a level of stress, it's a level of beauty. That has a deepening effect."

The guy seemed so in The Zone, I asked, "Do you think you're at a peak of your powers now? Do you, do we, keep getting better?"

"I've always felt like I was at the peak of my powers. So I feel that way now, sure. In the '60s and '70s I gave enormous numbers of poetry readings, but most of my life on the stage was in my plays which were being done all over. Some of them were considered quite scandalous — there were lawsuits, the actors and actresses were being thrown in jail at the same time I was getting theater awards. I like being political in the Chomskyan sense, the anarchist sense, not Democrats versus Republican shit, but I like going out for the politics of the spirit, and doing environmental poetry for young people. And they understand it.

"It's funny, sometimes you're performing to 25 people, and then other times like at the Human Be-In or some other large public event there's tens of thousands. In a way it doesn't matter. If you're reading in places where people have curiosity and intelligence and want to know what's new and happening, you're facing a lot of people.

"And then sometimes you go to a place where even the guy who booked you doesn't know who you are. There are places in the country where they've never heard of you, and they don't want to hear of you. And then there's other places where it's open arms, and, 'Can you do two shows?' It keeps getting better all the time. The audiences for my readings keep getting bigger. But really it doesn't matter the size of the audience, it's how engaged they are."

So I asked him what he saw as signs of optimism in the world today, and he laid on me an early version of a riff I'd hear him play many times in various interviews and documentaries over the following decades —

"These two young guys came up to me the other day and looked me right in the eye, proudly, with self-assurance in their own bodies, with their painted mohawk and their hair to their shoulders, and earrings, and tattoos, and wearing individualized clothes, and they believe in peace, and they understand that they're being propagandized by the government, and they're into the environment, and they say, right to you, 'Whatever happened to what you guys were doing in the Beats?' And I want to laugh. I want to hand them a mirror, and say, 'Take a look at yourself. Are you wearing a grey flannel suit? Do you have a crew-cut? You're calling me by my first name. I'm not wearing a uniform and you're not saluting me. You're not living in a tract home. There isn't a draft. And you're asking me what we did, and where what we did went? You're it.'"

"Great big picture answer!" I blurt out, and he laughed.

I'd heard him talking somewhere about "writing blindly," so I asked him about that.

"What I'm talking about is writing with the process of knowing through not knowing, like a blindness, and doing it deliberately. You have to get to that state and then write back. It's almost like writing a string quartet it becomes so complex."

"Do those moments come when you say alright, 'Tonight I'm going to go home and go blind and write'?"

"No," he says. "I do it many times a day. When I'm practicing my exercises, for instance. Or maybe just sitting in the afternoon, lying on a floor, I look for that state. I want to leave the room. Fuck the stereotype that goes with the personality that's been foisted on me, how do I let this whole thing go, and just be the blackness that's behind my own eyes. How do I let myself get there? How do I quit seeing things the way I've been domesticated into seeing? How do I let them just be?"

"So, you *do* write some poetry that way, and then edit it, sometimes in that mindset, sometimes not?"

"Some poems are completely spontaneous and have hardly been changed. I'm not necessarily *trying* to write spontaneous poetry, I am trying to **be a poet-athlete**, in other words, to keep myself in the condition that an athlete must keep himself in to perform what he or she does. And if I'm in shape, many of the poems will come out pure, clean, spontaneously. On the other hand, I can be in great shape and they don't (he laughs) and I have to work on them for months. But it's always been this way."

"But have you always been in this kind of shape, as you say?"

"Well, I am in especially good shape. I've had bad

times, too. There were many years of doing cocaine, which was not what I'd call empowering."

"Well, speaking of lines — what's the line that Jimi & Janis and Jack & Neal crossed that you didn't? You obviously got close to it and somehow saw it and walked back from it?"

"That's a real good question. But I crossed that line about as many times as they did, so there's a certain amount of luck involved. We were all living *on* that line."

I countered, "But even if some of those people would have had the luck to survive the early years, I mean, Belushi wouldn't've straightened out, Jack wouldn't have straightened out. They crossed over some line and were just gone."

"Okay, **let's just talk about different drugs for a minute**. Alcohol — is probably the most dangerous — alcohol and tobacco. Alcoholics don't quit drinking until they hit bottom. I had a higher bottom than some of those people. I hit bottom before Jack did."

"Well, what are some of the signs to look out for — how far do you think you can you go that it's still okay?" I ask in a world that spotlights William Burroughs and Hunter Thompson and Charles Bukowski.

"With drugs in general, there are quite a few people who shouldn't even experiment with them. And they usually know who they are themselves. There are many people who are simply too physiologically, and maybe also psychologically, sensitive to do so. Some of the most brilliant people I know have *never* taken drugs, and never should.

"And the other thing about drugs is they give new portholes to experience but if you continue taking them the porthole doesn't change. You *think* you're seeing more, or you think its more ominous, or less ominous, or more macabre, or more beautiful, but you don't need to take a psychedelic or any drug over and over and over. You only need to take it once. You don't *need* to take it at all, but if you want to take it for the experience, you don't need to habituate yourself. Drugs *are* deluding, and you fall into collusions with your friends who think you're going to triumph over time and space because you're dropping acid every day or something. It has quite surprising delusions. But I don't know how to warn anybody against such a thing."

I confessed, "I haven't been around long enough to have a friend turn into a Kerouac alcoholic or something. And I don't know at what point we're supposed to step in and say, 'Hey, brother ...,' ya know?"

"Most of my friends who've died of drugs have died of heroin. I have many very fine, strong, powerful, luminous, intelligent *dead* friends, who were extremely addictive physiologically and couldn't shake it once they had it."

"So, now you're getting high by exercising?"

"I don't even think about getting high anymore. I feel good. I guess I feel high all the time. And nature — walking in nature. My interest has always been in deepening and broadening myself, and I think that's the same for most of the people at this conference."

I looked around at the beautiful nature we were

surrounded by, so I asked him, "What makes the mountains such a spiritual place do you think?"

"Bishop Leadbeater, who was one of the founders of Theosophy along with Annie Besant, wrote a beautiful book which was a description of the ecology of spirits as you walk up a mountain and how it changes from Earth spirits, to treeline fairies, to pure spirit beings, to light as consciousness, to finally at the top of the mountain translucent angels holding one another in an immortal kiss. It's inherent in us to see the profundity of these high places, irregardless of our culture.

"And also, many times on mountains there's **waterfalls**, and quickly running water," he continued. "Like, if you go up here in the Rocky Mountain National Forest, the snow melt, the water running down to the waterfalls is *unbelievable* — there's so much snow up there that all year round these raging creeks and rivers *pour* from the melting snow. And of course this movement of water is giving off negative ions, which makes you very high, if you've ever stood by them."

"I stand by them whenever I can!" I gulped. "But didn't know why I liked it so much."

"One of the reasons you'll notice that people always hang around fountains in cities is because it sounds good, of course — running water makes a sound which is quite beautiful, like music — but also the flowing of water creates negative ions which feed our nervous system because we're living in such polluted landscapes. It's wild. Go stand by a fountain if you're ever depressed. Or by a mountain river, so much the better."

"Right on," I say. "I gotta go find some running water!"

"Yeah! Well, right down there," he points to the Boulder Creek we're walking by. "You can just sit by that brook and you'll get cheered up enormously. That's where I go and write — down there."

So that's what I did.

18

School's Out

Being Friday night heading into the final weekend, there was a definite end-of-school party vibe. And just like high school, somebody was throwing a big house party. I guess their parents were out of town.

It was in some quiet normal tree-filled middle-class residential neighborhood, and by the time I got there late in a car full of production loogans, we had to park about a block away, but you could hear the party as soon as you climbed out of the car. I think the house was actually owned by one of the teachers at Naropa, or a benefactor or something, but either way we seemed to have the run of the hood.

As we walked through the front yard and around the back, the first thing I came across was this big sloop of guys swaying in chairs in a little alcove harbor belting at the top of their lungs ... *a Canadian sea shanty!* Never saw them again, so I never did find out how the hell they knew Stan Rogers' transportive *"Barrett's Privateers"* — but suddenly I was sailing into the party behind a big gust of homegrown Canadian crazy right here in the middle of the Colorado Rockies!

In fact, music was blaring all night — but none of it from a stereo. Acoustic guitars, congas, small horns, there mighta been a mandolin in there, and out in the middle of the back yard, a pretty blond was playing violin on Desolation Row, with Ken Kesey quietly blowing harp beside her.

The house was fancy with stained wood moulding around the doorways and archways, kinda old-world rich, and lovingly cared for, but inhabited by a busy, messy, decidedly PBS, Beatles, Woodstock family. Lotta books.

And all the usual suspects were there — Allen, Peter, Anne, Gregory, Babbs, Micheline, Clausen, Carl Solomon, Ray Bremser, Diane, I think the Charters mighta been there ... and Arthur & Kit Knight who were looking decidedly straight and uncomfortable in the loud raucous scene with joints being passed around like juicy rumors every two minutes. I think the next time I looked they were gone.

Just like the day I arrived and the production crew immediately retired to the nearest bar, this party scene was indicative of the celebratory nature of just about everyone here. Although the official events were far from reserved, there was definitely an attempt by suit-wearing Allen to bring an air of respectability to the bawdy Beat aura. And credit to ol' Pops, he pretty much pulled it off, and largely when attendees and participants were at events they were pretty well behaved. Except for Puck, of course. But once it was nighttime and the righttime away from any stage or microphone — with none of the film crews around — everybody really got their Howl on.

Gregory was loud and always seemed to be disagreeing with someone. Loudly. Anne was colorful and flamboyant, and always flipping a long flowing scarf over her shoulder. Ray, lookin' gray, sat in the same chair all night chain-smoking cigarettes down to their filters. Carl Solomon was the insecure kid in school hoping someone would talk to him, but whenever I'd try he'd respond with something that didn't even seem to make sense, and I was way too insecure myself to ask, "What the heck does that even mean?"

Diane always had this beatific blissful smile on her face, with super long thick hair, she looked way more hippie than Beat — our Mountain Girl — and was definitely a matron at the madhouse, quietly talking Tarot cards in the corner, or loudly taking on Gregory in the middle of the room.

And good ol' Jack, the Micheline man, had enlisted the drummers and other players on the back porch to back him up as he riffed his rhythmic poetry from memory. Or maybe he was making it up on the spot. But that guy really took the "beat" in Beat to heart. He was a living tenor saxophone. Huge sound. And he delivered bebop solos with a punk rock edge.

Everywhere was a song and a celebration. And one thing I noticed was the way everyone was talking to each other — you couldn't tell if they'd known one another for decades or just met. Everyone was animated and open-faced and you were free to join in any conversation if you could keep up. Nuclear power and the arms race were huge subjects. I'd just stage managed the big Disarmament Rally in Winnipeg back on June 12th when simultaneous protests were held all over the world, including one million people showing up in Central Park, and many were pretty sure we were on the precipice of disaster. This nut-job Ray-guns was in the White House, escalating the arms race like a crazed madman right outta the movies even though Russia was collapsing and nobody'd seen Brezhnev in months. He appointed this insane loose canon Alexander Haig as *Secretary of State* fer chrissake, and was talking about reinstituting the draft. Mother Reagan over in England, Margaret Thatcher, had just gone to war over some tiny little Falkland Islands. The world had become unhinged ... and dangerous. And on top of all the warmongering, Three Mile Island had just melted down a couple of years ago, and now they'd opened a new one of these monstrosities at Platteville, not far from where we were standing. And this was in addition to all the reports of the also nearby Rocky Flats nuclear weapon facility covering up their plutonium contamination of the water and land. Which was coming on the heels of *The Atomic Cafe* movie that had just been released about the U.S. government's historical and hysterical safe nukes propaganda. So ... there was a lot to talk about besides Jack and the Beatstock.

At one point I found myself next to some cool bearded middle-aged Naropa teacher dude, and I mentioned the funny contrast between the suit-&-tie straightness of the afternoon events and where we were now standing in the middle of this freak frat party. The guy told me how it was Trungpa Rinpoche who'd gotten Allen to start looking and acting the part of the respectable poet if that was how he wanted to be seen. He was definitely no longer the flopping on the floor Allen from *Pull My Daisy* or walking around naked at his own party like John Lennon & George Harrison famously met him in London in 1965. And even tonight when the freak flags were flyin', ol' Allen was just as composed and in command as he was directing chaos backstage.

It made me think — I'd seen him every day since this started, but had never again laid eyes on Rinpoche since his mumbling opening night salute. I asked the prof about these two and how they ever came together, and he told me Allen and his dad Louis, and Trungpa and his assistant, were both trying to get the same cab in New York one afternoon in 1970.

"They met *over a cab?!*" I exclaimed. "What a fluke!"

"Or . . . perhaps not," said the Buddhist teacher.

19

Historic Meetings

Saturday was the last full day of workshops and lectures, so I stopped in at production headquarters at Naropa on Pearl Street to get my marching orders.

I was front-of-house managing the 2PM panel on the "Impact and Influence of Kerouac on American Literature," so I had to get the final attendee numbers and see if there were any last-minute changes and grab some flyers to advertise the evening show, then get to the room to make sure all the doors were open and everything was cool with the seats and all that — but when I walked into the Naropa office there was this weird scene going down where some guy was rather emphatically arguing with a couple staffers that he should be allowed to speak at the conference.

It was in such stark contrast to the grooving copacetic vibe all week — this New Yorker (I could tell from his accent and aggression) quasi-yelling how he knew more about Jack and the Beats than anybody on the panels and there was some big conspiracy to keep him off. I listened for a minute while somebody tried to explain to him they'd have to get the okay from Allen or Jane, but it didn't seem to be satisfying the guy, so I just sorta slipped on past the wacky voodoo before I got sucked into its vortex.

In the production office, I checked on my numbers and for any other daily production news or needs or updates and there was a bit of a party atmosphere, this being the last full day and we'd pulled off nine in row basically without a hitch. I'd seen this room go from a cleaned-up unpopulated unused virgin office pre-conference to what now looked like the morning after a New Year's Eve party — there was stuff everywhere — the walls plastered with flyers and notes, abandoned coats flopped over chairs, stacks of empty pizza boxes, various piles of backpacks and duffle bags and luggage of stray people in transit — and the phones were ringing and people were buzzing around like flies — so I just got my attendee numbers and no-news-is-good-news and to be honest I didn't wanna hang around there a lot because there was a never-ending flow of stuff to do that I didn't want to get stuck with and we had a bunch of student volunteers and things seemed well in hand so I split to get over to the school to prep the room, and just as I got to the stairs back down to the street, The Angry Scholar was leaving right at the same time.

He'd seen me in the room listening to the argument, and as we made eye contact walking down the creaky stairs he just picked it right up like I could make a difference. "I gave Kerouac the best press he ever got," the guy said.

And I was thinking, "No way! This is Gilbert Millstein?!" That made sense — New Yorker, scholar, knew lots about Kerouac. So I asked him, all excited, "What's your name?"

"Al Aronowitz," he said, sticking out his hand.

I knew I knew that . . . — wait a minute! — *"The guy who introduced Dylan to The Beatles?!"*

"Yeah, I did that, too," he said. "Hotel Delmonico, 1964. It was a blast," and he laughed a little for the first time.

As we hit we the street, he had a butt lit before the door swung closed behind us. Here was this hugely historic figure — but he looked like any middle-aged balding Jewish guy in New York that you'd walk right past a hundred times and never think anything of. And he talked with a slight lisp of some sort — just didn't seem like the catalytic ambassadorial type.

And another weird thing I noticed: all these mover-&-shaker guys around here carried an over-the-shoulder bag full of gawd-knows-what wherever they went. But Al's was one of those CIA-looking silver aluminum streamline briefcases with a combination lock like tour mangers carried. Whereas Allen's was all bright and colory and floppy, and farmer Kesey's was like a saddlebag, Al looked like he was up to some serious no good. Found out years later he was dealing in the devil's candy at the time — but here was this guy walkin' around the middle of hippie-town with a thousand dollar briefcase wearing ten dollars worth of clothes!

"What the hell was THAT like?" I had to ask him about the historic meeting.

He took a long drag on his smoke. "'Demure.' Allen came up with that, and he wasn't even there," he said. "Until we got high, then it was hilarious." And my own combination tumblers were starting to line up in my brain.

"Wait a minute — was that also the first time The Beatles smoked pot?! Is that story *true*?!" I asked, suddenly stunned at who I was talking to.

"'Course it's true. I brought Dylan, and I brought the pot," he said, as he puffed another dragon of his legal smoke.

"What was *that* like?" I blurted.

He laughed. "They laughed. We all laughed for about an hour. It was that first-time-getting-high laugh. They were funny anyway, but that night they didn't even need to say anything, we'd just look at each other and start laughing, and then laugh at the laughing. It was infectious. Went on for hours. From that night on, whenever John wanted to get high, he'd say, 'Let's 'ave a laugh.'"

"No way! So it's true ..."

"Yeah it's true. I also introduced Allen to Bob for

the first time. He seems to forget that. At Ted Wilentz's Christmas party in his apartment over at the Eighth Street Bookshop in 1963."

"No way! *I live right beside there!* Where it used to be — MacDougal and 8th Street, right?" He nodded. "Man, I missed some good parties! I was born ten years too late."

We both seemed lost in thought for a moment. I couldn't really think of anything else to say, so shocked was I at what I'd already heard. But I wanted to keep the conversation going and thought of his scene upstairs. "Well, what was your connection to Jack and the Beats? Did you ever meet him?"

"Meet them?! I wrote the stories that put them on the gawddamn map," he said, and I looked at him trying to think of what he was talking about. "1960. The [*New York*] *Post* sent me out to San Francisco to do a hatchet job on them. The editors *hated* Kerouac and Ginsberg, called them 'pansies,' thought they were 'destroying the youth of America' and all that.

"Kerouac was in Northport at the time, so I went and saw him first, expecting this wild-eyed monster to open the door, but here was this normal middle-class guy unpacking the groceries with his mother. And he was smart and well-read, and quoting Melville and Dostoyevsky, and being very nice to his mother. And she's bringing us sandwiches. It was the complete opposite of the impression in my editors' heads. When I realized what I had, I got them to agree to a whole 12-part exposé before I'd ever submitted a word. They thought, 'Great, he'll tear them apart for 12 weeks!'"

Al laughed at the memory.

"And . . ." I prompted.

"And . . . I wrote it. They were all serious and studious, but they were also funny and playful and really enjoyed themselves."

"You know, that's the hit I get, too!" I said. "Like, at these events ... I take lit classes at NYU, and it's that whole thing of sitting around talking about sentence structure and syntax and subtext and everything — but these classes at the conference it's like we're doing it at a party. For one thing, the sentences are way more interesting, but also it's the vibe from the teacher, not to mention the other 'students' in the room. This sure beats my Forms of Fiction at NYU!"

"And it sure beats a roomful of editors at New York City newspapers," Al said. "But these 'poets' can still be a bunch of backstabbing bastards," and he took another drag in thought, mumbling, "Fuckin Allen ..." before rejoining with, "But ... compared to a Hemingway conference, this is fuckin Woodstock!"

I laughed, "**Woodstock of The Beats!**' I love it! I missed that one — but glad I made this one! ... And no rain," as we both looked up and smiled to our lucky stars at the gorgeous Colorado blue-sky. "'Woodstock of the Beats' should be the conference t-shirt," and I actually got a little laugh out of him.

"They're not going to be holding Capote conventions in twenty years, I can tell ya that," the decade-surfing scribe kept riffing. "It's always more fun at Beat events."

"They're the rock 'n' roll of literature — that's the

way I see it," I said. "They're the bad boys breakin' the rules, but it's also got *a beat* — you can dance to it." And we both smiled s'more.

"'When you ain't got nothing, you got nothing to lose,'" he said, quoting that old friend of his. "They were never let into the academic halls in the first place, so there's nothing to be kicked out of. They never tried to fake it. And it's too late now."

"Oh shit," I just realized. "I gotta get over to the UMC. Where you going?"

"Yeah, I could go over there," he said. "Maybe that's where Allen is."

So we started walking. "Yeah, not fitting in ..." I said, trying to keep the conversation going.

"Well, they never did then ... not as people, or as a group. It was all about conformity then," Al said, as we walked through an outdoor street park party past safety-pinned punks and headbanded hippies and fire-eating buskers. We were both smiling at the surreal circus we were caught up in, and I thought of Michael McClure's "You're us."

"Now you can stick a fuckin' pin through your cheek or dye your hair green or set yourself on fire and nobody gives a shit," Al grumbled on. "Back then, if you wanted any kind of career, you had to be straight as a fuckin' Arrow collar. Forget being gay — you got blacklisted for smoking pot. Elvis joined the fuckin' army for christsake. A couple years later Cassius Clay said fuck this. ... For these guys to be themselves back then was a much bigger deal than people understand today.

"Back then," he went on as we went on walking, "Anybody who *was* having fun, stayed at home with the shades down. The Beats just had their party out on the front lawn. ... With Allen dancing around naked reading *Howl*."

"Yeah, ... and the cops came."

He nodded and took another drag. "That's where I interviewed Neal — in San Quentin — for two fuckin' joints. And it was a pot bust they were using to kick John out of the country. And Donovan. And they're still doing it ... John Sinclair, Leary, Kesey, Bob Marley, Neil Diamond, Paul in Japan, Tony Curtis in London, Cocker in Australia ... People need to be more careful ... until things change."

"But that 'not fitting in' thing," I said. "It's so widespread — I mean, you can see it here at the conference — like, there's rich well-to-do suits and hairdos and middle-class professors and poor poets. And also — I noticed it's not one gender. Like, if you look down the rows of the audience at the shows, it's nearly a 50-50 split between guys and girls. It's not all threadbare beatniks or something. There's doctors and publishers and authors and ..."

"The Beats came from that duality," he said. "Corso and Cassady grew up in foster homes, and Burroughs was in the adding machine family going to the finest schools, alright. And Jack and Allen were straight-down-the-road middle class. They come by their diversity honestly. It was quite a spectrum."

"To have seen a spectrum and everything!"

"And they affected a wide band of bands — from

The Beatles to The Clash. From the best then to the best now."

"Why do you think that is?" I asked.

"Well, Allen was a helluva promoter who nearly fell off the floor. And like I told you, they were smart. The *opposite* of that fucking Dobie Gillis caricature. If you only went as deep as primetime TV or *Life* magazine they were a bunch of lazy layabouts. But *if you read the books* ... you were on the road."

"Or 'on the bus,' as Kesey said."

"Yeah ... and as soon as you got on, there were a whole seatful for you of read. Didn't matter which one you picked up first, they were about real people, real-life characters from a bunch of good writers' points of view, including mine. It wasn't any one book or writer — it was the whole cabal. Lots of voices. Take your pick. There's so many different voices that became the basis for everything that came after. Once you're hooked by any one book, you're just at the launch pad of a multitude of trips that could take you anywhere. It never stops being interesting."

We didn't know it then, but we'd be picking up this conversation a couple decades later in New York when I was booking him at the Beat shows I put on in the Village.

20

Show Production and Film Crews

At some point we eventually got to the U. of C. building with the "Chem 140" room — the second biggest space we used — a theater auditorium with about a 500 capacity. I told Al that Allen was definitely not scheduled to be at this, and he went off to look for him in the store or the workshop rooms or wherever on his ongoing briefcase-carrying quest for recognition. Poor guy. "The Beat's Rodney Dangerfield," I thought as I watched him walk away.

At these panel discussions, there was always some last-minute change to the original setup — although occasionally we were removing a mic and chair, more often we were adding one for someone who was around that Allen thought would add to the discussion. (Apparently not Al!)

In the main Glenn Miller Ballroom, we first tried having the panelists behind long tables but it was too much of a wall between them and the audience, so right away we switched all the staged events to just having chairs with mic stands and little tables for water or their papers. Compared to a Rolling Stones production, this was Pete Seeger solo! And other than Gregory, there were no "rock stars" to deal with.

Normally when stage managing I would do the stage setup and mic checks, prep the backstage green room, start accounting for each panelist as they showed up, and making calls from the nearby staff lounge if they weren't on site. But on this last one I was just doing front-of-house which was making sure the house lights were set right, and the flyers were taped up outside advertising tonight's show, and the girls were there from the main office with their cash box to sell the $5 tickets to walk-ups, with enough volunteers on the doors to collect them or check for buttons. One bonus here was there was no band guest list because anyone who was supposed to be there had a ticket or a white staff / performer button.

And **there were a lot of film crews around**. I mean —
all the time ... you'd see little 2-to-5-person crews lugging
gear from one spot to another, setting up in the park or the
cafeteria or any room they could commandeer for an hour.
I've worked with a lot of film crews and most of the time
they think they own wherever they are, and I've seen some
pretty ugly egos and destruction of nature and historic
buildings, but I gotta say every one of the five crews here
was polite and unobtrusive and respectful of both the
"artists" and the attendees — and the environment. And
that's definitely not always the case.

This afternoon, Lewis MacAdams and Richard
Lerner and their sound & camera guys were covering this
one, and by now everybody had the routine down pretty
well. The crews would set up at the side or the back, and
we'd all found every outlet there was in the building and
were goin' through gaffer's tape like crazy, but everybody
was cool, and we were groovin' on Buddhist Time.

Of this pair, Richard was the business and
production guy who was always busy setting up sumpthin
or workin the phones, and Lewis was the Charlie Watts of
the band — calm, cool, grounding the Beat. He was really
soulful, smart, spiritual, genuinely curious and a published
poet in his own right. And who knew? but this pair would
end up making maybe the best doc ever on Jack at this
conference — *What Happened To Kerouac?*

I interviewed Lewis the interviewer about how
things were going and right away his face lit up and he
started gushing about the great Gregory footage they just
got. "This has been way beyond our expectations. We've

managed to get *every one* of them in one-on-ones. Jan ... Edie ... Burroughs ... Huncke and Allen together — oh man, wait'll you see *that!*

"And the whole time, here's Robert Frank walking around with his camera! Can it get any more intimidating?! It's a good damn thing we have the tripod or the camera'd be shaking the whole time. ... We've been so busy doing interviews we haven't caught many of these panels. How've they been?"

"Lively." And we both laughed.

"I bet," he said. "We haven't heard two people agree on anything *yet!* 'Jack was the same whether he was drinking or not.' 'Jack became a totally different person when he drank.' 'He was a Catholic.' 'He was a Buddhist.' 'He was an environmentalist.' 'He was a Republican.' 'He was the father of the '60s.' 'He had nothing to do with the '60s.' 'There *is* no Beat Generation.' 'We're *all* the Beat Generation.' I don't know how we're going to edit this! I've never made a movie before, but we've got enough for a mini-series!"

"Wow — that's great! Do you know when it's gonna come out?"

"No idea. We couldn't get any funding beforehand, so the new plan is, we'll just shoot it and use the footage to make a demo rough-cut to shop it. But unless we can get Jack Nicholson or De Niro or something I doubt Hollywood is going to touch this. In their eyes we might as well be making a movie about Hawthorne. They've never heard of Kerouac ... and don't care. Unless it's got explosions or aliens ... they think you're one for pitching it."

I laughed. "Sounds awful."

"Welcome to Hollywood," he said. "Richard's made a few movies — he knows more about it than I do — but we're really shooting for TV. Maybe it'll play in some film festivals, but ... when was the last time you went to a documentary in a theater?"

"Oh yeah. ... maybe never. Oh wait — *Woodstock!* ... And *The Last Waltz.*"

"Alright, the last non-concert documentary?"

"Right." I was caught. "Never."

"So ... maybe PBS or TBS or CBS Cable or something. At least with cable there's a lot more options than there were a few years ago."

"Right. ... Oh shit —" I suddenly remembered I was in charge! "I think we're ready to open the doors. You guys cool?"

I got the nod, and left Lewis to make his movie while I went back to making mine.

Today's affair was another powerhouse of brainiacs with two of the three Jack biographers — Dennis McNally and John Tytell, as well as Regina Weinreich who was yet another woman proving this wasn't an all-boys club, and my now old friend Arthur Knight who was publishing more Beat stuff than anybody else alive.

To be completely confessional, I don't remember a ton of specifics from this panel — I must have stayed outside for most of it or something — or maybe my mind was on the fact we only had One More Saturday Night, but I do remember Arthur echoing from the stage what Kesey and some of the university professors had said in private:

that "we might have to wait until the year 2000" for the old-school arbiters of taste to die off and for the legions of those who "get it" to assume the reins of academic and publishing power. But, y'know — nobody was even gonna be *alive* in the year 2000! He might as well have said 3000 it was so far away.

21

The Saturday Night Summit at The Summit

Then it was **the climactic Saturday night** — and the single biggest all-star reading of a helluva ten days — Ginsberg, Kesey and Ferlinghetti. And again, from a planning point of view, Allen thought through this whole festival masterfully, pacing it like a great book, and was even holding out a last-minute slot in tonight's closing show for Gary Snyder in hopes that the good word and good vibes would reach him and he'd fly out for the end. Not to be, but most noble-hearted planning.

Of course, for the final big event everyone came early and was milling about — including The Holy Trinity of Yin — **Jan Kerouac, Carolyn Cassady,** and **Edie Kerouac Parker** — each a sun in her own solar system of friends and fans.

Jan was 30 years old at this point. She didn't much want to be on panels or in the spotlight or anything and the only real appearance she made was at one of the group readings to riff from her first and just-published semi-autobiographical Kerouacian book *Baby Driver*.

She was shy and quiet. But stunning! I mean — gorgeous! A tranquil beauty. Thin, in tight jeans, with this super pretty tanned face and blazing light blue eyes, a to-melt-for smile, and cute shoulder-length jet-black hair. Almost Liz Taylor-like. Or definitely a young Jordana Brewster in more recent movie star casting.

Like many conference participants, this was her coming out party in Beatlandia. Besides being her first tentative step into the public arena, it was here in Boulder that she first learned from local Buddhist student and author John Steinbeck IV, the son of the novelist, that children are entitled to half of their parent's royalties, something she never knew or collected on before.

She always had a bevy of boys around her, and in my own young Canadian stranger-in-a-strange-land shyness I was too goo-gooed to go talk to her. Cuz also it was so weird ... you love this writer in a dude-to-dude hero mentor teacher master artist way — but suddenly here he was manifested ... as a babe! There's a funny Blake Edwards movie called *Switch* that this was like — where a guy becomes a girl (masterfully played by Ellen Barkin) with his old best friend trying to pick her/him up. It was this weird thing of being attracted to this girl who was really ... *your dad*. I know. Crazy. You couldn't take your eyes off her — she was hot as hell — but ... she was also ... *Jack*.

And if that wasn't freaky enough! It was kinda the same thing with **Carolyn**! — who was 59 years old at the time — and still intimidatingly gorgeous! Like a Sophia Loren, or maybe Grace Kelly if she'd lived; skinny, and blond, with a striking model's face and the cutest little dimples when she smiled; calm, and regal, and beatifically glowing, with twinkling eyes, and confident, and at peace. You sure knew why the ol' Beat boys fell for her! And ditto every cowboy at this rodeo!

I could start talkin' to Ginzy or Kesey or Huncke or just about any of these guys real easy, but sometimes I'm more Jack than Neal when it comes to jaw-droppingly beautiful girls. And to her lucky genes and healthy living credit she was probably the most attractive woman in the whole scene — while simultaneously being the oldest. When I was lucky enough to meet her again years later, I was well over the insecure shit and made damn sure I made up for my youthful Boulder shyness and went right up and became friends and remained so until the day she died.

The thing is about Carolyn ... she was consistently attractive from the time she was a girl. It was both a blessing and a curse, as it probably is for all who win the looks lottery. Just go ahead and try to find a heterosexual man who met her who didn't have a crush on her. You'll spend your life in vain.

How we first ended up arm-in-arm was somewhere in the '90s, at the Algonquin Hotel in Midtown Manhattan. Besides having met in Boulder and then elsewhere, like everyone else I'd been enamored with her since first reading Jack's descriptions. And to finally meet her! Crazy, man! I mean, it makes no sense. There was definitely an attraction ... but it wasn't about sex. She was hot — and also jazzman cool. She was petite, but loomed so large! She was Marilyn Monroe — but she was ... *my mother!* It was nuts! Positively Oedipal. Probably untreatable. But she was totally unBeatable!

So, we're down in a dark Dorothy Parker booth in the spirit-filled Algonquin lobby bar with Doug Brinkley, John Sampas, Dave Amram, and others hovering, then a few of us finally cut out and up to a top floor suite that one of the Greeks from Lowell had rented and continued the party up there with the big old windows that slid right up, and jazz playin' from a radio station, and drinks pouring, and big rooms to roam around in, and crazy late-night confessions and gossip. And after another round or two of this madness, Carolyn finally whispers to me she was ready to go back to her room.

We had bonded throughout the night to the point that she wanted me to be the one to walk her home. And so, the two of us left the party, this very odd couple, tottering down the hall, walking in a formal elbow arm lock like that first shot of her & Neal together on the streets of San Francisco, except drunkenly swaying on this lurching ship all the way to her cabin door, me freaking out that I'm in the Neal & Jack slot, but also playing with the moment, and we're having a hell of a time laughing at whatever was happening, and it hit me — *that's the exact same laugh Neal and Jack heard!*

She was around 70 at this point, and a lot about her had evolved — her brain, her body — but one thing that doesn't change about people is their laugh. And she had the most wonderful childlike joyous giggle. I loved it. And when I love a girl's laugh, I make sure I hear it as often as I can. So I'd make her howl till she was gasping! It was great!

And all that was born this Algonquin night. And when we got to her door — what did I do? Guess before you read on. What would you do? ... You know what I did?

I took her hand and kissed it, like an English gentleman. Little did I know at the time she had a whole thing for English gentlemen! — and in fact had moved there a year after the Boulder summit! But I let it go at that noble gesture. "Well, wasn't this a WONDERFUL night!" she gushed in unfiltered joy. A gentleman not insinuating himself on her, but rather just joying in each other's company. "We're all just walking each other home," as Ram Dass put it.

And that's what we did for the next twenty years.

When this conference came along, the only Beat story ever told on film was her *Heart Beat,* which had just come out a couple years earlier, and was based on an excerpt from her thousand-page memoir that was still unpublished. A good chunk of it, titled *Off The Road,* would finally see the light of print by the end of the decade, but this was all we had to go on at the time.

It was so funny how she referred to the movie as *"Heart Break"* (!) because of how inaccurate she felt it was. But for those of us who didn't live through those times, it was the only film adaptation of the events of the era in existence — other than the 28-minute black-&-white almost-documentary *Pull My Daisy* from 1959 — except nobody had a way to see that. (And we don't even *talk* about what Hollywood did to *The Subterraneans!*)

With Neal played by Nick Nolte, Carolyn by Sissy Spacek, and Jack by John Heard, *Heart Beat* also featured a secret surprise — Jack's only living blood, Jan, appears in an early scene about 11 minutes in, sitting in a small white-walled cafe, Beatnikly chain-smoking while her dramatized family cavorts at a table nearby.

Even though any halfway well-read Jack fan knew the movie was taking liberties with the facts, it's still a ton of fun — especially the scenes where the straight neighbors come by — and it's a rare treat to see a big-screen version of the dynamo '40s and '50s Neal in action. It's crazy, but it would take almost 20 years after that before any other dramatization of The First Family would appear on screen — *The Last Time I Committed Suicide* with Thomas Jane as Neal, in 1997. And that opened the floodgates. But at the time all we had to go on cinematically was Carolyn's *Heart Break.*

Jack's first wife **Edie** was the one I could talk to back then — and in fact would grow to become close friends with shortly after Boulder. She even enlisted me to write her autobiography with her, which seemed like the opportunity of a lifetime, until I learned she'd already scratched out a thousand pages ... and wasn't even up to where she met Jack! She was absolutely insistent that every detail of every moment of her life be included, and even at my young age with this huge opportunity before me I knew this would be an impossible task and we'd end up fighting over every detailed description of every piece of clothing she ever wore ... so I didn't end up joining her on the journey and we stayed friends instead. In fact it would be 13 years after she died, and only with the superhuman efforts of her close friend, the mighty Tim Moran, with key assists by (in sequence) Bill Morgan, Sterling Lord and Lawrence Ferlinghetti, that the epic 2,200 pages she'd amassed got pared down to the very readable version published as *You'll Be Okay.*

Where Jan and Carolyn were shy and quiet, Edie was a ball of fire — *always* talking, often to more than one person at once, telling stories, and relishing the spotlight. Where Jan didn't want to go in front of a microphone, Edie would eat them up like the six sauerkraut hotdogs she ate the first time she met Jack, the story of which she probably told 60,000 times over that week.

She was a hoot, a bona fide character, "a real pisser"

as they called people like her back in the day, a "dynamite broad," a catalytic woman, gregarious, a natural chatterbox — a female Neal in her confidence and making the party jump wherever she went.

She came with all these paintings she claimed Jack painted, but nobody was ever able to authenticate them. She had them displayed in her Chautauqua room and at an art gallery show that was part of the conference and she was trying to sell them or get them in a museum or something. Never happened.

She and **Henri Cru** were a real going concern for a while — until Henri made the mistake of introducing her to his friend Jack. That kinda put a damper on Edie & Henri's friendship for oh about 40 years. But the old lovebirds finally reconnected in 1980 and became fast friends again for the rest of their days. And I could sure see why after I also became friends with ol' Henri in the months following the conference.

These two birds were sure flappin' the same feathers — always workin' the angles to hustle a buck. And I don't mean that in a bad way. They were both generous, giving, loving, people people, but they always had some wild get-rich-quick scheme goin' and about 20 deals in the middle of being made at all times. Jack coulda written whole books about either one of these two.

The thing about Henri was — he had the greatest laugh in the world — but Jack already told you that in *On The Road*. And yeah — there was a pattern here among his old compadres. Henri was a born dry comic who loved to deliver drop dead funny lines totally straight and absolutely motionless like Mount Rushmore and only move his eyeballs to see if you got it. And if you did, he'd explode with this high pitched hee-hee-hee which would only make you laugh even more which would make him laugh even more.

He had these stock lines he'd deliver over and over — "You can't teach the old maestro and new tune." Or "Plant ya now and dig ya later." Or if someone wasn't talking, "You wouldn't say shit if you had a mouthful." And for years he'd been immortalizing these sayings into rubber stamps he had made at some little shop in Chinatown. He had hundreds of them stored in various old fishing tackle boxes — sometimes whole 3-sentence jokes he thought were hilarious but were really just extremely corny puns. Maybe this was his way of getting his words in print like his friend Jack, I don't know, but sometimes he'd send out whole letters to people that were nothing but pages of his stamped jokes and quotes of wisdom!

Unlike the people who'd made the pilgrimage to Boulder, which Henri couldn't do because he'd just recently been confined to a wheelchair due to losing half a leg to diabetes, but he also *wouldn't* do it because he didn't share the assembled's awe of his old high school friend. As Henri said, he "wasn't entirely pleased" with how Jack portrayed him in his novels (even though anyone who knew Henri knew Jack painted a vividly accurate and loving portrait), and he didn't care much for Jack's "fruity friends," or how rude he could be when drunk. 'Course, that didn't stop him from listing himself in the Manhattan phone book until the day he died as "Remi Boncoeur," the pseudonym Jack gave him in *On The Road*. What the old buddies were, more than anything, were two dashing young men on the town on the make. Neither of them, as it turned out, were really the settle-down marrying types (as Henri put it, "I don't breed well in captivity"), but they both loved to have a pretty woman on their arm and in their bed — and sometimes it turned out to be the same woman.

Henri Cru's 70th birthday -- April 1991. Henri in the chair -- me in the peacoat, Stringbeans Kurman & Tim Moran in the back, Mary & Alexandra behind Henri, outside the Blue Note Jazz Club after we saw Maynard Ferguson, West Third & Sixth Ave. in the Village, with the famous Waverly Theater over our shoulders, where On The Road would finally open in NYC 20 years later.

This gathering in Boulder was the first time Edie'd ever appeared anywhere to talk about Jack — but then that was the case for a lot of these people, this being the first major summit and all. **But she knew Jack before anyone else who was here** — having met him when they were both teenagers in 1939 and fallen in love not long after.

In fact, she had this whole thing she called "the '40s gang" — which was just her, Allen, Burroughs and Huncke — the core four who predated everybody. Neal, Carolyn, Holmes, Corso, Ferlinghetti — they all came years of youth later. You remember who your oldest friends are — who came first, who dates back the furthest. And same with Edie — acutely aware of who the original group was, and she made a point of reconnecting with each of them, but especially with Hunck who, for whatever reason, she seemed to dig the most. But then — he'd be my pick, too.

And just to be clear — **Allen was The Man**. This whole thing happened because of him, start to finish. As an event producer myself ... *you* don't get to hang with your friends and have fun. I mean, you do on a deeper level, but in the present it's all work, check lists, constant mental mapping of the upcoming minutes, hours, days.

And that's what old Allen was doing — starting more than a year before this happened, and then all during it, not only coordinating every damn thing that went on, but also conducting writing workshops, doing reading performances (where he *killed*), press conferences, conflict resolution, into leading actual meditation sessions, then back into administrative crap, and more hassle defusing, and croissant monitoring, and panelist rescheduling, and housing management, and dinner arranging, and most importantly — **Vibe Establishing**. It was *all* from his Tender Heart that this whole thing sprung and kept springing. And he was everywhere at once.

Neal Cassady + Bill Graham = Allen Ginsberg

But first came Edie — who introduced her brainy boyfriend Jack to this cool guy from her Columbia art class, Lucien Carr ... who in turn introduced Jack to his life-altering partners in crime Allen Ginsberg and Bill Burroughs ... making it pretty easy to peg the Beat Generation's inception to Edie's introduction and the all-night drinking, talking and phonograph playing sessions they danced across the universe in the four rooms of the Morningside Heights apartment that she shared with Lucien's girlfriend, then later Joan Vollmer Adams.

As much as Jack and the Beats were products and practitioners of the male-centric world of the 1940s and '50s, it was almost comically common for **the women to be the real catalysts of creation**. It was Jack's mother who gave her grownup son the love and shelter and stability to write and preserve his manuscripts. It was his last wife Stella who mothered him after Mémère had a stroke, and was keeping his filing cabinets and archives intact after they both passed away. It was Ann Charters who was the first scholar to take him seriously — and while he was still alive — showing up on his doorstep in 1966 to begin the work that would become his first biography. It was his second wife, Joan Haverty, who had the job that paid the rent on the apartment at 454 West 20th Street that gave Jack the space to write his career-changing scroll of *On The Road* in that 20-day shot in 1951. It was Carolyn who first moved to San Francisco, in 1947 — long before Ferlinghetti or any of them — and THAT's why Neal went there, followed by Jack, Allen and the domino tumble of history. And it was one wild fun-loving woman named Frankie Edie Parker from Grosse Pointe, Michigan, who chose to room with a like-spirited woman who would soon be Mrs. Burroughs just as she'd be Mrs. Jack and who together hosted the rented Eden from which an entire generation spawned.

Edie and me in her living room in Grosse Pointe with her Jack paintings.

The one woman who was conspicuous by her absence was **Stella Sampas**. She was the sister of Jack's closest childhood friend Sebastian who tragically died on the Anzio beachhead in Italy in 1944, and she became the third and final Mrs. Jack Kerouac for the last three years of his life. She was invited, but she didn't know any of the people Jack became friends with after he left his hometown as a teenager, and the word around town was she was a strict Catholic or something and had no interest in meeting any of them. Biographers and others were talking about all these books Jack had written that Stella wasn't letting be published, and that, plus the fact she wasn't there at his tribute, led to a less than favorable portrait of her being painted whenever her name came up. Which it did. It turns out she was keeping his writings and possessions intact, but little new material of Jack's would be published until after her death in 1990. And then there was a geyser of it.

Besides all the charismatic women who made (or didn't make) the scene, there was another curious subset of characters — older men in jackets and ties. Allen being disguised by choice in this establishment uniform, along with his mute sidekick Harpo Orlovsky, and Burroughs who seemed like he was born in one, they all gave cover to others to not stand out like narcs.

There was **Jay Landesman** in his dapper duds and big white fedora. This guy was definitely a player and raconteur — he knew everybody, and was always working the room and trying to pick up women wherever he was. He started *Neurotica* magazine in 1948 and was publishing Jack and Allen and Holmes before just about anybody. He was also, for a time, a nightclub proprietor of the most happening club between the coasts called The Crystal Palace, in St. Louis, which booked the likes of Lenny Bruce and Woody Allen along with jazz bands. He also wrote the satirical musical *"The Nervous Set"* which was basically *about* the Beats, and which actually played on Broadway for a short time with none other than Larry Hagman in the lead role. He became an ex-pat long ago, moving to London and immediately becoming a central figure in the swinging '60s scene over there. In fact, it was at this summit that Carolyn first met Jay and his wife Fran and it was in good measure their raving about how great England was that caused Carolyn to move there herself the following year.

Then there was the professorial one-eyed poet **Robert Creeley**, who you'd bet the farm was wearing a toupee, but you'd end up homeless if you did. He was always talking about the Black Mountain poets — the collective of Beat cousins named after their short-lived experimental college in North Carolina that closed in 1957. An interdisciplinary arts experiment whose faculty included such diverse minds as Creeley, John Cage, Merce Cunningham, Willem de Kooning and Buckminster Fuller, it was actually very much like what Naropa was hoping to do in Boulder — a place where poets and painters and composers and others would all share ideas and techniques.

It was Creeley who really spearheaded the

connection to the Beats, publishing Allen, Jack and Burroughs in their *Black Mountain Review* before traditional publishers would touch them. But it was the two groups' similar wide-open approach to the possibilities and interconnectivity of all mediums that was really their common ground. John Cage's "happenings," blending improvised dance, theater and live composing with audience participation, was really Jack's "spontaneous prose" set on a stage — and both were precursors to Ken Kesey's inclusive participatory convention-busting Acid Tests. Black Mountain poet Charles Olson had written about and practiced using the human breath as the basis for lines of poetry even before Jack did — as outlined in his influential poetic manifesto *"Projective Verse"* in 1950. But it wasn't a competition, it was a commonality, an idea whose time had come, and Black Mountain was the outpost halfway down the Eastern Seaboard doing it all at the same time and in many of the same ways the Beats were in S.F and N.Y.

And then there was the formal and proper **Ed White,** the Denver architect and Jack's close friend who had famously suggested he should sketch with words what he saw before him the way a painter does. This light bulb of advice in 1951 changed Jack's life, and in fact the very first sentence of the very next book he wrote after learning this, *Doctor Sax*, contains this very admonition — to not worry about words but just see the picture clearer. And evermore Jack became a sketchin' fool, painting Sistine murals across the ceiling of America the rest of his life. It was so strange that it was this unassuming middle-class middle-aged father-next-door guy in a suit who turned out to be the key confidant with the magic perspective that solved the puzzle and made all the pieces fit together for Jigsaw Jack.

Ed had the sketching idea in his head because as an architecture student he was instructed to carry around a notebook to sketch designs as he came across them in everyday life. Ed was always cheerfully intelligent — another real commonality among this close core of friends. He was the stable hard-working professional side of the family — he'd just completed the restoration of the historic Governor's Mansion in Denver — and had lived a life in stark contrast to most of his old friends. And around Boulder ... when E.D. White talked, people listened. He was a reliable straight voice of reason, and really knew his Jack history, quotes, books, dates and all.

There were tie-wearing others too, but much to my mother's everlasting chagrin, I've never bin a suit-n-tie guy. I blended like good Scotch on the free-thinkin' drinkin' team, and colors always made more sense to me than numbers, but I also respected those who dug the cool of life and could simultaneously master the hallway marching maneuvers and daily diplomacy of the capitalist topography.

Actually, the whole conference was a terrifically rich blend of people the whole time — the professorial suits standing next to dreadlocked Deadheads standing next to straight scholars working on dissertations next to old PBS types in frumpy secondhand clothes next to punks with short green hair and a shit-kicking attitude next to bearded back-to-the-land nature lovers next to players on the make next to starstruck autograph seekers next to inquisitive students who were always asking questions and taking notes next to radical protesters complaining about the admission prices and that everything should be free next to middle-aged housewives who had some profound awakening reading Kerouac long ago and had to reconnect with that moment next to enthusiastic Asian students who could barely speak English but for whom the Beats were more the cool soul of America than rock n roll next to calm quiet Buddhist students who were mutely blissed out by their yoga or sumpthin next to a hitchhiking hippie from Canada and on and on around every room on this merry-go-round of hardcore weirdos who made the pilgrimage and who were all appreciative and open to anyone else who successfully made the same effort.

And so, on that climactic Saturday night, the main thousand-seat Glenn Miller Ballroom at the university where we were doing all the big shows was packed beyond capacity and it was really loud and everybody had stories and ideas and new friends and a few drinks in them and knew this was the last night.

Oh, and a word must be said about **the giant painting that hung as a backdrop** on the main stage all conference. If you've ever seen photos or film from this summit, you will have seen this big painting of Jack in the background. It was a big deal.

The backstory is outlined in Jack's famous essay

"The Origins of the Beat Generation" (*Playboy*, 1959) and involved the most famous photo of Jack — the one you've seen a million times and was used for the conference poster and often as the author photo in his books with his hair messed up and he's wearing that black & white checked shirt, the shot taken by *Mademoiselle* magazine of all things, in the fall of '56 when he'd just come down from his summer on Desolation Peak to find that he and his friends were famous. Or getting there. The term "the San Francisco Poetry Renaissance" had just been coined — *"Howl"* had just been published by City Lights, *The New York Times* had just done a big story on them titled "West Coast Rhythms," *Life Magazine* was on the phone, and suddenly it seemed to all be happening for them at long last.

So, Jack's back just in time for this photo shoot, and while he's standing there with Allen & Whalen & Gregory, Corso takes off the silver crucifix he's wearing and puts it on good ol' Catholic boy Jack, and insists it hang outside his shirt. For whatever reason, *Mademoiselle* decided this was not appropriate to be seen on these bohemian poets and cropped the shot above the cross, effectively erasing it from the picture. And Jack was this guy who painted pictures of Christ on the cross and Popes and Saints and drew crosses all over his notebooks and was pretty serious about his Catholic faith, and the removing of the cross was the first of many heartbreaking disappointments he suffered at the hands of the American media. So, when he finally got a well-paying high-profile gig writing about the Beat Generation for *Playboy*, he used that forum to lay bare this visual censorship he suffered. So, Allen, God bless him, sought to rectify this not-slight slight to his brother, and commissioned Dutch painter Karel Appel to recapture the photograph *and put the cross back in.* And in fact they wrote in large letters right across the painting, "Here's your cross of tenderness they kept from *Mademoiselle.*"

So, whenever you see photos or just imagine that stage at Naropa, know that this massive painting hanging above and behind everyone was Allen's posthumous gift to Jack, safe in heaven dead.

And speaking of gifts, I should mention how we also had, just down to hallway from the ballroom, an official conference store, set up in a stray meeting room with stuff spread around on rectangle banquet tables manned by volunteers. It was pretty low-budg but always had customers when I looked in. They sold loads of conference posters, t-shirts, audio cassettes of the panels and workshops, books by all the featured speakers, and all sorts of Buddhist stuff. The whole thing was kind of a temporary prototype precursor to the permanent landmark Beat Book Shop that Tom Peters would open on Pearl Street a few years later. If I had money and an extra suitcase instead of peanuts and a backpack I'd have come home with a beauteous bounty of Beat booty. But as it was, I went hungry, bow bow bow.

Meanwhile, the evening show begins with Babbs coming out and acting as impromptu moderator and honestly, there was hardly an event all conference that didn't have somebody who wasn't previously scheduled show up and be part of it. That's why they needed stage managers like me. But this Babbs guy could have been a stand-up comic in a droll big-country way, and the audience was right with him, as they would be for all three performing readers this night, yelling out complementary one-liners in the artist-audience collaboration that the conference had bred. All three readers were in chairs on stage until their performance time came, then got up and rocked the house.

Ferlinghetti went first. He was probably the most respectable, straight and healthy of all the assembled Beats; word was he went swimming (!) every day at the university pool. He opened by stressing — like he did every time he was at a mic all week — that we should have another one of these gatherings in five years, and then every five years after that.

He was absolutely captivating, stalking the front of the stage like a prowling panther reading his "*Look Homeward, Jack*" tribute (that later appeared in *Wild Dreams Of A New Beginning*) and some other prose-poems he'd written for the festival's honoree and a funny one called "*The Love Nut*" and all sorts of other cool stuff. To all of our giddy glee, he also pulled out an unpublished book of poems that Kerouac had given him (but he told us Stella wouldn't let him publish it) called "*Poems All Sizes*" and read us a bunch of great Jack riffs no one had ever heard. It was definitely a pull-out-the-best-material kinda night, and he was very "up" and buoyant and projecting like a pro who could mesmerize the room even without a mic.

Kesey was next and once again told everyone about his Cassady-like non-stop drive from Oregon, and he brought out his giant ball of hemp twine — a prop he carried around for his legalizing marijuana raps. And although he was making his public service announcement playful and funny, he'd done a bunch of research and was making really salient points about the economics of the issue and saying to this Colorado crowd in 1982 whichever state legalized it first was gonna have a real jump on the rest of the country. Took 'em a while, but they eventually got the message.

Nobody knew what he was going to read, of course, and in fact he only made the decision at the last minute when he was already on stage reading the room, but I was happily stunned when, with everything he had in his trickster's bag of papers, he pulled out *"Now We Know How Many Holes It Takes To Fill The Albert Hall!"* — his personal moving tribute to John Lennon from *Rolling Stone* magazine last spring. I actually started tearing up right there in the room when he got to the murder part. Lennon was my hero. I was in Manhattan when he was shot, and went up to the Dakota that night long before the news trucks and rest of the world would arrive the next morning (you can read about it on my website), and in fact I was so moved by my other hero writing about it the way he did, I carried that crazy dog-eared copy of *Rolling Stone* with me all the way from New York to Vancouver, and for some reason also put it in my backpack and humped it On The Road to Boulder and back.

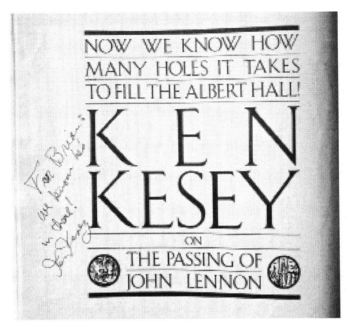

"For Brian: We know he's in there! Ken Kesey"

After Kesey managed to turn a tragedy against humanity into a comedy for eternity with 30 minutes of rolling laughter and getting the loudest sustained applause since the conference started, **Allen took the warmed-up room and set it on fire.** If this guy had this much boundless energy in his fifties, what kind of a bouncing kangaroo was he in his youth?! He was funny, talkative, playful, and totally in command of the room; this was his night to let loose after playing Bill Graham for two weeks. He rocked it and was laughing and loud and carried the room with every riff.

He read a new touching word portrait of Jack that he'd just sketched while sitting with artist Karel Appel as he painted the giant portrait hanging on stage, and a bunch of new pomes like the rhythmic *"Why I Meditate,"* as well as greatest hits like the personal *"On Neal's Ashes"* about his love for his Adonis of Denver. In fact, during the whole ten daze it was heartening to hear how often Neal was lovingly invoked.

Neal's ashes

Allen ended his set by bringing out this funk-jazz upright bass player and a trippy trumpeter from a band called Still Life to accompany him on a couple of numbers including his funny Schoolhouse-Rock-meets-Buddhism anthem *"Do The Meditation Rock"* with its triumphant refrains "It's never too late to do nuthin at all" and "Learn a little patience and generosity." This was the Beat version of all those cameos rock stars did on *Sesame Street* — taking often complex concepts or songs and breaking them down to their simplest childhood innocence and experience. It was beautiful, silly, joyous and truthful.

Then after this all heaven broke loose. Babbs and Allen got the audience to fold up all the chairs and clear the floor for dancing, the band Still Life came back out, Kesey strapped on an old black Les Paul — and somebody yelled out *"Dark Star!"*

Then ol' Ali Baba Ginsberg opens the door to the evening's climactic cave of delights with a tour de force *"Capitol Air,"* the very poem he'd performed with The Clash last summer during their 17-show run at Bonds in Times Square. And in fact that hang had gone so well, mostly between he and Joe Strummer, they invited him to their sessions at Electric Lady Studios a few months later, and he helped Strummer with his lyrics and appeared on the album they were recording — *"Combat Rock"* — which just came out this summer with *"Rock The Casbah"* blaring from every car radio in the country. And Allen was still clearly rockin' his punk chops and spitting out lines at times like Ginzy Ramone with these crazy guitars thrashing behind him.

Then Kesey led the way as they jammed a *"Gloria"* by Van Morrison, and "a Western in E," with Allen rippin' some wild Jew's harp and gettin' psychedelically tight with the mic, as they wove through some rambling blues. There's no doubt these guys should keep their day job, but what a wonderful raucous ridiculous riotous way to rocket us out of the final night like exploding Roman candles and everybody went *Awwww!*

Allen and Keez on stage
on the climactic Saturday night

22

A Sunday In The Park With Kesey

The next and final day was **the Sunday Farewell Awards Picnic.**

I got to Chautauqua Park, let off from hitchhiking or I dunno how I got there, and I spot the kegs of beer and people milling about, so I head over and cop a cup, and start lookin' around for familiar faces, except I'm way early and nobody's here yet. But I've got a full frosty and it's a beautiful sunny day in a tree-filled park in the mountains. Eventually this guy comes over and starts talkin' to me, and he says, "So, do you know anybody here?"

I look around. "Nope."

"Well, who are you, and why are you taking our beer?"

"Oops." Wrong party.

Eventually, wandering through a series of drum circles and pot parties and sunbathing bunnies in the gawd-damn '60s freak show that is a Boulder park on a sunny day, I finally find the right party, and before long Kesey comes drivin' up in his turquoise convertible with his turquoise-eyed beautiful wife **Faye** in the navigator seat, and Ken sees me and with his finger as an old six-shooter pops at me a couple of times, and I duck to avoid the shots and finger-shoot him back.

He lets Faye and the others out and goes to park the car, and she comes over, and she's really soft spoken and gentle and reserved and polite ... and really pretty — ironically, sort of like Louise Fletcher in *One Flew Over The Cuckoo's Nest*. And she comes over specifically to talk to me for the first time!

"You know, when Ken saw you just now, he turned and said, 'That's a really great guy.'"

What?!?! Ken said that?!?! I pretty much died and went to heaven right there on the spot. Faye didn't know me, but she knew what conveying something like that would mean, and went out of her way to do it. Random acts of kindness. And I was floating on air in the Rockies.

So — it's this big crazy "**Sunday In The Park With Kesey**" painting — peopled with Pranksters Babbs, Walker, Krassner, and Grateful Dead soundman Dan Healy's kid Michael; and Allen & Peter were there; and Jan and Carolyn both drawing the eye like candy-colored flowers in an alpine meadow; and Jack Micheline, and Andy Clausen, and Jane Faigao & Bataan and I dunno who-all else, but it was nearly the final event of the conference, and the Pranksters were giving out some awards, and there was beer and wine under the big old trees and it was your last afternoon to say Hello Goodbye to fellow pilgrims.

And there was a whole other funny subplot playing out on this tree-filled stage — of all things, there was *... a barbershop quartet convention in town!* And all throughout the park, whenever it got quiet for a split second, you could hear some crazy showtune being sung most enthusiastically by a bunch of very straight voices from a far away world. In the foreground there's these pornographic poets singing songs whose libretto gets confiscated by customs, and in the background we can hear Ivy League sweaters with manicured haircuts doo-wopping Pat Boone.

Yaaas ... surreality is a scrumptious stew. And for our next number ... with Allen's okay, Kesey & Babbs concocted these comical conference "awards," which really did seem appropriate since we'd all been living through these intellectual wars of illumination and literati for nearly two weeks — this was a silly and proper way to tie-dye a bow around it.

There was The Snappiest Dresser, and The Worst Dresser — both won by Peter Orlovsky! :-D And they had a Jack Kerouac Lookalike Award (won by Jan, but accepted in her absence by Paul Krassner since she'd wandered off somewhere), a Most Peculiar Award, a Hardest Worker Award — I can't remember who won any of these. But they also had a Dashiell Hammett Mystery Poet Award (for not showing up), and Babbs said, "This award goes to Gary Snyder. In fact, he's won this so many years in a row we're going to retire the award."

And then they announced **The On The Road Award** for the person who traveled the furthest by car to be here, and after hitchhiking 1,500 miles from Vancouver, and after the Kesey car gushing comment earlier, I started straightening my metaphorical tie to go up and accept it, already sensing the laser beam of people's attention on my soon-to-be-famous self, and as Babbs gets to "and the winner is ..." I'm plotting my way through the crowd until ... he says somebody else's name! Aaaaa! And the guy only drove from measly San Francisco!!

It was the one bummer of the whole trip. And then they started this Loudest Poets Contest which I wasn't much into at this point where each person gets to do up to a three minute poem (which was also won by Peter, even though Jack Micheline and Andy Clausen were way better, and all Peter did was go "Om" really loud), but I just thought fuck it, and while this was happening, I went backstage, which in this case just meant under a tree away from the microphone, and I was like, "Hey Babbs, um, you know I hitchhiked here from Vancouver."

"Oh my gawd, Brian! You're right!" he roared in that huge bear's voice of his.

And before the next poet, he went to the mic and announced, "Okay, Breaking News, everybody. Listen up — we have *two* winners of the On The Road Award! Brian here hitchhiked all the way from Vancouver, Canada. But Raymond *drove* the furthest, so we're gonna give 'em both awards cuz there's more than one way to make it, ha-ha-ha," as he laughs loudly like he's wont to do at the end of just about every sentence he speaks. And there it was, Boom — my 15 seconds of fame!

And then the whole thing ended with a Worst Joke Competition, which really lived up to its name and there's no need to tell you about it in mixed company, and then Babbs boomed, "And this concludes the Jack Kerouac On The Road Conference," with a laugh at his own faux formality, and we all dug the silliness. The wrap moment really had no sadness because there'd been so many events, so much happened, so much still to be digested, that even though it was only ten days it felt like forever ... and plus, at least for me, this was nowhere near over ... as you'll soon see.

And so, **the herd slowly begins to thin** as figures dissolve away into the park, returning to the land from whence they came, but the mighty oak hardcores still stood not giving any ground. Allen, Peter, Krassner, Carolyn, Jan ... all there for the Pranksters hitting The Road right outta the park — heading to Yellowstone to soak in some waterfalls and get smokey with the bears.

And with Kesey's comment from earlier and me now being a proud award recipient, I was feeling most comfortable with these former idols. I'd been accepted into their world, and now it was just family packin' up and wrappin' up. And Babbs and I got to talking, and he's like, "*Briiiiian!*" he bellows in his grizzly bear roar. "I forgot you said you hitchhiked here! Man, that's great! You're doin' it Jack style. (ha-ha-ha) He'd be proud. (ha-ha) Are you hitchhiking back to Vancouver? You should stop by and visit us at the farm. Right on the way. I'll give you directions."

Whoa! "Yeah, I'd love to. I'll do that. It would be cool to see where you guys live."

"It's beautiful, you'll love it, wouldn't live anywhere else. We're just down the road from each other," and he nods to his other Ken.

"Oh boy!" I'm thinking, as Kesey brings the big 1966 Catalina convertible around, and the boys start putting in the last of the gear from the show, and Babbs says to Kesey, "He's comin' to visit us at the farm," nodding to me, and Kesey looks up and goes, "Greeeaaaat!" and smiles in that big warm way he does.

My dream plan was coming true. After meeting and getting to work with some of my biggest childhood idols in New York already in my young life — Bill Graham and Alice Cooper for two — I wasn't scared to talk to heroes. I *wanted* to talk to them, get to know them, spend time in the orbit of their world. You gather something from everyone you meet, some little something or lots of big somethings transfer from them to you, and it's all these transfers, all these somethings you soak up that make you who you are. And the better people you can be in contact with, the better you'll become.

Every person has their own unique series of transfers and influences. For me, it's always been about event production — basically putting on Acid Tests in one form or another. And you don't need the LSD to create temporary moments of magic — a night or series of nights of euphoric freeform chaos — and that's what my whole life had been about — creating that magic, with a big crowd or small.

And now I was finally going to the birthplace of the purpose of my life.

Allen thanking Ken, finger-locked
— the Beats and Pranksters entwined in eternity —
with George Walker & Ken Babbs, about to go furthur

23

The Realist

And so finally the ship-size sea-colored convertible sailed out of port to a coastline of waves, and slowly disappeared over the horizon, and all the faces sorta turned downward in silence as minds started processing past pranks and future chores, which for most people consisted of their own departure, but as usual I didn't want the party to end, and another guy who didn't seem to be hurrying off was Prankster **Paul Krassner**, the editor, publisher, writer, and political rabble-rousing leader in the spirit of Abbie. In fact, he was sticking around to do some benefit show the next day for "the incarcerated poet and the second black hippie, Jerome Washington. ... Jimi Hendrix was the first," he made sure I knew.

Even though he kind of scared me when I'd been around him earlier in the week — he has this rough tough crass (wink-wink) veneer, sort of a Corso meets Larry Flynt — but he's actually really funny, soft spoken, thoughtful and gentle one-on-one. If you've ever read or heard him speak you know he's super-smart and well-read — almost a Garcia mind that knows so many things about so many things. And we started talkin' and right off he's like, "I didn't know shit about Kerouac."

"Yeah, *I know!* ... But what do *you* mean?" I asked.

"*Visions of Gerard, Tristessa*, ... even *Visions of Cody* —
I still haven't read that for some reason," he said, listing
some of the books he hadn't read. Then, "*On The Road,
Dharma Bums, Big Sur, Subterraneans, Mexico City
Blues* ... I'd read more than most people, but I've just
scratched the surface. It was great Allen did this. There's
so much more to Jack than most people know."

"Yeah, it was like I'd only been listening to the
'Greatest Hits' but suddenly somebody finally started
playing his whole albums," I said.

"Right, right," Krassner laughed. "Perfect."

"It seemed like kind of this whole rehabilitation
thing," I said. "Like Jack was finally being released from
prison or something after serving some long sentence for
the crimes of his youth, and now he was being released and
making a new respectable life."

"The Allen Ginsberg Halfway House For
Rehabilitating Poets," Krassner cracked.

"And this whole Duluoz legend thing," I added.
"I had no idea about that. The whole 'one vast book like
Proust' routine. Now I want to go read the whole story in
order."

"Yeah, yeah, right," he said as he motioned we start
walking through the lily fields towards the exit. "And it
was the effort, man. The dedication, the volume of work,
the discipline over those years to keep writing when
nothing was getting published ... and that he never pulled
a Faulkner or Fitzgerald and just went into the advertising
business or Hollywood or some fuckin thing. Even after
On The Road came out he could have written ten of those

and cashed in but he stuck to his vision. Like *Leaves of Grass* except it was a *bunch* of books."

"Yeah," I said, looking into the thick leaves of dark green mountain grass we were shooshing through. "John Clellon Holmes was talking about that commitment thing — and how Jack'd go into physical training before he'd start a new book — do push-ups or go running or whatever and approach it like an athlete starting a season. The seriousness and uh ... like scholarly or professorial or like a scientist's approach or something."

"He was like a jazz musician always learning his instrument," Paul riffed on. "Like Buddhism or enlightenment — always *becoming*, never there. He should have called his book '*On The Path*'. (I laughed) It was that fucking booze that killed him. If he stuck to pot he'd still be writing."

"Yeah. And I was thinking about Lennon after Ken did that piece on him," I said. "How John totally embraced Jack and I guess Neal's idea of your life as your art, autobiographical — like '*The Ballad of John & Yoko*' and even '*Help*' or '*God,*' and everything on '*Double Fantasy*' ... it so sucks ... that Jack never got to write about growing old, or older, either, you know, cuz of the booze, and John cuz of that fucking asshole ... that the two best autobiographical artists only got half their story written."

"That's true," he said. And after we both walked a bit in silence, "But not everybody died. You didn't. Ginzo didn't. The Dead. Ken. There's still voices. Maybe in the wilderness, but you can still hear them. They're still out there."

"Yeah, I guess. And we just heard a bunch of them," I smiled to him. "Abbie was great."

"Wasn't he?! So glad he's back. That's another one," Krassner said about him finally reemerging after six years in hiding. "We could sure use him right now. Or a thousand of him."

"Right. Man, he was *on fire*, eh?" I burst. "I'd never seen him in person before. What a speech!"

"Yeah, he can do that," and he smiled at me, us both beaming over an old warrior in such fine fighting shape rejoining the battle.

And by then we were reaching the edge of the park and he was going one way and I the other, and we parted ways, but we'd end up reuniting a couple years later with The Dead, The Band and Kesey at The Third Eye Ball in Toronto, and he was part of the ceremony in Amsterdam when I inducted Jack into the Counterculture Hall of Fame, and I ended up booking him onto a couple of the shows I produced in Greenwich Village, but this was the day that yet another friend-for-life bloomed in that flower-filled alpine poet's field of Boulder.

24

The Oracle

As if we hadn't done enough damage in this town already, the location of the final climactic event was the big theater of *a high school* fer gawdsakes! — a setting I was only a couple years removed from.

Allen dubbed the summation of the summit **"Oracles: An Agenda For The Found Generation'"** ... which is so Allen ... and he made it the wordsmith's equivalent of the all-star jam at the end with everybody stepping out for one last solo. It was a visionary idea from a visionary soul who could not only out-poet just about everyone, but proved he could out-design and execute a festival rivalling Michael Lang or Bill Graham.

The idea was to have all the all-stars and also-stars come out prophesying briefly where we're going from here. From a show producer's point of view — what a brilliant collective closing chorus concept. And it all worked n everything but ol' suit-n-tie Allen didn't take into account the celebratory imbibing he himself should have been swept up in ... but No. He's The Man! General Ginzo! Our fearless leader out there gamely herding cats, who all seemed to be in heat at this point. I know I was off the clock, and from the looks of things most everybody else was, too.

At some point Paul Krassner took over as host. Again. He never even mentioned he was doing it when we were hanging just flashes ago, and yet here he was once again The Man at The Mic, the Beats' play-by-play man callin' the game.

And Gregory saunters out — I picture him with a whiskey glass in hand, but maybe it was just his Sinatra-cool swagger I remember. He admonished us to make the right choices in life — this coming from a guy who knows what it's like to make the wrong ones, but who somehow slipped through the decades of jaws of myriad rumors of Death to still be swingin' the soulful truthful spirit journey.

He was the most Beat of this entire submersion we were swimming in, and here he was pulling it all together for one last "shot." It's up to you: you can be a fuck up, you can be a corporate suit, or you can follow the voice that's already raging in your head. "Everything is right here and now, that's where you are . . . and it's a matter of choice," he said, abruptly walking away from the mic to at least a few standing ovations.

McClure read a trance-inducing poem about our interconnectedness with the environment. Anne Waldman did her new mega-mega-mega song-poem "*Uh-Oh Plutonium*" to a musical backing track. Diane di Prima also did a no-nuke poem, written on June 12th for the worldwide Disarmament Rallies. And come to think of it, Jan Kerouac also did a brief ominous oracle warning about plutonium. And just like Jan, Carolyn Cassady came out to huge whoops, and used her time to defend Sissy Spacek's portrayal of her (but not the movie). Ted Berrigan read a bunch of funny fortune cookie fortunes he'd written. Ferlinghetti said (again) we should do this every five years, and read a prose-poem about how artists today need to be more activist. Harpo Orlovsky came out and mostly just stood there for the two minutes, occasionally looking at his watch, and then just turned and walked away. Both the famous actors, Paul Gleason and Max Gail, stuck around for this closing night party and each read an original poem. Arthur Knight reminded us all to "Be in love with your own life," as Jack taught in his "*Essentials*."

And lots of the second and third generation Beats who hadn't gotten enough or any microphone time got up and let 'er rip for their two-minute shot, including this Dan Barth guy I never heard of (but did later) who rocked a riff on Whitman's children and mentioned not only Jerry

Garcia but Steve Goodman and Neil Young! — the only time my fellow Kelvinite from the Peg was cited all summit! The whole endless crazy night was a jamming jukebox of joyous Jacksters sharing their love just like John Lennon oracled.

Oh, and this one funny-priceless thing happened that was totally twisted and all in the family spirit of the whole climactic night. I mean, everyone had a good buzz on as the final peak folded in. I'm not saying it was immoral but it was certainly illegal in a high school — everyone smuggling in their Kerouacian Tokay in their pocket, which come to think of it prolly wasn't that different from every other graduation dance this building hosted.

Anyway, **ol' Al Aronowitz comes out**, and anybody who was at that "Jack and The Beatstocks" Living Room show I put on in New York when Al went on ... and on ... will get a kick out of this. So, The Outlaw Journalist, as he called himself, never did get any stage time all conference, but Allen agreed, late in the final night's proceedings to let him go out for a two minute oracle. Meanwhile ... Al's written this whole report on the conference that he right off informs us won't get published anywhere, so he begins to read the thing! I mean, the *whole thing!*

And about three minutes in, you can hear Allen yelling, "Two minutes, Al!" But he just keeps going. And I don't know if he planned it, but he was right in the middle of this great part that was actually an astute and loving tribute to Allen being a prophet and poet promoter, "the talent scout, the recruiter, the proselytizer, the missionary, the clown and the straight man," and he's getting rounds of applause, but Bill Graham knows we're now pushing five minutes and he's in the wings getting louder and louder, *"Two Minutes, Al!!!"*

But Al just keeps reading sentence after gushing sentence about the very director who's pacing back and forth on the side of the stage becoming a forehead tapping *Woody* Allen freaking-out trying to get the attention of the star he's put in the spotlight who's running amuck!

Eventually he comes out with what looked like Burroughs' cane and starts pantomiming a vaudevillian "getting the hook" routine. The audience is howling! **"The hook! Al! The hook!!"** he starts yelling since Al's ignoring him — this whole crazy comedy improv playing out in front of the whole theater — a real-life Shakespearian comedic setup with an actor stealing stage time by praising the director who's trying to yank him off it!

Finally Allen goes right out to center stage and they're standing mano-a-mano, muse-a-miscreant, Allen saying within mic range, "We're gonna turn the microphone off," as Al keeps thumping away on his pulpit, the other hand's finger raised in emphasis — "He's a visionary who spins his web with the patience of a spider! A teacher who has forged a new link in the chain of knowledge! A holy wanderer through eternity ..." — as Allen's *pleading* with him to *stop talking*. Finally the head of Beat Security comes out, Jack Micheline, and now that he has backup, Allen actually puts the cane around Al's neck while Micheline bear-hugs him and they drag poor Al off the mic and off the stage!

Gawd it was funny! And God bless 'em all. One

last lively family reunion memory-moment played out at a microphone.

After ten days of pomp and panels this may have been the most authentically unruly Beat event of the bunch — loud, messy, improvised, chaotic, open-miked and multi-voiced. The audience was drunk and hooting, the poets were drunk and Howling, the assembled were channeling and wailing, and the mad ones were clearly prevailing.

It was a long and winding evening with people wandering up and down the aisles, gathering in little clusters, conversing at the back of the house, and a large collective of revolving smokers out front. How and why we picked a high school to throw the final party is beyond me, probably because it was cheap and available in August, but I was thinking how so many of these practitioners of the page never even graduated from these haunted hallowed hallways of metal lockers and over-waxed linoleum — and for so many it was their first step back inside the homework hub since they were thrown out of their neighborhood High for getting high.

But here we all were graduating together from The School of Jack, with round berets instead of square mortarboards, secret stashes instead of sacred sashes, clutching bookmarked diaries instead of ribboned diplomas.

Hard to say which school would take us furthur, or even which was more fun, but what was different here was the collective passion of commitment, the uniformity of purpose without uniforms, the poetry of memory over the prose of memorization, and the practice of play over the perfection of performance.

And there was the right honorable Dean Ginsberg next to Dean Moriarty (in absentia) passing out the car keys to these new knights of the American Road that they may go forth and capture The Spirit and tenderhearted visions of the Adventure of Life for the rest of their lives.

The Gang's all here!

Front row, left to right — cross-legged on floor unknown;
on couch: Fran Landesman, Carolyn Cassady, Jay Landesman,
Gerald Nicosia, Regina Weinreich, William Burroughs

Middle row — standing: Paul Jarvis, Anne Waldman, Lawrence
Ferlinghetti, Nanda Pivano; sitting: John Clellon Holmes,
Robert Creeley, Peter Orlovsky, Allen Ginsberg, Al Aronowitz

Back row — Clark Coolidge (btwn Anne & Ferling), Jack
Micheline, Ann Charters, Sam Charters, Paul Krassner,
Timothy Leary, Leary's girlfriend, unknown man in glasses,
Abbie Hoffman

Taken: Saturday night, July 24th, 1982

Photo courtesy of the great Lance Gurwell.
You can get prints of this and tons of other Boulder '82 shots at:
stores.ebay.com/lancescollectibleslair/

25

Paradise To Heaven

After a few daze of decompressing in Denver and rock climbing in the Rockies, it was time to go On The Road again. But before hitting Kesey's, Brother Tom had insisted I go stay in his house in Marin just north of S.F. And it wasn't just *his* house, it used to be Grace Slick and Paul Kantner's mansion on the hill when they were rock's royalty leading the Jefferson Airplane.

Tom was always going on about how great Marin is (pronounced ma-rin — like "ma" as in Martian, "rin" as in Rin Tin Tin), and how the Dead and all the musicians live there now, and there's this tiny club called Sweetwater where they all play when they're not on tour — which Tom and the Dead still were all summer — but he had some cool hand dude taking care of the joint and insisted I go make it my base for as long as I want.

So, **I hitchhiked from Paradise to Heaven** — I mean, Boulder to Marin — using my well-read Jack thumb to flip me through.

Adventure Host Cliff and I jumped in the Rat Pack Cadillac for the last time, and he dropped me off on 104th Street on the outskirts of Denver, and **before I could even get my first sign made, some Air Force guy honks and pulls over!** This is startin' easy! My mom's first husband, who was killed long before I came along, had been an Air Force pilot and somehow through The Great Osmosis I could relate to this guy's world and he to mine. He was a straight-up dude out dudin' the right thing, pickin' up some guy on the side of the road who was going somewhere just like he was — the wild blue yonder, other places, other spaces, other faces by the graces.

We were a helluvan Odd Couple, though — Bobby Brush-cut and Prince Valiant. Close to the same age, I was digging on the incredibly different lives we led, and had led, to this point. I couldn't imagine being told what time to go to bed and what time to get up and what to do every minute of every day; and I don't think he'd know what to do without the structure of someone telling him. Yet we were totally simpatico, and had a symphonic jam as we crossed the simple land.

He dropped me off outside Fort Collins, another Colorado college town where the pick-ups are easy and the roadside breezy. Of course I was jamming on this being the place where Dylan's Rolling Thunder tour was filmed and recorded for "*Hard Rain*" and halfway had a notion to go find the stadium, but figured there prolly wasn't enough of a payoff for the hike involved. And besides, in about 10 minutes this old Ernest Borgnine-looking guy stopped, telling me he's heading for Cheyenne, and right away in my Kerouacian head I started replaying Jack's bar-hopping girl-chasing visit with Montana Slim during Frontier Days in *On The Road*. So I asked the guy if he ever goes to it, and he damn near slams on the brakes and throws me out! "Why the hell you askin' me that?" he says.

"It was just mentioned in this book I was reading."

"Well, that can't be much of a gawdamn book, cuz yer a week late, thank gawd," he says.

"You mean it just happened?"

"Yeah, of course it just happened — you an idiot?"

"Well, I was just at this writers conference in Boulder," I say, hoping that'll chill him a little. "We weren't getting much news from beyond there."

"Boulder? You some kinda hippie?" and he looks over at me. "Yeah, you look like a hippie." And suddenly I'm flipping from *On The Road* to *Easy Rider*.

"I don't know. I just came down from Canada for some writers courses," playing my Northern card and studentiness to see if that will get him off whatever problem he had.

"Canada? Never bin. Why would you live there? What the hell is there in Canada?"

"Well," I said, looking around. "A lotta land like this," as we were surrounded by the vast views of nothingness, and there was suddenly silence as we High Plains drifted across the tundra.

"Yeah, I suppose there is. Well, as long as you weren't here for that gawddamn Frontier Drunks."

"Why's that? Is it a bad thing?"

"Gawddamn right it's a bad thing. People pissing all over the fuckin' streets for two weeks. I get the hell out and live with my sister in Collins every year when that buncha idiots comes to town. Turns the whole gawddamn place into Disneyland for Assholes. Woo-woo-woo-woo-woo," he goes, making Indian war path sounds.

And we went on like this for a while, and I learned everything that was wrong with people, and the country, and the world, although I got the sense the guy'd never been out of the Mountain time zone in his life!

He finally dropped me off outside Cheyenne, assuring me how lucky I was that the "fuckin' tourists" from the East were all gone, and he smiles and waves goodbye like he was the friendliest guy in the world who'd just made a new best friend.

After about an hour of nothing happening under the blazing midday August sun of Cheyenne, Wyoming, I started to lament the lack of tourists at Disneyland, and suddenly remembered this was the least populated state in the country or something, until finally this guy in a fancy tan Caprice Classic pulls over, and I'm thinkin he's gotta be more civilized, as Huck would say, than ol' Ernest Borgnine. I throw my pack in the back seat, jump in the front, ... and the guy's got a bucket of spit beside him, and a Colt 45 on the dash — and I don't mean the beer.

He turns out to be okay. That is, he doesn't shoot me, and drives us clear across Wyoming from the desolate endless grey High Plains into the foothills of the Rockies again. Right away he notices me lookin' at the shiny long-barreled six-shooter, and lets me sweat it out a while. We talk about whatever, but my eyes are prolly always flashing over to it, so eventually he says, "I see you notice the gun. Don't worry, it's for niggers and assholes. You don't look like either."

That's one of those lines you don't forget. Boulder, of course, was a liberal mecca of tolerance, not that I ever saw any black people there, but in *Denver* I'd heard "the N word" several times and other comments I'd never heard firsthand before. And they thought nothing of it. Coming from Winnipeg and Vancouver and lately Greenwich Village, Manhattan, I'd never experienced authentic inbred totally-accepted racism before. In my world, people would name-drop some hip band or philosopher or author to convey their cool to a stranger. In these parts, it seemed like you wanted show how much you hated the n-words to prove your cool. Very weird. I would let it just pass through the air and not say a goddamn thing. When in Rome ... get out alive.

This guy seemed to have a lot of hate for other

people, too, and I figured he just wanted somebody to listen to his rantings. You have to become a different character to survive each of these different road plays. I don't wanna think about what would happen if he knew what I thought about what he was saying. But it's part of the world — and that's what I was digging on. Who *are* these people? I'm sure not gonna run into one on MacDougal Street! They hate every person in government except Ronald Reagan, and any person who's not a WASP, and they're angry, and probably go through a lot of ammo shootin' at gawd knows what every week. It really is still the Wild West out West.

So, old Ku Klutz Krazy drives me all the way to Green River, and I laughed as John Fogerty's riff started to wipe off the dirt on my mental windshield with just the push of a memory button. "Let me remember things I love..." Johnny's singin' in my jukebox head.

Suddenly I was standing in a gorgeous mountain town surrounded by windblown buttes with rivers and lakes and green trees, a full-blown oasis after the desert we'd just crossed. I could see doing some serious hang time here, but I was on a mission from God — or at least from Tom, and Ken, and Jack, and the Saint of Wanderlust. And before long a semi picked me up and we're heading across the hump, back into dreaded Salt Lake City, a place I vowed I'd never come back to. Unless I did.

And to make matters worse, by the time he drops me off on the outskirts of town — it's dark. What I was doing hitchhiking through the Wild West in the middle of the night I'll never know, but I did it. And now it was this crazy challenge to get the heck outta there as fast as I could

— but who the hell's gonna pick you up at ten o'clock at night — except maybe a baseball player who's just finished a late game and is heading home still in his uniform and jazzed that they won and telling me about every play in Roger Angell detail; followed by two drunk girls who'd just left a bar and didn't think much of the guys there, or me either, as far as I could tell; followed by this Texan dude who'd come up there just to make money and was workin' two jobs and layin' low; followed by this older woman who was going in to work the night shift at the "76" truck stop on the far side of town where she dropped me off and was certain I'd get a ride with a trucker from there, and she was right, and I was back inside another semi-trailer headin' West my friend, with Salt Lake Shitty in the rearview mirror.

And in the silent semi thought-time of the nighttime void I drifted back through the foggy ruins to everything I'd seen and everything I'd heard in the daylights just past, and was loving how I was living the subject of the book that was the subject of the conference, and playing back the tapes in my head if not my cassette deck, and suddenly in the darkness a bright light bulb came on!

"Wait a gawddamn minute ... Salt Lake City ... through Nevada to S.F. ..." and I climbed back in the belly of that bouncing beast to my backpack, fished out my *On The Road*, and with the trucker's nifty little nightlight, started flipping through its notated pages and sure-a-damn-nuff! — we were following the exact same route that ol' Jack described in the book! Mind you, they were driving *to* Denver on the big trip after Carolyn had thrown them out of the house which led to the travel-bureau Cadillac and eventually New York where Neal would meet Diana Hansen and father Curt and they all would live tumultuously ever after.

But that whole damn adventure started with the travel-bureau trip in the "fag Plymouth" with the eponymous driver and the two scared tourists as Sal and Dean sat in the back and talked so excitedly about "IT!" they started rocking the car, completely forgetting about the people in the front, but bopping up and down about knowing *TIME* and how they know they're going to get to where they're going and you can choose to worry the details or simply *know* you're going to get there and lock in on the joys of the journey. Which they did, and thanks to Jack writing it down, I did too.

Old Yosemite Semi Sam bounced us all the way to the far end of Utah to a little place called Wendover, right on the border of Nevada, when I suddenly heard the air brakes whooshing the big rig to a stop, and he says, "Alright I'm gonna have a sleep here," as I looked out at a roadside rest area in the pitch black desert in the middle of Nofuckinwhere, Utah. *Greaaaaat!*

This is your one-car-an-hour midnight highway, and I'm not even at any kind of a stop, just a freakin' dark rest area that everybody zooms past as they're gettin' the hell outta Utah. The only thing goin' for me is there's a full moon tonight! But it sure ain't workin' its magic! And of course you immediately start thinking about the rattlesnakes and scorpions that you heard come out at night and lie on the cool pavement in the total freakin' dark. And I'm thinking a frickin' flashlight would be handy right about now. Note to self.

After about 7,000 years of fears and no beers, of sitting on top of a picnic table scared of the bloodthirsty ground, but still getting up to run to the road whenever car lights would appear on the horizon, until about 5AM when a car finally swerved over to the shoulder. It was some guy who'd just won a jackpot in Nevada and had run home to Utah for some supplies and was dashing back "to the go-go girls" in the Sin City state. The guy was amped and talkin' a mile a minute about how he just won at blackjack and how when you're in the zone you have to keep playing. "I knew I had it, this full moon, baby, it's all comin' together. Ride 'em when ya got 'em! Wooo-hoooo! America! Love it or leave it, baby! Hey, you smoke?" he asks, pulling out a joint. And we made that Nevada highway sing like Duke and Gonzo. I'd traded my paperback *Las Vegas* for *Road* way back when — and now I was trading back.

So we blast n blaze across that straight line through the night with that big holy spotlight beaming down on us, and like life, we could only see a little ways ahead at any time but we could race into the future as fast as we wanted to push it. We finally got to Wells, the apparent base of his debauchery, and he was jacked for more of his same, and I was Jacked for more of mine.

Although it was still dark, at least this kind of drop-off wasn't the blackened hell of Nofuckinwhere, Utah — and now I was in a state more to my liking in more ways than one, and in fact there was a 24 hour beer store right there on the highway! *Mmm-doggie!* With nuthin' but my kinda lawlessness ahead — Nevada into California into Oregon — I opted for a can or three of the lager champaign to celebrate breaking the back of this badboy. It was gonna be a coast to the coast from here, Mr. Beer — now soaking in the full moon cheer and not wanting the night to end.

Full moon over Nevada, 6:00 AM
August 4th, 1982

But I still had many miles to go before I sleep, and just as the dark fun of the Nevada night was ending, without much work at all, a VW van came in for a landing. They're the best. The side door slides open and it's a couple way older than me, God they coulda been 30 for all I know, but they were Lefty hip and Weir right in synch. She's running the tape deck, a boombox perched between them, cuz this is a '66 Volkswagen window van, with everything original including the smell, and all it's got is a classic 5-button AM radio in the old-school dashboard. "You like Van Morrison?" she asks as she clicks off the nocturnal Pink Floyd and puts on the mellow Morrison morning music as the highway and desert slowly begin to reveal themselves — the wide highways of the West, 2 lanes here, 2 lanes across a wide boulevard going the other way, and easygoing low mountains lopping along the horizon.

And Van's singing to us in the van, some album I hadn't heard, and all of a sudden — something familiar. Wait a minute! "The smell of the bakery from across the street, got in my nose ..." Hold on! No way! "*This* song!" I fairly scream! It's Van's first good single in years! — "*Cleaning Windows*" — "This song mentions Kerouac!!" I blast them loud enough for the rabbits to cock their ears along the roadside!

"Oh yeah, I guess it does," she says, already boppin' in her seat. "It's the best song on the album. That's Mark Knopfler on guitar."

"No way! That's Knopfler?!" I blurted.

"Yeah. And Pee Wee Ellis on sax," the drummer driver fills in. "Great song to play drums on," he says as he bangs out precision beats in the air, two handed, cymbals and all.

"What album **is** this?" I ask, and she hands me the cassette case of his new release — "*Beautiful Vision*" — but I'm too jazzed to really look at it. "I've got this song taped from the radio in New York — it's *amazing*!! They play it on WNEW. You had to pick me up off the floor the first time I heard this!"

The song's an autobiographical reflection by Van on the books and music that made him who he is, and the three of us are suddenly locked right in like we're playing it with him. "I'm a working man in my prime, cleaning windows," we all sing together. And then he gets to the climactic verse, "I went home and read my Christmas Humphrey's book on Zen, *Curiosity Killed The Cat*, Kerouac's *Dharma Bums* and *On The Road,*" and I'm freakin' out! Here's Jack *on the road with us* — unbelievable! The Grande Synch continues! Live and in person!

And after it's over I begin to tell them at a million miles an hour about everything that just happened in Boulder. And the sun was now freshly beaming just like the three faces of Van in the van as everything turned into an epic God-given Beautiful Vision.

We're all bopping along, soaking in the gorgeous movie playing on the windshield before us, when this VW Beetle cousin coming towards us in the opposite lanes — suddenly veers off the highway and onto the grassy meridian straight towards us! But it cut so fast it suddenly flips over — and starts rolling sideways like a ball across the boulevard! "HOLY SHIT!!" we all scream in harmony, none of us turning our heads from the rolling dust as we pulled to the shoulder and stopped nearly at the same time it stopped flipping over.

Jump out — run over and there's this dead bug on the side of the road with its legs in the air — and people start crawling out of it. One, two, three, four, *five* of them!

Geezus! And they're all beat to shit and bleeding ... but they're moving. The next car coming the same direction slows down, it's some solo woman, and we yell, "Call an ambulance," and she yells back, "Okay," and speeds off — because the only way you could call one was to drive to the nearest place with a phone.

And we start doing triage, but they're all sort of stumbling around in the wide boulevard like zombies, totally in shock, and we have to corral them one by one and get them to stay near the damn car. Then it got even worse — at least for them and whoever owned the car. The driver was the only guy who knew what happened, because everybody else was stone cold asleep, and apparently he inadvertently joined them, and he tells me how it's *a drive-away car*, and they signed a contract that they wouldn't drive at night, and wouldn't have more than two people in the car. "Oh man, this is not good. ... We're fucked ..." he's saying over and over again as he's pacing back and forth around the car, and he's got this huge bump the size of a golf ball already growing on his forehead, and he doesn't want us to call the cops, and asks if I'll help him tip the car over so they could keep going!

"Uh-huh . . . um . . . you might have a bit of a ding on your head there. And . . . I really don't know if this car's going to be able to . . . um . . . drive right now," I try to get through to him.

Miraculously, and high praise to whoever makes these Bugs, the thing tumbled like a Daytona crash and the roof never caved in and everyone walked away alive.

Pretty soon we heard sirens, and pretty soon after

that we were back On The Road in the VW van, driving much slower, with no music on, and it was a much different morning.

They finally dropped me off in Winnemucca, Nevada, can you believe it? The kind of place you'd never know existed if you didn't hitchhike through it and get stuck there. Tiny, like Gimli where we had a cottage in Manitoba. Nuthin' but a highway goin' past. But it was in this empty space that a bus came by and I got on — a station-wagon from Minnesota goin' all the way across the Sierra Nevadas to Sacramento! The ride I was waiting for! California here I come!

And suddenly I was back home. Minnesota is America's Manitoba. Mayberry writ large. Cottages in the summer, hockey in the winter, and fishing holes in both. For the next five hours of picturesque California mountain road trippin' I was *home*, talkin' Jets vs. North Stars, Carter & Minnesota's Mondale vs. Rayguns & Texas's Bush — and which of us remembered the coldest winter. There's different things valued in different parts of the world. And those of us from a certain part of the continent, well, we got a peculiar sense of pride.

We were laughing our heads off, tellin' stories of all the crazy places we've been, and without saying it, this theme emerged of how us Manitoba-Minnesota boys can fit in anywhere. It's an honesty and a trust and an enthusiasm for life and people, a curiosity — a show-me state, except we don't mean "prove something," we just mean *show* me something! Anything's interesting after you've trapped inside half the year!

And being two hockey boys heading to California, I asked, already knowing the answer, "Did you see that Miracle on Manchester game?!!"

"Oh my God — *how does that happen?!*" he said about the greatest comeback in NHL history that just went down a couple months ago, where The Great One's Oilers were up 5–0 *in the third period*, but somehow lost the game and then the series to the nobody L.A. Kings in the playoffs that just ended. "Who the hell loses to *L.A.??*"

"I *know!*" and we were both suddenly bouncing in the front seat like boys who grew up with ice in their veins and under their skates are prone to do whenever our greatest passion's evoked.

"I was blown away by how *into* it the L.A. fans were," he said.

"Yeah — and think about the fans who *weren't!*... who left after the second period when they were down five–nuthin? Right? Gave up ... to beat the traffic ... and then listening to it on the radio in the car."

"*Br-uuutal!*"

And for the next hundred miles we cooled ourselves in the blazing hot dry desert by evaluating every team in the league. Then I suddenly remembered — this is the place in *On The Road* where Neal took the wheel and balled that jack across Nevada and freaked the straight-streets right out, so I pulled out my road-worn copy and read The Nevada Road section to my Minny driver as we ripped that blacktop all the way to Reno!

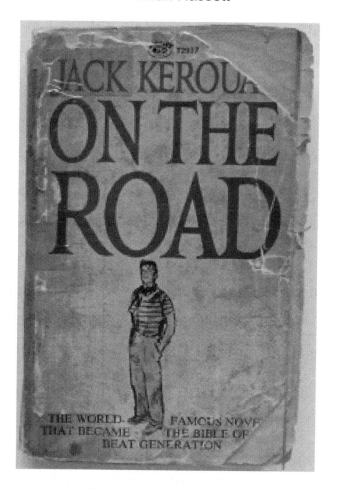

My road Road — a 1965 edition copped from a sidewalk bookseller in the East Village in 1981 for a buck. It was the second copy I got, cuz I wanted to have one I could Beat up and keep sacred my first copy.

Then suddenly — Boom! The Sierra Nevadas were staring us down from all sides. And what pretty eyes they have! Faces of sculpted natural beauty surround us like fashion show runway models, with every minute or two a completely new and different beauty appearing before us, pirouetting for a good view, and disappearing again, all day long until you became numb to it.

And in a before-ya-know-it, we're in the Capital of Cool, Sacramento, California, where the laws of this beautiful land-of-the-free are set forth, and I feel like firing up a doobie as soon as Minnesota Mike drops me off. But before I can soak up even a ray of California sunshine, some State Trooper pulls up and tells me to get the hell off the freeway! Welcome to Happyville! Think I'll go back to Salt Lake City, I do believe I've had enough! And oh yeah, right — this is the same town Dean got hit on on their trip and made things weird — maybe this joint *wasn't* the cosmic bop groove after all.

But before I could even walk to the bottom of the ramp, some guy in a 4-wheel-drive jeep makes a sharp pull-in to the shoulder — and we're off! It's about 2 in the afternoon, well more than 24 hours since Cliffy dropped me off in Denver, and this guy's heading nearly to San Francisco! To Vallejo to be exact, which sounded like Valhalla to me. And to top it off, he figures it's a good idea we stop and get some beers for the road. Boom! — California — just like I pictured it! Beer for sale at every lemonade stand, fruit at every gas station, dreams on every corner.

My head was bouncin' in circles taking it all in, while Eddie at the wheel was calm as a cactus with roots as wide. He grew up here and had seen it all — the Dead at the Fillmore, Janis at the Carousel, the Airplane at the Matrix, and he's makin' me just about sick. I start cursing growing up in Winterpeg a million miles from anything cool, and he says, "Yeah but, you are who you are." And whaddya gonna say to that? "And you're here now," he winks.

The student was ready and the teachers were appearing!

And somehow we got to talking about our parents, and I explained how I got along with my mom but not my dad — that she was an artist and he was a conservative farmer-cum-banker and we'd never seen eye-to-eye. And Eddie says, "Talk to your dad. You have more in common than you think. You seem like a levelheaded kid. He's probably more scared to talk to you than you are to him. Did he go to college?" he asked, seeming to already know the answer was no. "He won't admit it, but you probably intimidate him. Talk to him. It's going to be up to you."

Between Kesey's benediction and Eddie's admonition, and thinking how both ol' Neal and Jack lost their fathers in different ways and spent the rest of their lives trying to resolve it, I pledged then and put into practice ever-after a dialog with my distant dad. Even though we only got part-way there, I spent the rest of his years giving him all the time and attention I could, and even if he couldn't articulate much, his tears each time I left told me the effort was worth it.

Eddie may have driven me to Vallejo, but he also took me a whole lot furthur.

And as this California prophet dropped me off on the burning shore of that bay by San Francisco, I knew I was knockin' on the heavenly door of Marin.

Not a minute after saying goodbye and stepping onto the roadside in this Holy Land of Hip, some young short-haired guy in a fancy red sports car going about a million miles an hour pulls over to a silent instant robo-stop. This snappy young brainiac was driving all the way to the Dead's home base of San Rafael, next door to Brother Tom's! Right away he began talking about computers, which I knew nothing about and was picturing the banks of giant machines in the underground bunkers of James Bond movies. He explained, no, he was talking about personal computers that you'd have at your house. "Why would you want one of those?" I asked. "I don't want to become a computer."

He laughed, "Okay, what do you do?" I told him I produced shows and I wrote. "Okay, for example you could keep track of all the specs of all the venues you work with so you could instantly search and find the best room for whatever show you wanted to do. And — " he stopped, "Wait, you're not still writing on a typewriter are you?" Uh, *yeah*. "Ouu. What if you have to change a word or add a sentence or something after you've finished? What do you do? You retype the whole thing?" as he looks at me like I'm an idiot. "With word processing, you'd just change whatever you want and print it out fresh and clean and only have to type it once."

I'm sort of starting to hate the guy now, because that does sound pretty cool ... and sort of ... impossible to comprehend. But ... but ... computers run robots and I won't become a robot. He laughs and starts making R2D2 sounds and moving his arms around. "You are riding with one now," he speaks in robot. "Robots are friendly. You just tell us what to do and we obey." The guy's freakin' me out. I'm supposed to be in the land of organic music and anti-materialism and back-to-the-land living — and here's this Hugo Suavé in a fancy sports car talking about computers and robots!

He dropped me off in downtown San Rafael right on Francis Drake Blvd. heading to Brother Tom's house with my head spinning more than that good reefer in Nevada. By the time I got back to NYU that fall, the Commodore 64 had been released and I started noticing these things they called computers in a few students' dorm rooms, and saw these class papers being handed in that weren't typed by the hand of man. And these computer people didn't seem to be robots at all. In fact, a couple of the girls were kinda cute.

A month later, The Grateful Dead would play the US Festival, entirely paid for by one of these San Francisco computer guys, Steve Wozniak, and I'd end up buying my first IBM clone a year after that. But for the rest of time I'd always wonder if that was Woz or Jobs or Gates or one of those neighborhood whiz kids who first opened my eyes.

In a California minute, I was picked up — for the final and once again exactly 17th time (!) on this journey from Boulder to Marin — by a former navy warrant officer who bailed on that and started baling homegrown weed instead. Looking out into these lush dense mountainous hills and valleys of Northern California it was sure easy to see how it would grow here and never be found. And with every twist of that weird & winding road we climbed higher into the mountains and grew smaller under the trees, until he knew exactly where I was going, pulling into the Woodacre General Store along the edge of the highway, and I was a 10¢ payphone call from the next basecamp on this long strange trip.

26

The Airplane Hanger in Marin

Brother Tom's gatekeeper, Lee, drove up in The Official California State Vehicle — a VW window van, an identical twin to the one Allen bought in the early '60s and visited Kesey & Neal with at La Honda not far too from here — and this young David Crosby lookalike proceeded to weave us up some unnamed one-lane tree-suffocating shadow-and-light mountain road to the peak of a cliff with a wooden gingerbread house hidden behind trees and perched on the rim.

This had been **Grace Slick and Paul Kantner's house** in the early '70s — definitely the kind of place nobody could find — in fact, I'm surprised *they* could in the condition they were prolly in most nights — but it was your all natural, au naturel hideaway. Made of lightly varnished wood, it looked like a plain little cottage from the dirt lane they called a road, but once you walked in, it kept expanding with room after room after room.

And because it was built on the edge of a ravine, out the whole main back wall were the tops of the trees that were growing way down below, so all the windows looked directly into crowns or mid-trunk foliage — the same trees Jack marvelled over when he was here. And all along the watchtower cliff side was a labyrinth of decks and balconies and walkways and sitting areas and the requisite outdoor California hot tub surrounded by redwoods — a scene I hadn't seen very often in Manhattan or Manitoba.

Inside was the secret writer's hideaway I'd always dreamed of living in. Every room was like a giant cedar closet lined with strips of fine wood that smelled like it had just been cut. There was a huge stone fireplace in the living room, giant ferns and other greenery in every corner, and tall bookcases with glass doors built into the walls. And everything else was built-in, too. Ornate carved cabinet doors hid the elaborate stereo system with speakers camouflaged into the ceiling corners of every room so you never saw them but could hear Jerry everywhere all the time. And if you pushed on one of the boards on the wall in just the right place, a giant hidden well-stocked liquor cabinet opened up, which Lee couldn't be more pleased to show me.

In fact, due to Tom's um "occupation," he was an extremely private person, and with the Dead touring so much of the year I got the feeling ol' Lee didn't get many visitors. "Oh, Tom had me put this together for you," he said, as he led me into my designated guestroom, and on the waterbed was a huge baggie of California's finest that I couldn't smoke all of if I stayed here till Christmas, plus this outrageously gorgeous Grateful Dead rose t-shirt that I've kept to this day, and an assortment of Dead stickers in all different shapes and sizes. Much like him giving tickets away, I'd also seen him after a show buying one or more of pretty much everything that was for sale on the way to his car — it was his way of funneling money back into the family and giving generously to Jerry's Kids. His hotel rooms were always full of this stuff — he musta bought truckfuls over the years — and then he just gives it all away.

And here we were in his prankster's paradise hideaway, with Jerry playing in the trees and nuthin left to do but smile smile smile.

Lee, the Old Hermit of the High Ground, was naturally interested in the backstory of the person behind this rare invitation to the inner sanctum, waving his hand across the bar wall for inspiration. In keeping with the Kesey tradition, I selected G&Ts as the tonic of choice, Lee picked up the clear pyrex baking tray half filled of gummy Humboldt buds, and we retired to deck number one to begin the fun. If you've never come across these freshly picked nugs, the mind-pleasing resin is so thick the flowertops stick to your fingers like honey, and the aroma gets you high before you even light it up.

And thus began a rather indeterminate number of daze at the Airplane Hanger on Mount Tom.

Does anybody really know what time it is? Were we ever here at all? Everybody's dancin' ... or at least I was.

It was Mission Accomplished at Camp Kerouac, and I was safely back on the coast of homebase Vancouver, living in the hills of my heroes, breathing in their air of moist evergreens and flowering dreams in the pungent August of the redroad earth.

In fact, it was neighboring Marin City that first launched Jack *on the road.* He called it Mill City in his book, but it was where his old friend Henri Cru was living with the promise of a job shipping out from San Francisco Bay that gave Jack the destination and purpose and confidence to cross the country for the first time. Of course, the whole thing turned out to be a comical disaster, as befitting Henri and his wild schemes, and as portrayed by Jack in his wild book, but if this mysterious outcropping of redwoods and hills was home enough for them it was good enough for me.

And of course we were also just a few minutes from the sacred ground where Jack's glorious nature novels were born — the hills of Mill Valley where Gary Snyder lived in his "Marin-An" shack behind Locke McCorkle's house on the slopes of Mount Tamalpais (Tam-al-pie-iss) where Jack got back to the land and set his soul free in *The Dharma Bums* and *Desolation Angels.* This was the magic place on the planet that turned him onto the Earth, the environment, the rucksack-Jack mountain climb — and is where he told Edie he wanted to retire: "I'll take Mémère out to California and get her a little rose covered cottage, and get me a shack for half the time, in the wild hills beyond Mount Tamalpais."

It was easy to see why he and George Lucas and the

Boulder *Kerouac* documentarian John Antonelli and Van Morrison and David Crosby and all these cats were gonna make these mountains be their home. Paging – The Great Planet Earth Rock 'n' Roll Orchestra! In fact, when that all-star amalgam of the Dead, the Airplane and CSNY got together in San Francisco to record among other things Crosby's masterpiece *"If I Could Only Remember My Name,"* they named the album's glorious transcendental instrumental, *"Tamalpais High,"* in a loving ode to their inspirational earth force overseer.

And this was all in the wake of the flood of Bill Graham, Peter Coyote, Janis Joplin, Carlos Santana, Steve Miller, Mike Bloomfield, Jessie Colin Young and half the musicians on the West Coast all migrating to these meandering, mindful hills and hamlets of musical Marin. And as if that wasn't enough, and by golly it should be, even John & Yoko came and lived here in a home near the Mill Valley library in the summer of '72.

You've got the mysterious mountainous terrain and old growth redwood forests including Muir Woods a couple miles North; dramatic, rugged ocean coastline with hidden sandy beaches to the West; Mill Valley, the Deuce, the Sweetwater and other smalltown clubs and adventures just down the hills to the East; and all "the mad ones" and jazz joints of downtown San Francisco about 30 minutes to the South — and all the while you're living in some kind of fairy tale woodland wonderland that's more densely populated with trees than New York is with people. But unlike Manhattan, this is a local-centric place — no numbered street grids for outsiders to find their way around — maps and directions have to be in your head and a homing instinct in your heart to survive this Pollock of paved pathways.

It's where the Dead first moved their scene from the Haight — to the legendary exotic Rancho Olompali camp in nearby Novato, then scampering and scattering into the hills of the surrounding countryside. It was the site of the famous Muir Beach Acid Test that in fact Kesey would write about in his eulogy to Garcia. And it's where Jerry did that first historic interview with *Rolling Stone*. As local visionary rock 'n' roll heart Jann Wenner tells it, by 1970 the magazine's in-depth interviews had become part of the national conversation, but his S.F.-based counterculture flag-bearer had never gotten The Big One, the driving force behind the music that made their city famous, in part because Jann (pronounced "yawn" even though he never yawned or said a commonplace thing!) couldn't find anyone up to the task — until a Yale anthropologist named Charles Reich walked in one day and asked why there hadn't been a Garcia interview. The two of them drove up to Jerry's mountain hideaway with Mountain Girl who was not long removed from being Kesey's girlfriend, and the two *Rolling Stoners* and the two stoned rollers hung out on the Captain's bridge with a panoramic view of the ocean, communicating so clearly, so richly, that Yes! This was not just an interview — *this was a book!* Of course! *A Signpost To New Space.* And so it was.

And besides everything else this fertile land birthed, it's also where the very first outdoor rock festival was held! Yep. Not only pre-Woodstock, but pre-Monterey

Pop. Halfway up Mount Tam at a little amphitheater in the sky bands like The Airplane, The Byrds, The Doors, Country Joe & The Fish, Captain Beefheart, Canned Heat and a couple dozen others (but not The Dead, who were off playing their first-ever shows in New York City that week) gathered for two days of fun and music, and nothing but fun and music. Appropriately called the Fantasy Fair and Magic Mountain Festival, it grew organically out of San Francisco's free festival spirit that also gave the world the Human Be-In six months earlier, and it cost all of $2 a day — *which* was then donated to a children's care center.

Not only would the Dead go on to set up their permanent and legendary office on Front Street in San Rafael, but according to *High Times* publisher and herbal historian Steve Hager, that's also the town where the now-ubiquitous term for smoking pot — **"420"** — came from. "It was 1971 at the San Rafael High School," he said, after much research. "A half-dozen or so students were looking for an abandoned pot field that they thought they had a map to. They'd meet after school let out — at 4:20 PM — by the Louis Pasteur statue near their school to go looking for it. They called themselves The Waldos. They never did find the pot patch, but '420' became a term they could use in front of the their parents and teachers meaning, 'Let's get high.' Many of the Grateful Dead crew and extended family lived in the area along with the band, and they were always of a mind to mine whatever's cool and new, and the phrase worked its way into the Dead culture, and from there it spread nationally and ultimately internationally into the code word for — and time of day to — get high."

The beauty of both the land and the people also inspired tragic Beat poet and fellow mountain resident **Lew Welch** to write his wonderful *"The Song Mount Tamalpais Sings"* that hymnfully concludes, "There is nowhere else we need to go." A minor character in Jack's *Desolation Angels,* Lew is also immortalized as Duluoz's drinking buddy Dave Wain in Kerouac's masterpiece of madness, *Big Sur.* Lew was college roommates with Gary Snyder and Philip Whalen at Reed in Portland, Oregon, got separated from them for awhile, but once he found them living here in Marin, he stayed on for the rest of his short life. It's also where he hooked up with a woman and became a terrific stepdad to her son, who grew up to be a singer known as Huey Lewis — who's been quoted as saying, "The Beats were the original rock stars."

And to add to that spirit land's end — **Alan Watts** lived nearby until he passed away in his cabin one night in 1973. The author of *The Wisdom of Insecurity, This is IT, The Joyous Cosmology,* the Buddhist master and new world thinker, was writing and exploring at the very same time in the very same place in the very same space as the Beats, in fact Jack writes about discussing Buddhism with him in *The Dharma Bums,* and he shows up too in *Desolation Angels,* and was orbiting in Planet Snyder's same Buddhistic Tamalpaisian trajectory, and was a major cat in this cool clowder that was Mighty Marin. Watts was part of the psychic psychedelic British Invasion along with Aldous Huxley, Aleister Crowley, George Orwell and the rest — the British Evolution Revolution that presaged and pre-raged the soon-to-be Beat-les. And at the root of it all Watts was a Zen scholar (though of course he'd call himself a student) when Jack was discovering Buddhism. This place was one giant party of practicing pranksters and prophets, and the hills were alive with the sound of magic.

It's no wonder . . . "That *Mork and Mindy* guy grew up just down the road," Lee mentions in passing. "He's still got a place here."

"Really? ... Wait ... what? I was just *in* Mork & Mindy's town! You mean Robin Williams?! I love that guy! He *lives* here?! You ever met him?!"

"No," he says a little down-tinged. "He's in some movie coming out this weekend though — *The World According To Carp* or something. Heard it's not really funny, but it's supposed to be good."

And after another long pull on a Tom stogie of California's finest, he says, "And if you wanna go hear a band we should check out The Dinosaurs."

"Oh yeah? Never heard of 'em."

"It's Robert Hunter and John Cipollina's new band."

"WHAT?!?!"

"Yeah. Cipollina lives just over the hill. He and Tom are pretty good friends. And it's got, like, Barry Melton from The Fish, ... oh and Spencer Dryden from The Airplane ... and Merl from Jerry's band."

"*What?!*"

"Yeah, I know! They just played their first gig at the Marin County Fair last month. I missed it but heard they were Grate."

"Man — you guys got it made in the redwood shade

here. No wonder Tom raves about it."

And after another long pause, "And Stewart Brand," he kept going. "Y'know, the *Whole Earth Catalog* guy? He just moved into Gerd Stern's houseboat there in Sausalito. They just put out a new edition last year I think it was — we have it here somewhere. But the guy's getting way into computers n shit. ... I'm not into that Big Brother crap."

"Yeah — me *either*," I said. "Some guy who just gave me a ride was trying to sell me on that shit. What's with people around here and computers?! I didn't expect an IBM Inquisition!"

But it all kept coming back to *Jack* — the refraining chorus in this ongoing songscape — including everything digested and not yet from the past two weeks at Camp Kerouac.

I was thinking how I was Neal's exact age when he first met Jack and their *On The Road* adventures began. And how it was only the beginning of August and this year I'd already been adventuring in New York, Winnipeg, Gimli, Vancouver, Boulder, and now Marin and San Francisco, and soon Kesey's in Oregon, before going back to Vancouver and Winnipeg and Manhattan to start a third year at NYU running the school's concerts. *"That's keeping a Cassady pace,"* I'm thinkin'. But what I wasn't keeping was a Kerouacian writing schedule, and somehow I had to work that out, because even this trip was worthy of a book. But how could I get there? Turns out, I'd spend the rest of my life coming up with solutions to that badboy.

And I was thinking about how Allen and Gregory and Kesey and Abbie and all of them were now the age of my parents' friends ... but these guys still seemed like teenagers in their enthusiasm and energy and optimism and playfulness. And I decided that's how I wanted to be when I grew up. You didn't have to be straight and boring. These guys were proof that I was on the right path. Look at them! They were all great friends and have been doing crazy shit together for decades — *and they're still doin' it.* That's the way I wanted my movie to roll out. And I had time to direct it.

This was a young person's game — but you didn't have to be physically young. I had that numerical advantage at the moment, but they had the crazy wisdom of the playful ages. And we could work together — giving each of us what the other didn't have. It's not like these guys were dead and gone. And also, now that the vision had been confirmed — that is, my not-commonly-accepted view of life and art and the world — now I knew for sure and for firsthand that this path doesn't kill you and in fact makes you smarter and there's art at the end of the tunnel.

To a man, these guys were so confident. And their vision, as they so proactively executed it, was constantly reinforced — sometimes financially, but always aesthetically and connectively rewarding. They kept getting more experienced — and I wanted to be cool like them. Fuck this 21 shit. I wanna grow up and be *weird!*

And I thought of my new essential reading list just assigned at summer school ... Whitman, Hesse, Faulkner, Blake, Nathaniel West, Henry Miller ... and how I couldn't wait to get back to ol' New York with my well-read friends and cool professors like Walter Raubicheck who knew this stuff inside out. Like the Dead (in whose hills I now sat) turned me on to Jack, now it was he who was springboarding me into the next level of life-altering authors and philosophies — and I wondered where *that* was gonna lead!

I was charged with the energy of eternity — realizing we're all just single notes in a long melody that's been playing brightly, dancing lightly, since the first song & dance, man. There was a harmony of spirits I'd just met, and now I knew for sure how this song would go. And there were lots of voices. We're out there. "Oh, so out there." And it was empowering.

And I thought about **the collective** — "the whole" being more than the sum of the parts — and how Jack and the Beats thrived on their *scene*, their friends, and how their interaction was so important to each of them; that Kesey had the bus — not a car ... a *bus* — full of fellow Pranksters, and threw acid parties with hundreds of them, and then as the Warlocks became the Dead with thousands of them; and that Abbie and those guys had their underground network and organized events that brought streetsful of people together, whether protesting the war or chanting to elevate the Pentagon ... which is all just following the tradition established by the Florentine artists and their confraternities of the Renaissance, and the Bloomsbury Group in England, and the surreal Surrealists, who themselves evolved out of da loopy Dadaists. But it was always about solo artists *working in tandem*.

Each of these individual people strove for — and thrived in — large collectives of like-minded artists in an interconnected array of disciplines. They could help each other and push each other and challenge each other and hug each other in the downtimes when the unsupported and unconnected might give up the ghost in the mindful machine. But by having a community and a collective there were always teams of people pitching in and coming up with new ideas. And new reading lists.

And that's what I saw at Camp Kerouac. A crazy collective of nonconformists getting along really well together and still functioning — in fact at a higher level than they did before. No way these goosey Lucys could have pulled off ten days of organized *anything* back in their younger daze. As Garcia says, "With a little practice we might get it right one day."

And this was the space we flew in at Tom's Airplane hanger in the sky. Pacing time on the deck, notebook time in comfy chairs, hiking time in redwood forests, and dreaming in the immensity of it.

27

The San Francisco Adventure

Somehow we managed to extricate ourselves from this paradise mountain and took a drive down to the Paradise City. There were some Beat sites I had to experience in person after only seeing them through Jack's words. Even though it seemed like an eternity ago, it wasn't even 13 years since he left us, so we weren't that far removed from the world he roamed.

Dig the virtually nonexistent midday traffic circa 1982!

Ol' Lee n me — who I'd taken to calling Croz cuz he looked so much like David, and he'd taken to calling me Neil cuz he thought I looked like Neiler, and especially after I told him we grew up in the same neighborhood and went to the same high school in Winnipeg — we hit The Road on a double-doppelganger rock 'n' roll mission in The Official State Vehicle — Crosby and Young jamming in the birthplace of jamming!

Luckily, he knew everything about the drive and loved to show off his hometown, so I just beatifically rode shotgun in the jump seat of joy. We naturally followed the beacon right into the **City Lights** of North Beach — the pilgrim's touchstone and safe home base since 1953 — and it was just like I dreamed it! — old and rickety with crooked walls and mismatching bookcases and narrow aisles crowded with colorful people and cosmic pages.

Sadly, ol' Ferling wasn't there, but the whole scene was overwhelming — like a condensed Disneyland all in one house with twirling rides spinning up to the starry dynamo ceiling while poet's voices were creaking up from the history-worn wooden floor below.

And of course their massive Beat _section_ knocked me for a blithering loop ... after it taking six stores to find a single *On The Road* in Vancouver! — suddenly every Beat book ever printed was staring me in the face!

I didn't have much money, as y'know, but there were two Jack poetry books I'd never seen — *Heaven & Other Poems* and *Scattered Poems* — and a nice *Lonesome Traveler* — all 3 bucks each! Plus I had to get an iconic copy of *Howl* from the very place they were published and banned but still sold — for $2.50! They were all small paperbacks that could nicely fit in a backpack, and made fine traveling companions for the rest of this trip and life.

Then I'd always heard about this legendary bar next door — **Vesuvio's** — including how Jack famously and boisterously went drinking there instead of going to visit Henry Miller on his way to secretly hiding out at Larry's cabin in *Big Sur* as per their elaborately laid plan.

It was the middle of the day but we had to hoist a pint in Jack's honor you understand, so we went in, and after coming from the overwhelming Beat Disneyland of City Lights it was such a shock to see nothing about Jack or the Beats *anywhere!* There was one small photo by the bar, but I was imagining a Kettle of Fish or Folk City with rows of framed 8x10s of their picaresque patrons. Mind you, the joint seemed to be doing a booming business without my help. It's right on a corner with floor-to-ceiling windows so it's really full of light, city light, with big doors standing open in the August afternoon warmth of a California city, and it kinda felt like a French Quarter bar open to the street and all the characters who people it.

We snagged some frosties — "Anchor Steams" — Croz insisted. "The pride of San Francisco." And he knew about the semi-secret second floor via some hidden stairs in the back where we could cop a table with a view, which we did, right in front of a big window open to the streets of San Francisco blowin' right over us.

I immediately started flippin' through *Lonesome Traveler*, and feeling the iron pull I was drawn right to the *Railroad Earth* — which I knew from the original *Black Mountain Review* collection I'd found at a library sale in New York — and Boom! right in front of me were the opening lines about the little alley in San Francisco at Third and Townsend — and I knew right away where we were going next.

Croz sez, "Yeah, there's cool little alleys all over this town," as we were sitting right beside one between Vesuvio's and City Lights. He pointed to the wall below us, "That's where that picture was taken you probably know with Dylan and Ginsberg and Robbie Robertson standing against a wall," as he points to the exact spot.

"No way! Really?! *I know that picture!* Wait — McClure's in that as well! Yeah, that was the whole Beats-passing-the-torch-to-Dylan thing ... so cool they got together for that," as I'm staring in awe and envy at the history this city oozes that I missed out on. San Francisco is one of those places that makes you wish every minute you were born earlier. And of course a few years after we sat here ol' Ferlinghetti would spearhead the effort to get this very passageway officially renamed Jack Kerouac Alley. But here it was, breathing its history and telling its stories when it was still just a regular old hideaway cut-through.

And just then the only other person sitting upstairs came over to our table. "You guys talking about the Beats?" he asked and we nodded. "I just drove up from L.A. to get some books at City Lights. You can't find a fucking thing down there."

"That's L.A." Croz says derisively. "Why would anyone live there?" To a Canadian, the entire state of California seemed like a God-sent fantasyland, and I know they had some big Civil War in this country, but I swear the North hates the South and vice versa more in California than anywhere else in the country! They're just too high to fight about it.

"I'm an actor," the guy says. "That's where the work is."

"Oh yeah?" I bounced. "Have we seen you in anything?"

He said his name was Steve something, and rattled off some TV shows and movies neither Croz or I had ever seen, but now that he mentioned it, it was obvious: good looking, extrovert, big booming voice, dramatic gestures — and he was certainly working the room, which at this point was an audience of two. He was a few years older than us and really knew his Jack, so we had him drag a chair over and join us.

At first I thought he was drunk cuz he was so zooming and animated and excited, almost wild-eyed, but I quickly realized this was natural juice he was running on. And right away he started pulling out the books he just bought at City Lights and bouncing like a kid on Christmas morning — every gift making him more excited than the last. "Look!!!" as he shows us each, one by one. "*Gasoline* by Gregory! *Reality Sandwiches* by Allen! The new *Holy Goof* Neal biography! *Visions of Cody! Desolation Angels! Old Angel Midnight! Scripture of the Golden Eternity*, man!! Can you believe it?!" And he stacks them up in front

314

of us, reminding me of that professor who wanted to make a pile of Kerouac biographies in front of his department heads. This guy was obviously on some similar castle-building mission.

"Hey-Zeus, you guys are both Kerouac crazy!" Croz says, and we all laugh in the happy Christmas of it all.

"You too?" the actor looked at me.

"Yeah-yeah," I confirmed. "I was just at the Boulder conference. Were you there?" I asked, immediately regretting it.

"No. What conference?"

Oh no. Never should have mentioned it. Poor bastard hadn't heard. I barely had the heart to tell him, but now I had to, and even downplaying it, he was just about hari-kariing right there in Vesuvio's. "*NOOO!* You met *Jan?!* And *Gregory?!!*" he screamed like Stanley for Stella.

I couldn't lie cuz that gets you nowhere, so I pulled out a couple Boulder stories like books from my bag, and in no time he went from depressed to excited again, cheering the riffs like a great troupe member.

And after I'd soloed plenty, I wanted to pass the spotlight back to the real performer in the house, so I asked what his story was — and sure glad I did! You could tell this guy came out of *the womb* delivering a soliloquy!

"I was bored shitless by the crap they were feeding us at UCLA, and somebody told me about this Vietnam vet who sold used books out of his basement. So I finally went over there one day and it changed my life. His name's Basil and he just sits down there smoking cigarettes and joints all day long surrounded by *crates upon crates* of books that are barely organized. He sits at this tiny desk, in a creaky chair, and the desk drawer is his cash register, and when somebody comes up to buy something he'll just look at the book and make up a price. So, we got talking, and that first day he sold me *On The Road* and *Factotum* by Bukowski. And my head just went ..." and he made that explosion sound as his hands showed his head blowing apart.

"That's great! What a first find story!" I told him, and he knew it. And then he went all Big Picture on us.

"If you look at most all great movements, starting with Father Walt rolling forward ... Village Bohemians, Lost Generation, Beats, hippies ... they all blow on the heels of war — the Civil War, the World Wars, Korea, Vietnam ... especially atomic bombs at the end of World War II, reinventing the cosmic wheel and becoming the birth of the Beat blues really, the true genesis of post-mod thought and the Be Here Now of what becomes Western Zen."

And after barely a whole note rest . . .

"I think Jack is the same thing Judy Garland is to people — open and wounded. Anybody who can *feel* can't help but feel for him. He was a wounded warrior. He just *felt* too much. He was truly empathic — he felt everything, all the time. The guy was too good for this world. It was just too painful to live. And anybody who reads him knows that right away and identifies with it. Universal suffering. And Jack turns it into beautiful poetry.

"And Cassady is the Paul Bunyan of American literature," he riffed on. "I mean, the full cartoon caricature that we love. The mythic giant. America needs heroes. And tragic heroes all the better. JFK, Lincoln, James Dean, Marilyn ... And Neal dying too soon is right in that larger-than-life heroic mythology. He gets women like Jack Nicholson. He's driving a stolen car with a wild chick next to him like Bonnie & Clyde. He's the center of attention like a rock star. But he's also the real-life stunt driver like Steve McQueen."

I'm raisin' my eyebrows, thinkin', "Riff forth and beautify, man!"

"And it was Kerouac who did the heroic work to capture the mythic figure. It was his eye, his lens, his script. He's the Woody Allen to Diane Keaton. Or Scorsese to De Niro. The one artist who captures the other. And by Jack doing that work, he elevated *himself* to heroic," the actor said, ending with this dramatic silence that left the entire audience speechless.

"Great stuff, man!" I finally blurted out, and Croz broke into applause. "You should be a teacher!"

"Or a talk show host or *something*," Croz chimed.

"It's all about myth-building," the song-&-dance man started again before the shining faded. "If Kerouac had been universally loved when he was alive, his story wouldn't be nearly as heroic and we wouldn't be sitting here in Vesuvio's right now. The fact that he had to suffer is key to the myth. Like van Gogh. Or Jesus. Or Sylvia Plath. People aren't going to mythologize Norman Mailer or John Updike."

"Yeah, that's true," I said, suddenly remembering how I always thought Hollywood actors were dumb. But this guy was ten times smarter than me! And a movie star to boot! I hated him already — and I hadn't even *seen* his movies!

"Somebody said at the conference Jack died with $62 in the bank," I brought up, trying to show I knew *something*.

"It's America, man," he said. "We don't love our outlaws till they're dead. And if you challenge the system they're gonna Lenny Bruce you."

"Well, so … what we do about it?"

"Just keep fighting, man. Walt Whitman made it to old age. Just keep winning every battle you can. Change every mind. Reach every person. I do poetry readings in L.A. whenever anybody can rustle one up. In fact, I have to run over to a club right now about getting on tonight. You should come."

"We're actually just heading down to that little redbrick alley by the Southern Pacific station at Third and Townsend from *The Railroad Earth*," I told him with a beatific beam.

"Oh right, *Lonesome Traveler*. Great. Yeah. The railroads, man. That's another central character in American myth-making." This guy didn't stop! "They brought the people who built this city. In the *whole world* they were important — how nations were built — I mean, they predate the highways Jack rode on. And how they spark the imagination. A train whistle at night. The clack of the tracks. Poetry in motion. You can hop on one of those iron horses and ride it to towns you never even heard of. And Neal worked on them — and Jack rode them.

They were totally plugged into that icon of wanderlust and imagination."

I wanted this guy to keep hanging with us all day! What a tour guide! And he wasn't even *from* here! "No, I have to go see if I can get on tonight," he said when I suggested it. "Then I gotta see a couple casting agents and get them to come out," and he held up another bag with head shots in it. The life of an actor. I wanted to grow up and be weird, but now I also wanted to grow up and be smart like this guy. I'm thinkin this is gonna take a bit of work.

Eventually we poured ourselves back into The Official State Vehicle and headed for the train station ... but ol' Croz wanted to make sure I got a Jerry tour as well as a Jack, so he was a big help on the way taking me from **Beat Wonderland to Dead Winterland** — the historic shrine, so named cuz it used to be an ice skating rink that good ol' Bill Graham turned into a 5,000 capacity open-floor concert venue where every band in the world played including The Boys about a hundred times (okay, 60, but still) right from the very beginning until its closing night New Year's Eve '78 — which was so Grate they made a movie of it! And of course it's where Cassady passed out the diplomas at the Acid Test Graduation, and The Last Waltz was danced — with every major rock giant alive and a smorgasbord of Beats on the side to go with the Thanksgiving dinner Bill Graham served the entire audience.

We parked and went walking up to it, cuz ya have to,

and I just about had a bird(song)! There, painted right on the side of Winterland — not a temporary ad or anything, but a permanent painted-on billboard — was the Dead's logo, and written in fancy large calligraphy,

"They're not the best at what they do, They're the only ones that do what they do"

Couldn't believe it! That Bill Graham'd do this! — of all the bands he ever booked, of all the musicians that ever came out of this city — it was *these* guys, *my* guys, left blazing on the wall of music's greatest shrine in one of rock's cornerstone cities.

This whole trip was continually reinforcing that I wasn't alone chasing some mirage, some irrelevant minor artists or wanky writers or illusionary visions. I was finally in places and with people who got it, and not just a little bit. Proof! The world had *whole bookstores* full of Beats, and whole shrines for the Dead, and whole Boulders full of bards!

Then on top'a this, ol' Croz walks me a couple blocks over to **the original Fillmore!** — the place McClure was talking about! — the early pre-Fillmore West psychedelic incubator where Kesey and the Dead did their first large-scale Acid Test, where the psychedelic light shows were born out of the room's regal size and high ceiling, where Bill staged the seminal Mime Troupe benefit that launched his career as a "dance hall" promoter and where he would later book Allen opening for rock bands and put on both McClure's *The Beard* and LeRoi Jones' plays, and the place where Hunter Thompson famously first dosed and "BOOM ... [became] a victim of the drug explosion," as he tributed the joint in *Fear and Loathing In Las Vegas.*

Then falling backwards in time, we drove off in search of some nameless red brick alley with only Jack's story for a Road map. And sure enough, channeling our inner Intrepid Traveler, we found it in half-a-jiff, and of course it's just an empty alleyway — **But there it is!** Right where Jack left it, in back of the railway station at Third & Pete Townsend, a dead-end alley for dead-enders to hide off the Beaten path. But by now all Jack's drinking buddies were gone and we came across an empty space; I trembled and exploded at the bus stop in its place.

 With nothing left to do but click our heels and smile three times, ol' Croz and I decided to walk the length of it since we came this far, and suddenly that McClure riff about the power of hearing something read aloud came to me, and as we walked along the alley I read Croz the opening of *Railroad Earth*. Imagine my surprise a year later when I met Henri Cru and he lent me his Jack record with Steve Allen and it *opened* with this very piece!

There was one other place I had to experience — from a key part of *On The Road* that I call "the San Francisco epiphany" — which I would end up reading years later at St. Mark's Church in New York as part of Viking's massive *On The Road* 40th anniversary all-night marathon reading and celebration — after Dean drops off Sal & Marylou penniless in the big city and Sal starts hallucinating from hunger and having flashbacks and visions. Maybe the wildest craziest coolest prose in *OTR*.

'Course I'd brought my ragged road-weary copy, all notated for easy lookin up, and off we zoomed for the site of **the infamous drop-off on O'Farrell Street**. An' right away ol' Croz starts giving me The Tenderloin Talk — that this is definitely not the kinda place we wanna go stumbling around drunk on Burgundy wine. And boy was he right! It still looked like the scene Jack described being dumped into with all the hustlers, pimps and whores with their "end-of-the-continent sadness," and now with modern crack-desperate eyes fixed on these two very white guys who took a very wrong turn into their hood. We didn't even wanna stop at a red light. At least I got a real in-your-face look at the sour "lemon lot" that ol' Jack found in his darkest hour.

But I still wanted to try to see the fancy apartment block that Marylou came out of when Sal was waiting in the doorway across the street at Larkin and Geary. I knew 'ol Croz wasn't gonna be up for much more of this, but I spotted the only fairly nice building near the corner, and this block didn't look nearly as bad, so I got him to stop for a sec so I could take a pic, and jumped out of the van, and

shot the nice beige building,

then turned around to take one of the doorway across the street when suddenly out of nowhere this scruffy wiry black guy dressed all in black is in the middle of the street headin right for me and just about on me. As I start back for the van, he's goin', "Hey, wait a minute, I just wanna talk to you for a second — I just gotta ask you a question ...." an' as soon I got touching distance from home base I bolted for the door, and Croz stuck his head out the window so the guy knew there was two of us, yelling, "We're good, man. We don't need anything," and I jumped in, and Croz was drivin' off before I got the door closed.

    "That was close," I said looking back at the guy still

in the middle of the street waving his arms at us like the madman he was — and that little putt-putt of a VW motor never sounded so good!

"Had enough Tenderloin?" Croz asked, shakin' his head like I-told-ya-so, which he did.

"Whoa, yeah, it's like New York out there. Didn't expect that here."

"That's the slit-your-throat-for-a-dollar bunch'a bananas, for real. Can't believe I let you talk me into coming here!" he says, staring straight ahead, driving us the hell outta Scarysville to I-Don't-Care-Wheresville. "That's why we live in Marin, man. S.F. was getting bad by, like, '68. That's when the Dead and most of the bands moved out. Like, a big reason Bill closed the first Fillmore we were just at was because that neighborhood just got too dicey to be bringin in thousands of blissed out hippies every night."

And the furthur we drove from that scene the more it started to look like San Francisco again — all the funky Victorian houses and colorful little street-level shops and smiling tourists hanging off slow rumbling cable cars. And ol' Croz was puttering us along pointing out various historic events that happened in various fast-passing now-changed places and I was just letting him play Tourguide after my bright ideas nearly got us killed.

Eventually, "This is The Panhandle," he says with a sweep of his hand toward the park beside us. "The Dead played here a buncha times, you prolly know, doin' all those free shows with the Diggers and Peter Coyote and those guys ...."

And I'm nodding at the green and tie-dyed history, having flashbacks of trips I never even took, and suddenly my spider sense was tingling. "... The Panhandle ... wait a minute ... we gotta be close to ..." I'm thinking as he wheels the bus around a corner onto ... "Ashbury Street!! No way! 710!!" I blurt out like a kid who's just spotted the candyman's store, as Croz glowed a mischievous Prankster springing-a-surprise grin.

"'710' should be the code number, not 420," I say, as we pull up in front of the Grateful Dead's famous house — where it all started — the communal pad a block from the corner of Haight & Ashbury that was featured in issue #1 of *Rolling Stone* after the band's famous bust, where Neal bunked in with the boys, and McClure & Garcia attempted to turn *Love Lion* into a song and on and on and on.

We double-parked right in front, on what was now a quiet residential street a century removed from the high Haight heyday, and we blew a spicy bomber in honor of all the jazz that joint doth sprung. The defiant post-bust photo with the band on the steps holding the rifle and Billy giving The Man the finger is so emblazoned in any blazing Deadhead's brain that I could superimpose it over the current image and transport myself back to that day in 1967 — another flashback to a scene my bean had never been. But sacred places come with that transportive power, and I carry an adaptor wherever I go.

After we did our due diligence of herbal remedies, we stopped some friendly local who knew exactly why we were there, and scampered up on the steps for him to take a quick snap of the terrapin.

Then of course there was the other famous residence in San Francisco — 29 Russell Street — the Cassadys' historic home where so much happened that was covered in *On The Road* — Neal and his tire recapping job, Neal and his broken thumb, Neal and his domestic loveproblems and Carolyn throwing the two of them out which put them on the road trip that comprised the second half of the book — but to be completely confessional — I didn't know the address in both my and the Beat World's much younger years. No one did. There were just those couple biographies, *if* you could find them. No *Off The Road*, no published letters, no notebooks, no walking tour guides, and 29 Russell, and for that matter the site of the historic Six Gallery reading, had not entered the cultural mindstream like 710 Ashbury had.

And anyway ol' Croz was wanting to get back to the house before dark — so we left the city of hills for the town in the mountains.

And with this San Francisco treat now behind me, I was suddenly picturing the fruits of Kesey's farm ahead.

28

On The Road To Kesey's

I was On The Road again by the next morning, and after a couple quick short rides outta Marin, damned if another VW camper van didn't pull over! And the guy's goin' all the way to Washington! BOOM! Done.

It's Richard, a 40-something West Coast camping back-to-the-land nature guy who was heading to the Olympic Peninsula for a week in the rainforest. He had a kind-of proper Dudley Do-Right thing about him, yet was sporting a short Ginsberg beard, and as he gradually confessed, was sadly without a collective of like-minded people in his life. Terrifically nice guy, but too shy to talk to the world around him — so some total stranger on the roadside was safe. Early on I was wonderin' if ol' ShyGuy was gay, so I quickly worked my gorgeous girlfriend into the conversation, and it turned out, man, he was just nuthin but great! Ranger-Smith-meets-Gary-Snyder drivin' all the way to Basecamp Kesey! And with a cooler of cold beers to boot! "Help yourself."

"Don't mind if I do."

And after a while of yakkin' the flora and fauna of the universe, he goes, "Do you smoke grass?" And I'm like, "*Alriiiight,* thought you'd never ask!" as I reach for my ample Tom road stash. But he got all quiet.

"I don't," he finally says all grimly and weird. Aww . . . so sad . . . cuz ya knew deep down he wanted to know what it was like, but his straight side was so dominant, and mind-altering was a binge too far, and you felt for the guy. But of course every time we'd stop I'd nip around the corner to Bogart some Humboldt and come back giggling like Buddha at the grand joke, and he'd know.

And it was so perfect to be driving northern California in the Official State Vehicle, with the thin doors and roll-down windows and knee-side air vents and puttering old-school motor, and nobody's in a hurry. In fact, he said he was planning to camp for the night at someplace near Mount Shasta. He was gonna get some steaks to bar-b-que on the fire. He could either drop me off if I wanted to keep goin', or he was hitting a campground with all the amenities if I wanted to stick around. Hmmm ... steaks ... beer ... a campground ... arriving fresh at Kesey's ... yeah, alright, *if I have to.*

And there we were in the setting shadow of "cloud-flirting Shasta" as Jack called it, this Dharmic Desolation mother mountain dome towering above everything around her — a blaring reminder of something much bigger than us. But here we were, so small, scurrying along the ground scavenging fallen gifts to make a fire, cooking the earth's bounty of corn and potatoes in the embers, washing utensils in a fast moving stream, and remaining humble in the golden eternity by the fire near the mountain.

And that wasn't the only thing that was burning! Ha! With a few beers in him and nowhere to drive and no one he knew around in the safe heaven's earth of the remote mountain forest, whaddyaknow but ol' Richard The Feint of Hearted decided to take a couple coughing pulls off me after-dinner smoke! And lo, it was good. In fact it was grand! He got giddy-blasted and started laughing for the first time all trip, and at one point going, *"You bastards! So this is it! You bastards!"* to everyone in his past for not *really* explaining or sharing the herbal delights before. And of course this was some particularly golden delicious gummy-bear bud so the guy went from his puttering VW into a racing Ferrari in two tokes. Couldn't shut him up! And *everything* made him scream-laugh like a baby, the lucky first-timer. I'm sure the neighbors for campsites around were wondering what the hell was so funny in the woods in the dark. But ol' virgin Richard was howling at the moon and just about anything I'd say! Whadda night!

Then a morning shower in minimalist campground facilities is all you need to hit The Road in the cleanliness of Godliness, heading to a god's home, who'd recently become a friend.

After regaling Richard with my righteous destination, he surprised me with a detour off the highway and right to the sideroad leading to Kesey's. I God-blessed the brother, and palmed him a handful of buds and some papers ... as we both shared that grateful look of having taken the other so much furthur than expected.

In this flat glowing Oregon farmland of the lower Willamette Valley, I decided to just walk and meditate on the moment the rest of the way. Maybe that Buddhist stuff did sink in a little. How could you thumb or ask for anything now? What a blessed gift this whole trip had been.

After making it to the conference and meeting all my other heroes, this was the audience with The Big One. The Chief — as Neal Cassady called him. **The guy the summer's Mission began with**.

And as I walked along that flat empty rural road that led to the Prankster bullseye, there was some fellow farmer out working the yard in front of his house. He stopped, resting on his rake a spell, watching this young skinny guy with a big blue backpack walking determinedly down the middle of the road in the middle of nowhere. Eventually, after we'd been watching each other for quite a walking while, he called out in a slow but friendly farmer's drawl, "Where ya headin'?"

"Ken Kesey's place just up the road," I hollered.

And he just kept watching me walk. Then after another long Farmer John pause, he finally called back, "Yeaaaah . . . a lot of people do that."

29

The Chief

Following Babbs's minimalist directions I don't know why the hell I was so confident I'd find the place, but I was, and a left turn here and a right turn there and a crunch crunch crunch and suddenly there was an old-fashioned rural roadside mailbox painted in crazy splashes of bright psychedelic Day-Glo colors.

And sure enough — **Ken Kesey lived on a farm!** And not a faux farm either. There was a big red barn and some other giant storage buildings, and cows in a pasture with bales of hay for dinner, and a tractor, a tinker, a tailor, a sailor's song, a pick-up truck, a bunch of farm implements, and miles of flat wide-open space like the farms of the western prairies from whence I knew and my father grew.

Walking up to Kesey's farm

And there was the big red barn-house combo set among the trees, seemed like a story-and-a-half, and I bet it was. I walked up the well-packed driveway to the old worn screen door — couldn't see a soul in any direction — or a doorbell for that matter — and after another couple deep breaths of that dusty summer air I knew, "This is it," ... and knocked with conviction on the wooden slat, then took a step back to give them some space. Right away Ken's wife Faye came to the door, frowning and perplexed at first. "Hi, I'm Brian from Boulder, Ken said I should come by," and a big smile crossed her pretty face.

"Yes, I remember you. Come in," she said so gently it was almost a whisper.

Into the Castle of a Kesey. Once you pass through a short gear-filled hallway, the whole house opens up into this enormous space — The Great Room they called it — that didn't look possible from the outside. Going all the way down one wall was the kitchen stuff — and then in front of that was a long wide island — it looked like a mess hall or something, like this place fed a hundred people at a time!

On the other side, next to the long island, was a giant living room — with green wrestling mats taking up nearly the entire floor! And there were dumbbells and other gym flotsam scattered around the outskirts — and it made ya wonder how many other major American authors had a wrestling gym for a living room!

The whole long wall beyond the mats was all huge windows, and at one end was a bunch of electronic gear — a video monitor, a rack of tape machines & mixing gear, mic stands and tape boxes and cables and stacks of different colored gaffer's tape and all manner of production essentials. At the far end of the long island countertop runway were a couple steps up to a raised alcove dining area with Kesey and George Walker sitting across from each other with a nest of papers and blueprints scattered between them.

"Ah, young Hassett," Kesey calls out. "You made it. Knew you would," and he's got his huge smile on. Then he dropped the bomb. "Your mother just called. She's looking for you."

"What!?!? *Awww geez*," I'm thinkin, completely deflated. You try to be cool, try to fit in, try to be happening, step up, get an audience with The King . . . and your mommy's calling you home for dinner! *aaahh!* ... Of course! — she musta remembered how I was able to find his number, and went and did it herself. She'd do anything, that woman. But I was totally humiliated ... *and I'd just stepped up to bat!*

"You better call her. She has every right to worry — and you should be glad she does."

What?! Kesey's siding with *my mother?!* Where's the acid punch? Where's the liquid lunch? Who *is* this sober bunch?

But I was just beginning to learn about the solid family and home life behind the curtain of this Wizard of Wild.

And I didn't consciously realize it then, but it was my mother who got me On The Road in the first damn place. Her dad was a railroad engineer in the '30s and '40s, and they got passes and could travel all over — which was *very* unusual in those years. So she knew The Power of The Road. And got me on it right from the get-go. And we became a masterful traveling duo, lemme tell ya.

So, from a wall phone with a handset cord that could stretch to the next county, E.T. phoned home. "Yes, I'm having a good time. No, I'm not hitchhiking. Yes, I'm staying at this famous writer's house. No, I'm not coming back till the end of August. Yes, I'm still going to school in the fall. No, I didn't turn gay in San Francisco," and on and on the way conversations go with worrying mothers of thrill-seeking kids.

After the grilling, I join George and Ken at the table where they had all these schematic drawings that turned out to be The Bus or the bus engine or something. Walker seemed to be the mechanical guy, and he's explaining how things work. "The this goes down to the that which connects to the whozit, and I think we can rig up a belt around the whatzit to make the tickler work with the tockler, and if we add in a modified buzzer to the nuzzler this should work."

"You think you can make the modified buzzer fit the nuzzler?" Kesey asks.

"We should be able to pull a juicer off the old Ford and solder on a sprucer with a double trick whammy bar, and that oughta do it."

And I'm just — *"What the yibiddy doobity . . . ?!"*

Turns out they're talkin about firing up old Furthur again to take a little Prankster Field Trip. It's been ten years since the last one, and with Cassady surging through their veins after the Road mission to Kerouac Mountain they're thinking it may be time to rally the tribe again.

After the mechanics of the matter were resolved for the moment, we all leaned back and began laughing about all the crazy characters and happenings back at summer camp. And like any old friends debriefing, we were pokin fun at ol' Allen sayin Jack was a Buddhist when he was really a Catholic, and all the old wives and girlfriends confessing their pillow talk — but this was family, and maybe we were jibber jabber goofy goofin behind closed doors, but I just saw the best minds of my generation standing united against The Combine, as Ken called it in his *Cuckoo's Quest*.

I chimed in about my organizer days in Winnipeg and how you couldn't get two activists to agree on the weather. We were all simpatico on who and what we were rising up over, but nobody had remotely the same idea of how to fix anything. Similarly, even though everyone in Boulder was there because of their love of Jack, it was cool that everybody had their own very personal angle. But apparently I'd struck a nerve with Kesey. "That wasn't all benevolent love, don't kid yourself. These pornographer biographers showing up and sniffing through his bedroom trying to paint their own take on him to rip some money out of a dead man's pockets when he ain't here to defend himself. Didn't he leave enough? What's enough? 20 books? 30? 40? How much does a man have to leave behind before these vultures stop picking him dry?"

Geez. I was thinking about doing his "Cassady" show at NYU, and the thought just struck me, so I blurted it out cuz that's what ya do around this First Thought Best Thought crew — "But ... how's that different than what you're doing with Cassady?" I was kinda scared as I gulped it out, but by the time I finished the sentence and he wasn't freaking out I was kinda sure he'd have a good answer.

"Cassady didn't leave behind the work Kerouac did. If he wrote 20 books we wouldn't have to do a show because everybody'd know him. There's only Jack's couple novels, but they were young, and *The First Third* is when he was even younger. The full story of the man has never been told."

"*The Holy Goof* last year," Walker chimed in.

"Yeah, and it wasn't bad," Kesey kept rolling. "But Cassady needs more than a book. The only way to capture him is with the footage and tapes — you were there — the books aren't enough . . . we can do it better now — you gotta hit the audience head on," and he punched his fist into his hand at the end of my nose and we both laughed at the impact.

So we started talking about an NYU show — some sorta de facto Acid Test. I told him how I was completely in control of the whole space and how they'd just given me the university's Programmer of The Year award a couple months ago and we could do any damn thing we wanted. And *some*body had to bring Cassady back to New York.

Ken called out to Faye, who'd been an orbiting spirit guide fluttering nearby the whole time, to bring him his datebook, which was this big old leather-bound thing he seemed to have had forever but would put in a new diary calendar each year. And Faye was just the nicest, most accommodating person, making you think of the old "behind every great man ..." as I was seeing it manifesting before these too-young-to-*really*-know's eyes.

My girlfriend and I were striving for it, beginning as 17-year-olds — somehow we knew equality was the answer and were supporting each other and challenging each other and 100% equals, and we were still going strong four years into it, sort of basing our love affair on John & Yoko, and she was teaching me about Simone de Beauvoir & Jean-Paul Sartre, but whatever the models — here was this couple right in front of me *living it*, this Captain

Crazy who'd instigated the Acid Tests and changed the world, and was the non-leader leader of the psychedelic enlightenment expedition across the universe, and created the culture the Grateful Dead grew out of — and behind the scenes here he is with *his* high school sweetheart in a loving partnership just like I always imagined and believed it could be. And when he caught me stealing glances at her, he smiled, and said softly, "My keel."

And we started jamming on what kind of a show it would be, how I wanted to have the Flying Karamazov Brothers, then maybe Rick Danko or Country Joe for the musical part, and Ken was totally into it and saying he'd also do a straight reading to open it — and through it all the running theme was we have to "produce the spirit" — that was his mantra that guided every sentence of thought.

All of a sudden there was a bustle at the door and Babbs The Friendly Giant was stompin' through the kitchen in his war boots, "Weeeeelllll, Mr. *Briiian*," — he always said it dragging the out the "i" — "You made it! Ha-ha. What took you so long? Ha-ha," and he gives me a slap on the shoulder that nearly sends me across the table.

Suddenly the volume's turned way up. Kesey says, "We're talking about doing 'Cassady' at NYU."

"Yeah, let's do it. Fuck Columbia, ha-ha-ha. I think I have something in Buffalo ... and maybe Boston," Babbs says, and turns to me suddenly sternly serious. "We have to work out a tour. Can't bring it out for one show." And I see right away who the point-person is gonna be on this show. I tell him about the hall, and what we'd have at our disposal, and how I could get a ton of psychedelic clowns and poets and dancers and artists from the Village to fill in the atmosphere and make it fully multimedia, and we're all on exactly the same page about how to stage it. **Functioning chaos**.

But pretty soon Babbs goes, "Ah shit, I gotta go. I just stopped in for a minute, Gretch's got some meeting in town. I'm with the kids. Why don't you come back to the house and get yourself set up," he says to me.

And I look over at Ken who goes, "Yeah, George and I gotta run get some parts," and I realize in a liquid flash I'm staying at Babbs's, not Kesey's, so I jumped up to get my pack cuz I knew I'd be back.

30

Babbs and The Bus

$\mathbf{A}$ speedy bouncing 3-minute pick-up ride and we're at **the sprawling Babbs Plantation** — a large rambling all-natural-wood farmhouse with multiple porches surrounded by apple trees and swing sets and half-a-dozen bicycles in a jack straw pile by the door. Turns out he has a whole nest full of kids. And it was funny how Pops was bringing home this dude they'd never met before who was gonna stay a couple days and none of them even blinked.

The madness these kids must've seen on an ongoing basis ... I felt like I must've been about the 7,000th stray Dad brought home.

And right away it's clear sumpthin special's goin' on here. His three youngest boys come scrambling down the ladder from their loft fort bedroom as soon as he comes through the door, and he holds one up on one arm, and picks up another to use like a sword against the third, and they're all screaming in laughter. And there's a huge mural along one wall called "Creation" painted by all the kids, and intricate models of airplanes made out of matchsticks. And there's toys and books and clothes and kids' stuff everywhere — they musta ranged in age from about 6 to 18 or so, so there was a huge spectrum of stimulants for growth.

And Babbs himself was just a big kid. That ringmaster playfulness he has at a microphone was perfected in this circus. And the whole time he's carrying on multiple conversations with multiple kids, almost jumping between languages as he switches from the youngest to the eldest and back again — and flash — *right!* — Cassady carrying on multiple conversations at once! As Hunter said, "It was hard *not* to be Neal after he was around." Like a musician passing on licks. "Here's the tricks." And the ripple in still water exists.

"Mom's not home tonight so come help me make dinner," he says to his two eldest girls, who I don't mind sayin' were knockouts. And the three of them started working together like a long-playing trio, falling right into the rhythms, anticipating moves, but still calling out cues.

And I noticed people 'round these parts all seemed to have kitchens you could park a bus in! Maybe it's cuz they're always feeding small armies. Anyway, once the massive mess manifested, everyone just grabbed a plate and took it back to whatever they were doing. And none of them were watching TV. But me and Babbs did.

"C'mon, the ballgame's on," as he walked towards the giant couch for about 12. And just like Kesey's, the enormous living room was an extension of the giant kitchen. And speaking of giant — it was the San Francisco Giants at Candlestick Park! And the second the tube comes on, like a master musician he's right in on the beat in the middle of the song, running his crazy comic commentary, calling pitches before they're thrown, and plays before they happen. "He'll drop it," he says of some fly ball, and the guy does, and Babbs laughs and says, "Told ya, ha-ha," without turning his eyes from the game or his fork from the plate. I was wondering why he even watched these things if he knew everything that was gonna happen. And it was the same routine with regular TV later — he'd say the punchline before the character did, and be laughing his head off before the actor even delivered the line.

And that's what life with Babbs was like. He could see around corners, that guy. Like somebody else I heard of.

The next day we went back to the other Ken's, but first we ran a few errands, and I noticed everywhere we drove he waved to every person we saw along the way and gave me a one sentence bio on all of them. When we got to his rural

General Store, it was a kinda busy parking lot, and he gets out and leaves the windows rolled down with all his stuff on the seats without a thought of anything being stolen, which to this New Yorker was just crazy-talk. And walking through the parking lot it was a steady series of, "Howdy Ken!" "Morning Jim! Gorgeous day." "Sure is." "Hi-ya, Ken!" "Hey there, Bob! How's the kids?"

And we go into the store and it's a whole new chorus of Howdy Kens, and he's doing a running commentary with all of them at once as he zips around the narrow aisles of the old dark country store filling his arms with stuff. And he's still talkin' by the time he gets to the counter, and the Mr. Drucker in the apron goes, "Whatcha got there, Ken?" And he rattles off whatever's in his arms, and the guy says, "Alrighty then," and Ken just walks out.

He sees me lookin' perplexed, laughs, n says, "He puts it on my tab. I just pay him at the end of the month." Yet another thing you won't see in ol' New York. And I'm thinkin', boy if this guy ever needed a character witness he could get a million of them.

And we get to Kesey's, where of course **today's mission is: <u>See The Bus</u>!**

Babbs just walks right in the door, hollers out sumpthin' crazy, and Ken comes down the little wooden staircase from his office on the second floor. Right away they're talkin' about farm stuff and car stuff and I-dunno-what stuff, so I wander into the living room to look at the artwork and woodwork and goodwork of decades of creation. There in the corner was the giant hemp ball he brought on stage in Boulder. And of course every inch of every wall had *something* — a Dead poster, a funky old mirror, an abstract canvas, a framed award for one of his kids, or a photo of the expression-filled faces of '60s New Yorkers taken from the roof of The Bus as they drove through Manhattan tootling the multitudes.

Scanning the bookshelves, among other things there were all these great atlases and I suddenly remembered I wanted to figure out how far I traveled on this Road trip. I found one with mileage graphs in the back and went over to the kitchen island and started looking up the distance numbers between the major cities and notating a list in my notebook.

Kesey walked over, looked at what I was doing, smiled, didn't say a thing, and walked away. I kept looking up each city-to-city distance in sequence, then had to manually add up all the numbers, and the split-second I could see the result, I hear Kesey call out, "How far?"

I was starting to get used to this telepathy thing. "3,508 miles."

And both of 'em broke out in cheers and applause, Babbs bellowing, "Alright! That's our *On The Road* man! Captain Canuck! From Camp Kerouac! Ha-ha-ha." The guy cracked himself up. And us too. Whatta crew. I could get to like these guys.

I put the atlas away and they were still yammering on about farming or some such I had no idea, so I said, "I'm gonna go look at the International Harvester." I don't know why, but for some reason I thought I should specify the make of the vehicle I wanted to check out! And Kesey stopped. He had this great trick where ... see, he was always moving or talking or in action, but he'd also mastered this theatrical maneuver where he'd freeze in place like a photograph while things kept whirling around him, perfectly frozen for just a second or two, creating this mental snapshot — a way of registering the moment, and wresting control of the action, of *time*, breaking the rhythm of the room, a silent and motionless action that got your attention and captured the scene by him doing . . . nothing. Then he broke into his big wide smile and walked me to the door and stepped out and pointed to where it was out behind one of the barns, and said, "Have fun!!" in his super happy way before setting me free on The Farm.

The first thing you notice is all the farm tools from rakes to tractor implements are painted in bright psychedelic Day-Glo swirls and splashes like the bus — an Expressionistic collage of colors — "The Prankster motif," as Babbs calls it. In fact, as soon as I got home from this adventure, I proceeded to paint my hockey stick in the team colors.

It was like following a trail of psychedelic bread crumbs . . . past the first barn, past the second barn, hang a right — and suddenly! blazing in an orange ball of fire in the field was The Magic Bus, The Mighty Bus, The Real Bus!

Finally. I was here. After first reading about it *sooo* many years ago — gotta be at least five by now! — a quarter of my life ago! — here I was at last one-on-one with the psychedelic magic carpet!

It was like Stonehenge or The Great Pyramid or something — this giant man-made creation outdoors with some intangible magnetic mystical mythical reverential *presence.* And yes, damn it, it *does* look alive, it *is* alive — the windshields for eyes, the front grill for the nose, the fat bumpers are the smiling cheeks, the mirrors the ears, and it's wearing a round white cap on its head. Or maybe it's bald. But there's no doubt it's a person!

Of course the first thing I do is climb inside to see Neal's Wheel.

If only we had his '49 Hudson to put next to it, or maybe that travel-bureau Cadillac — but until then this is the only wheel we know of that that trans-generational driver ever worked. Maybe this wasn't a church, but I'm not gonna say it wasn't a shrine. There was something sacred, spiritual, transportive and weird about being in the Holy Goof's cockpit, this Cody Pomeray of The Next Generation, this muse for two masters.

And it was funny how the thing was paint-covered from stem to stern — just like the graffitied New York subways I rode every day — every square inch covered in some crazy color. In fact layers and layers of crazy colors!

And I began hearing Keith Moon's claves bringing *"Magic Bus"* into the soundtrack, as The Beatles' *Magical Mystery Tour* began screening on the windshield. I looked out the side and there was the Partridge Family driving by singing *"C'mon, Get Happy."* I saw the school bus that delivers the cast of *Jesus Christ Superstar* into the desert in the opening of that cinematic masterpiece. And there was the Green Tortoise pulling out of San Francisco for New York. And suddenly I flashed on my own old school bus trip across the country in 1978 with a bunch of Winnipeg musicians and pranksters — and how all of that and so much more was inspired by this exact terrestrial spaceship I was standing inside. "I'm *on the bus*," I blurted out, and laughed at myself makin' sure The Spirits could hear me.

The author in white t-shirt standing on hood in center, age 17

I couldn't believe I was here. Then I started thinkin' nobody else would either. I had to get a picture somehow ... somehow ... ah-ha! A mirror! The only shot. The whole shot. The Gregory shot! But the inside rearview was already gone, so I went back outside and begin to twist ... *petrifiedly ... carefully ... slowly . . . soooo slowly . . . could you imagine?!* Yikes! ... Neal's ancient delicate driver's side mirror in its swivel until my frame could perfectly fit in its.

And I started thinking about all the lessons I'd internalized from Kesey, and from "that book about him" as he coyly refers to *Electric Kool-Aid Acid Test*, and having just seen him on TV a few months ago goofing with Garcia on that goofy Tom Snyder's show ... **"You trade off"** ... and reading every interview or article on him in *Rolling Stone* or anywhere else I found — and how my time with him these past few weeks had reinforced every preconceived great notion and then some.

And about how every event I'd produced since I was 16 years old was inspired by the Acid Tests, how my whole life had been a way of recreating that group spirit of collaborative crazy unrestrained fun. How he taught me it was okay to go beyond what you were scared of — not only going through the door but *playing* when you were on the other side. The openness of possibility. Embracing the goodness in everyone you meet. Engaging them. Playing with them, pranking with them ... tootling the multitudes all road long.

And how there was a responsibility that came with the gift of Magic. If you got the Cosmic Giggle and could see the Golden Light, let alone knew how to dance in it, it was incumbent upon you to share it with as many people as you could. Not everyone sees the Grand Prank of Life, and it's our job to shine the light in the strangest of places for people to look at it right. If you "get it" you have to grab it — share it — push it a little bit Furthur than it's gone before. You have to lead. Yeah — that's what Kesey taught me. Leading. Inclusion. On the bus. Which is a *bigger* concept than on the road. This was about all of us, not just some of us.

Jack writ The Road — but this is The Road writ large. And it's our duty to write on, and drive that bus furthur.

Yeah . . . it was all comin' together . . . but this was also a get-together, and I'd been out talkin' to ghosts for about an hour and thought maybe I should head back to talk to the living who were *really* on the bus.

On my recon meander back, out behind the house I spotted a cool little dark-wood cabin down by a pond, which they later told me was where Ken did most of his writing. The perfect getaway without leavin' the farm.

As I went back in and joined them at the round

table, Kesey said, "It's a good thing you're not coming in stinking of cigarettes. If I didn't tell ya, there's no smoking that shit around here." I had no idea, and it's a good thing I didn't smoke, but boy he sure was adamant about it. Only time I ever heard him lay down a rule. "Stick to the good stuff," he winked. "And while we're at it, don't ever touch anything white," he sternly instructed with his father-figure finger.

"Yeah, don't worry, I don't," I kinda lied. "But um, speaking of taking good care, why's the bus just sitting outside with the windows open and everything? Shouldn't it be in the barn or something?"

"We might fire her up one time yet," he said. But then gave me an early version of the answer he'd later give a million times because everybody asked — his "It's returning to the land, nothing lasts forever" riff / philosophy. It was his bus, and I didn't want to argue with the guy, but I wasn't too crazy about that philosophy.

Then out of nowhere he hits me with, "My brother Chuck and I are going to Alaska next month!" he says with fire in his eyes. "The last frontier. Where it's *really* wild. Forget New York — this is the real survival of the fittest," he grinned. "And *Life* magazine's payin' for the whole sh'bang," — the same bunch who picked up the tab for Jack and "that kid" (as Jack called him) Robert Frank's trip to Florida in 1958 to pick up Mémère. Who were those guys?

And it was hilarious — in the multi-page super-cool photo-essay feature they did on him and his Alaska trip shortly afterwards, in the one shot they published that was taken at the farm, Ken's standing by the bus, and you can see the rearview mirror still twisted outwards. :-)

Actually, Ken was writing his first novel in *years* when I was visiting — and he never even mentioned it! It came out as *Sailor's Song* . . . and is set in Alaska. (!)

Thinking about all the books recommended at JackFest, I asked him, "What do you think should be the first non-Kerouac book I read when I get home?"

He gave me this long look, sizing me up and down, then finally said, "You read Herman Hesse's *Journey To The East* yet?"

"Nope."

"He was a huge influence back then. Another overlooked writer. You should let him in," he twinkled.

"Thanks!" I said. "Okay here's-another-one" — as I scrambled for questions to ask him — "What do you think Jack would be writing about now if he was still here?"

"Kerouac wasn't meant to still be here. He wrote it all down and was done. There was no more writing left in him. It's 'the Hemingway hump' — once the fire goes out and the power's gone, what are you going to do? Sit there in the dark waiting for some fan letter to come through the mail slot? His work was done and you could feel that great sigh at the end of *Vanity of Duluoz*. It was time to go."

This whole time I'm simultaneously freaking out that I'm talking to Ken Kesey ... *in his house* ... while rackin' my crazy brain for what else to ask him cuz I knew I was leaving tomorrow.

"Do you still go to Dead shows?" I blurted out, like

some barely-21-year-old idiot.

"Only every chance I get," he winked.

And Babbs had just come back from somewhere, and boomed in, "As Bill Walton says, 'My favorite Dead show is the next one,'" and he laughed louder than any of us.

Then I asked, in my scramble, "Well, where else do you think a person can find that spirit these days?"

"In the small places. It's off the beaten track, where it's always been. The Oregon Country Fair's in a couple weeks," he said. "You should come back for that. They finally bought their own land, and that's a fine scene. You'll find it there. The Boys are comin' around to do a benefit for 'em at the end of the month."

"And there's more naked girls than you can shake your stick at," laughed Chico Marx from the cheap seats.

"*Alright!* What's the date on *that?!*" I tossed another ripple in the laugh pool. But I was gettin' the sense we were winding down, and Boom right on cue, Babbs jumps in with, "Alright, we gotta go. Young Briiiian's leavin' tomorrow, and you and I gotta get on whatever we're gonna do for the Fair."

I was just goin' with the flow, just happy to be here however this played, and as Babbs and I are clomping towards the door, Kesey tosses out, "Stop in tomorrow on your way outta town."

31

Follow Your Star

Back at Babbs's palatial palace, all the kids were playing or creating in different ways simultaneously — like a noisy fun factory. And there was Gretchen, and yeah, still fetchin', as all these Beat and Prankster women seemed to be. There's definitely sumpthin' in the water fer sure.

And besides the telepathy and sweetleaf — there was also the birdsongs that filled the air, and Babbs's constant conversation with them — whistling to his parrots and talkin' back to his parakeets, and in the next breath asking his kids if the fish were fed and the grass got mowed. After another collaborative dinner for the comical masses, and a combustible encore for the coming attractions, we settled in for tonight's feature — *Hell On Frisco Bay* — starring Edward G. Robinson and shot on location in San Francisco in the mid-50s. Perfect.

And there was Babbs running his commentary. "That's Jayne Mansfield the guy's dancing with," he says, pointing out some uncredited cameo, as both of us spend the entire movie calling out S.F. sites enough times we coulda made a drinking game out of, "Oh, look! That was shot before [something changed in San Francisco]."

And as the final credits rolled I knew they were on this trip, too. While I was packing the pack for the final leg back I came across a coupon I'd torn from a *Whole Earth Catalogue* or someplace for the first five issue's of Kesey's *Spit In The Ocean* series of short books for $5. "Glad I found *that!*" I thought. "Wonder what the hell else is in here?!" dig dig dig ...

In the background — another beautiful thing about being there — Babbs didn't just find himself funny, but when he was in his room reading at night, these random thunderclaps of laughter would explode in the dark silence and shake the foundations, filling the house with his enjoyment of life.

The final morning unfolded like I imagine every morning around Basecamp Babbs. The farmer is up with the sun and the roosters by 7. One of the kids goes out and brings in the newspaper from the mailbox by the road, and Ken makes some strong country coffee, plopping in a dollop of homemade ice cream while classical music plays the soundtrack from speakers rigged up in the ceiling corners of every room in the house.

We hit The Road and crossed the Grate divide between the two Kens with Jerry playing the electric violin as the Morning Dew flowered into a Sunshine Daydream, and **all was alive with colorful greetings at Camp Kesey**. Everybody was up in more ways than one, and a vote for Jerry is a vote for fun.

Gathered around the round alcove table once again, we talked about lots of things including the "Cassady" show, which ultimately never happened (they never made that Eastern tour), but I did manage to pull together Rick Danko, Paul Butterfield, Country Joe, Blondie Chaplin, Bob Holman & some other poets, along with the Joshua Light Show and San Francisco LightWorks, the only time those two ever psychedelicised together, and dancers and jugglers and magicians in a full-on multimedia Acid Test show that people talked about for years and won me another Programmer of The Year Award.

Then I suddenly remembered that coupon for five issues of *Spit In The Ocean* for $5, which seemed ridiculous, and truthfully I think it came out way back when they'd first released the initial issue and were looking for subscribers, but I thought I'd at least, I dunno, ask. Ken didn't even glance at it while I'm pointing and going, "See, it says right here I can get them for five bucks," point point. He just nodded some vague "Mmm," as we kept riffing on about all these other things, and at one point he gets up and goes speaks to Faye and she goes away.

And we're talkin' about my route outta there, and I said, "Oh yeah, I gotta make a sign. Do you have any cardboard?" And we go find a nice piece because — as internalized now — selecting the right size, quality and cleanliness of your cardboard is essential. As is scripting the calligraphy, of course. So, I pulled out my trusty elMarko pen still with me from Portland, and started making the sign, and Kesey goes, "No, no, you're doing it all wrong."

And he goes and gets s'more cardboard n says with faux anger, "Gimme that," and yanks away the pen and starts drawing this wild "Home to Vancouver" sign with a giant cartoon thumb. Ha! "That'll get me home!" I smile, as I hold it up like a rehearsal for my roadside attraction.

And just then Faye wisps into the room carrying all the *Spit In The Ocean* issues *plus* the new special $10 "Cassady" tribute, *and* a hardcover of *Kesey's Garage Sale*!! I'd never even *seen* one before! — don't know as I have since. — And with a beatific glow, she whisper-says, "Here," and slides them across the kitchen island with my eyes bugging out and bouncing off it.

"*Whoooa!!* Thanks for the reading, Ken!"

I made it home with all of them and to this day still have everything . . . the conference poster, my holy notebooks, the cassettes, the ancient-even-then Kodak Instamatic X-15 camera, Brother Tom's t-shirt, and that cool old John

Lennon *Rolling Stone* issue I carried with me everywhere that Ken read from and I had him sign — but speaking of signs, my Mom didn't cotton too well to me hitchhiking, and one Christmas I went home and that Kesey sign wasn't there anymore.

But the memories and changes still are, as we jumped in the car, and Babbs drove to a bar, and said I'd go far if I followed my star.

And for the rest of my life I did just that.

Then — BOOM !!!

Look what I found ! . . .

doing a deep archaeological dig through the ruins of my
life in 2017 . . . at the very bottom of the very last box
stored under the basement stairs . . . .

32

Song of The Road I Sing

Out on the highway, the fireworks started to go off ...

Pranksters ... and writers ... and Deadheads ... and
Jacksters ...
Poets and players and teachers and teammates ...
Adventures and strangers and shows and family ...

Flashing snapshots
of learning and loving
mythical tales and magical pages,
lessons imparted in sacred places —

City Lights' floor
    worn to the core,
Red Rocks carved
    by the hand of God,
Pearls of street wisdom
    crazy with love
of diamond mind sutras
from diamond mine digging
the cats in the cradles
of culture's creation,
sharing the tricks
of rabbits from Hatters,
of joy from Paradise,
and passion from lovers
of words and visions and music and candor.

The Road is The Life
The Path to The Light
the first steps of a thousand miles
for a good conversation,
or sharing your diary
with simpatico strangers,
and having your heroes
share their lives back atcha.

Keseys in cars
and scholars in bars
and Holmes in classrooms
and homes in mountains
"gonna make them be my home"

as Jerry & Croz ripple in harmony,
with more mountains of books
building castles to heaven
warding off devils
in blue dress suits
and nay-saying no nopers
who've never flown the coop,
while painting in crosses
and filling in pictures
of visions first danced in sugar-plum heads.

Dancing now on the shoulder of life,
thumb outstretched for the next car's light,
canvases blank and lips upcurled,
seeing for miles like Neal around curves,
a Prankster twinkle
with a Grateful sprinkle
of spontaneous music meets spontaneous prose
in an endless tale — who knows where it goes?

But I'm loaded for bear cuz now I've been There.
It ain't just me in this rainbow glass tree
with shimmering prisms and dancing refractions
of a million reflections of the Walrus and Whitman,
surrounding me, covering me, delivering me from evil,
For this is the kingdom,
and the flower of power,
and the glory of the story,
for ever and ever,
Amen.

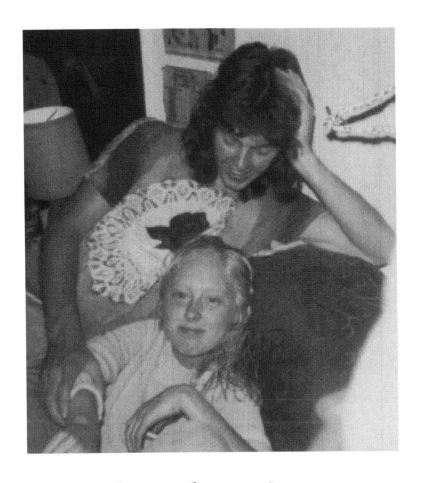

Safe in Heaven Home with Super Sue in
Vancouver, wearing Brother Tom's t-shirt
from the Airplane hanger

2015

and now . . . here's . . .

The

DESSERT

Menu

Where Jack Went After Boulder

Boulder '82 turned out to be not only a turning point in
your young narrator's life, but it was a turning point in
Jack's, too. This Summit of Spirits was the key correction
in the long road trip to respectability for Kerouac. It
marked the deepest darkest low water mark (the end of
the '70s and the beginning of Reagan, when you couldn't
even find *On The Road* in bookstores) before the rising.
From this point forward, Jack's fortunes and public
perception would begin a steady ascension to where he's
now an accepted part of university curriculums, and
virtually every bookstore on the continent has multiple
titles on their shelves.

But — there are a lot more choices now. At
the time of the Conference there had been maybe 20
different books by Kerouac in print over the years, *if*
you could find any of them. Today there are nearly 50
available *everywhere*, and in more languages than you
knew existed — including letters, diaries, short stories,

collaborations, juvenilia, "sketches," a haiku volume, a play, and a couple Buddhist treatises. Before Boulder, you could count the Kerouac biographies and Beat histories on one hand — now there are *hundreds* of them.

By 1982, all Hollywood had done was butcher *The Subterraneans*, and more recently Carolyn's book *Heart Break* (at least according to the author), plus rip off *On The Road* for the hit TV series *Route 66*. And there was one 28-minute movie by Robert Frank that nobody'd seen. And that was it. Now, two of Jack's masterpieces, *On The Road* and *Big Sur*, have both had the Big Screen treatment (and in the same year!), and both directed by sympathetic Beat auteurs; as have Allen's *Howl*, Bill's *Naked Lunch*, and Neal's Joan Anderson letter (under the title *The Last Time I Committed Suicide*), and there's even been offshoot big screen movies like about the killing of David Kammerer (*Kill Your Darlings*) and the shooting of Joan Vollmer (*Beat*).

And documentaries! Don't even get me started! But they all got started at Boulder in '82. Not one, not two, but FIVE documentaries were filmed over the course of the Conference (see full coverage of each later in Dessert). Other than late '50s / early '60s short TV news stories on "the beatniks," to my knowledge there had never been a Kerouac (or even Beat) documentary before the ones that were shot at The Summit. Now think of how many you've seen? You prolly couldn't even count them all.

Besides the big-production all-star documentary masterworks like *The Source* or *The Life & Times of*

Allen Ginsberg, there are literally hundreds of them, by everybody — both the BBC and Channel 4 out of England, the CBC and National Film Board of Canada, PBS, Bravo, the History Channel, the Biography Channel … you name it. And for every one made in English, there's been another made in German or Dutch or Portuguese or French or any number of languages in productions all over the world. The Beats have become so ubiquitous, Anthony Bourdain devoted nearly an entire episode of his CNN show *"Parts Unknown"* to "Uncle Bill" as he called Burroughs in his episode set in Tangiers. And … Harry Potter is playing Allen, the *Twilight* Queen is playing LuAnne, and with three big-budget film dramatizations in the same year, there spawned an endless stream of news stories about a guy that no one on any news show in America could even pronounce the name of when we first answered Allen's call to the Mountaintop.

And then there's the flood of recordings that have come out — from elaborate box sets of Kerouac's three albums or Allen's retrospective collection *"Holy Soul Jelly Roll"* to the Burroughs-Kurt Cobain collaboration on *"The Priest They Called Him"* or Allen making a video for MTV for his hit single *"Ballad of The Skeletons"* with Paul McCartney doing most of the music or Michael McClure recording and touring for years with Doors' keyboardist Ray Manzarek, not to mention numerous audio versions of all of their major works being recorded by an awards show worth of famous actors and released on every format from vinyl to iTunes.

And then there's all the conferences and similar

summits of like-minded souls that came from this good idea and its word-of-mouth. There's the now-famous gatherings like Quebec in '87, the Ginsberg *"Beats and Rebel Angels"* call-to-hearts back to Boulder in '94, and the mega-conferences at NYU in '94 and '95 ... but there are smaller ones going on every single year at universities all over North America and Europe.

And then there are the *annual* gatherings! ... like Lowell Celebrates Kerouac! every October, the Neal Cassady Birthday Bash in Denver every February, and the European Beat Studies Network conference each fall, that have not only not fizzled out, but actually keep getting **bigger** every year.

And then there's how Jack went from being essentially blacklisted in university curriculums, to now being taught in classes that fill up immediately from the Pace business school in Manhattan to the University of Iowa to the most prestigious institutions all across the U.K. and Europe.

And then there's the whole women & the Beats thing — and the correction of the misconception of misogyny in Beatlandia, which was actually the opposite of true in the relativity of their times. If you could keep up with the boys, and *stand* up to them, you were in the poet's circle — just ask Carolyn Cassady or Edie Kerouac or Hettie Jones or Diane di Prima or ruth weiss or Helen Weaver or Joyce Johnson or Lenore Kandel or Joanne Kyger or Anne Waldman (all of whom have published various accounts to this effect) — and everyone from fans to scholars are now enriched by hearing their perspectives and voices, many of which were only first heard or heard widely after this Boulder blossoming. In fact, entire books are being published now that are nothing *but* women Beat writers. So there's that.

And somewhere in this same garden is the truth that — when I was at the *On The Road* movie premiere in London, well more than half the audience was female, and I went around talking to as many as I could (naturally), and they were all there for Jack and no other reason. There may have once been a time when being Beat was "a guy thing" . . . but Anne Waldman runs the Jack Kerouac School of Disembodied Poetics, and Nancy Peters was the executive director behind City Lights until well into the 21st century, Ronna Johnson & Nancy Grace founded and run The Beat Studies Association, and Ann Charters and Joyce Johnson are probably the two biggest-selling writers of things Beat this century ... so, as The Grateful Dead sang, "The women are smarter, that's right."

And speaking of them — that band also continued a rather steady upwards trajectory! When I first saw them a couple summers before the Conference, it was in an 8,000 capacity general admission arena. My last shows 15 years later, were two sold-out nights in a row at an 80,000 seat stadium. They went from something that was whispered between music lovers to ... well ... I guess the word got out.

And you could almost peg Kesey's reemergence to this '82 public prank of him first putting on the "Cassady" show On The Road. Within the next few years he'd published a play, a short story collection, and two novels — his prior one having been over 20 years earlier.

And your friendly narrator ended up producing a massive Acid Test that fall with Country Joe, Rick Danko, Bob Holman and a ton of others, and reunited with Kesey & Krassner at The Grateful Dead's "Third Eye Ball" show in Toronto, and become close friends with Edie and Henri shortly afterwards, including finding the Henri-Jack unpublished manuscript in Henri's historically hysterically pack-ratted apartment, then become friends with Carolyn and John and McClure and Brinkley and Sampas and Tytell and Mellon and Amram and almost writing his book with him while simultaneously doing about a hundred shows together, and producing all these Beat poetry & music shows in New York at places like The Bitter End, Bowery Poetry Club and The Living Room, and appearing at all sorts of other festivals and readings, and helping put together *The Rolling Stone Book of The Beats* then being Holly George-Warren's go-to person for the public readings, into inducting Jack into the Counterculture Hall of Fame in Amsterdam, and shepherding Carolyn & John through their first-ever on-stage appearance together as we inducted Neal, and then producing/stage managing that huge LitKicks 9-hour anniversary show at The Bitter End, and those 50th anniversary of Jack writing *On The Road* shows in New York and L.A. with S.A. Griffin, and John Cassady & I sneaking up to the Hollywood sign, then staying at Carolyn's in the later years, and becoming good friends with Walter Salles and going to five different premieres of

On The Road ... it's been one helluva Beat journey since first hitchhiking to Boulder!

The point is — there's a never-ending road of new events and miles of new material being released every year in multiple mediums all exploring this vast empire of ideas.

But even bigger than all the new releases and individual stories and *stuff* — with the Beats in general ya gotta think about how America thinks about gays now compared to the '50s, when they were simply and naturally an accepted part of the Beat world; and how Jack was one of the rare white authors (following in Twain's footsteps) to write so glowingly and with such dignity about black Americans — and now one has been elected President a couple times; or how the Beats were the most overt group of American artists in *any* medium to be openly advocating marijuana — and sometimes taking the fall for it — but being way ahead of the curve of where most of America is now with so many states now decriminalizing or outright legalizing it; and how they were creating an environmental movement before there was such a thing; and how Jack (in particular) was championing Charlie Parker and Dizzy Gillespie when they were still unaccepted outsiders in the jazz world, but are now recognized as giants, "as important as Beethoven" just as Jack prophesied ....

You think about all these aspects of America that the Beats wrote about and *lived* ... and how today America has become the Beats writ large.

IN MEMORIAM

or ...

Love The Living
In Your Life

As of early 2017, here's the sadly long list of some of the conquerers who made it to The Summit who have since gone on to that great artists' salon in the sky ...

Al Aronowitz — May 20, 1928 – Aug. 1, 2005 (age 77)

Ted Berrigan — Nov. 15, 1934 – July 4, 1983 (age 48)

Justin Brierly — Sept. 3, 1905 – April 22, 1985 (age 79)

Ray Bremser — Feb. 22, 1934 – Nov. 3, 1998 (age 64)

Brother Tom — May 24, 1943 – Aug. 1991 (age 48)

William Burroughs — Feb. 5, 1914 –Aug. 2, 1997 (age 83)

Carolyn Cassady — April 28, 1923–Sept. 20, 2013 (age 90)

Sam Charters — Aug. 1, 1929 – March 18, 2015 (age 85)

Gregory Corso — March 26, 1930 – Jan. 17, 2001 (age 70)

Robert Creeley — May 21, 1926 – March 30, 2005 (age 78)

Henri Cru — April 2, 1921 – Aug. 25, 1992 (age 71)

Jerry Garcia — Aug. 1, 1942 – Aug. 9, 1995 (age 53)

Allen Ginsberg — June 3, 1926 – April 5, 1997 (age 70)

Paul Gleason — May 4, 1939 – May 27, 2006 (age 67)

Abbie Hoffman — Nov. 30, 1936 – April 12, 1989 (age 52)

Jim Holmes — May 11, 1926 – Dec 4, 2002 (age 76)

John Clellon Holmes — March 12, 1926 – March 30, 1988 (age 62)

Herbert Huncke — Jan. 9, 1915 – Aug. 8, 1996 (age 81)

Edie Kerouac Parker — Sept. 20, 1922 – Oct. 29, 1993 (age 71)

Jan Kerouac — Feb. 16, 1952 – June 5, 1996 (age 44)

Ken Kesey — Sept. 17, 1935 – Nov. 10, 2001 (age 66)

Arthur Knight — Dec. 29, 1937 – Sept. 7, 2012 (age 74)

Joanne Kyger — Nov. 19, 1934 – March 22, 2017 (age 82)

Jay Landesman — July 15, 1919 – Feb. 20, 2011 (age 91)

Fran Landesman — Oct. 21, 1927 – July 23, 2011 (age 83)

Robert LaVigne — July 15, 1928 – Feb. 20, 2014 (age 85)

Timothy Leary — Oct. 22, 1920 – May 31, 1996 (age 75)

Jack Micheline — Nov. 6, 1929 – Feb. 27, 1998 (age 68)

Brent Mydland — Oct 21, 1952 – July 26, 1990 (age 37)

Nanda Pivano — July 18, 1917 – Aug. 18, 2009 (age 92)

Peter Orlovsky — July 8, 1933 – May 30, 2010 (age 76)

Carl Solomon — March 30, 1928 – Feb. 26, 1993 (age 64)

Warren Tallman — Nov. 17, 1921 – July 1, 1994 (age 72)

Chogyam Trungpa — Feb. 28, 1939–April 4, 1987 (age 48)

Joy Walsh — May 3, 1935 – Oct. 9, 2011 (age 76)

Peter Warshall — Dec. 6, 1943 – April 26, 2013 (age 69)

That's one helluva choir!

Love the ones you're with.

Love The Living

Here's what some of the survivors have been doing since they reached The Summit — whose lives you can still appreciate and support while they're here to know about it . . .

David Amram has continued to compose and play music, and make appearances for Jack and Neal at events all over North America, keeping the pace of a man half his 86 years.

John Antonelli has continued to work in film ever since finishing his conference documentary in 1985 — lately based in Mighty Marin no less, with a focus on The New Environmentalists.

Ken Babbs has kept the Prankster torch blazing in rainbow colors, turning The World's Mightiest Home Movie into DVD releases, staging events, and is represented by Jack's old agent (the also still-living Sterling Lord), and writing novels like *Who Shot The Water Buffalo?* and an upcoming memoir called *Cronies* ... wink wink. You can find him at — SkyPilotClub.com

Len Barron, the hugely popular public radio host who talked to half the conference speakers on air, has remained an active artist in Boulder including writing, directing and producing plays like his landmark *Walking Lightly, a Portrait of Einstein.*
You can find him at — LenBarron.com

Dan Barth, the wild poet I remember citing Neil Young and Jerry Garcia on closing night, went on to publish several books of poetry, write for *Beat Scene* & loads of other literary magazines, and became an official Poet Laureate in Mendocino California.
Check him at — AcesWebWorld.com/danielbarth.html

Douglas Brinkley went on to lead student-filled bus trips around literary America, captured in his *Majic Bus* book, as well as edit Kerouac's diaries and Hunter Thompson's letters, and become a leading Presidential historian, writing numerous books on a wide range of them.

Ann Charters continues to do important research in Kerouac and other Beat studies, editing numerous anthologies, publishing her own photo collection, overseeing the legacy of John Clellon Holmes, and releasing the magnificent *Brother Souls* about John & Jack.

Tom Clark continues to write and publish poetry, as well as biographical works including on the major Black Mountain poet Charles Olson, and he just recently completed a 20+ year stint teaching poetics at The New College of California. He's at — TomClarkBlog.blogspot.ca

Andy Clausen continues as a raging Beat poet, one of the most energetic, forceful, powerful performers in the business, while also releasing numerous poetry and prose books. He spent many years teaching at the Jack Kerouac School For Disembodied Poetics at Naropa, and now calls Woodstock home. Check out — WoodstockBeatPoet.com

Cliff continued to live in Colorado, and the next winter met his wife to-be, and at their wedding I met the next love of my life! But that's a whole other book. Brother Cliff ended up going back to B.C. and among other things started this Test Of Metal off-road mountain biking competition in the Rockies that's become world famous.

Clark Coolidge spent a lot of time traveling the globe while continuing to write and publish his vibrant Language poetry, including some 26 different books since the conference, as well as playing jazz drums.

Diane di Prima continued for many years to write her poetry and teach at Naropa and other colleges, was named the Poet Laureate of San Francisco in 2009, and is still publishing new books like *The Poetry Deal* as recently as 2014.

Larry Fagin continues to write and teach poetry, and is still based in New York City where he's also been an editor and publisher of John Ashbery, Clark Coolidge, Charles North etc., as well as tending to crops of younger writers. You can find him at — LarryFagin.com

Chris Felver has continued capturing *Angels, Anarchists & Gods* as he calls them in a half-dozen photography books and as many films that have illuminated the Beat brotherhood as well as their cousins like Cecil Taylor and and John Cage.
You can find him at — ChrisFelver.com

Lawrence Ferlinghetti is still swimming, bicycling, painting, writing and overseeing City Lights, and among the million other things he's done, saw to it that San Francisco renamed many of its streets for the writers who made it famous, including creating probably the most visited Jack "site" in the world — Kerouac Alley in between Vesuvio's and City Lights.

Janet Forman has continued to use her cinematic eye and storytelling to capture stills and films for *National Geographic Traveler* and other such globe-trotting publications, and has won a ton of awards for exploring and capturing the planet.
You can find her at — JanetForman.com

Robert Frank has made a dozen more films since his *This Song For Jack* at the conference, and continues to live as he has for decades in Nova Scotia, Canada, where he still takes stills and occasionally helps put on a retrospective of his work like the one at the National Gallery of Art in Washington in 2009.

Max Gail continues acting in a ton of TV shows and movies — you've prolly seen him a bunch of times and didn't recognize him — and he's a *really* soulful guy and lifelong environmentalist who also runs a film company that does docs on Agent Orange, Native Americans, and other enlightened subjects. Very cool guy then and now.

The Grateful Dead continued to get more popular every year after the conference, until Jerry died in 1995. Since then all the surviving members have extended the musical journey both together and separately in various configurations, celebrating with three 50th anniversary shows in Chicago in 2015.

James Grauerholz continued to live with Burroughs and take care of him right through the end, and then has done a masterful job managing his legacy, and helping facilitate all kinds of both direct and offshoot projects.

Tim Hunt continued to pave the road to Jack, keeping his magnificent *Kerouac's Crooked Road* in print all these years, while also championing the great environmentalist poet Robinson Jeffers, as well as seeing his own poetry published in nearly a hundred different journals. You can find him at — TAHunt.com

Joyce Johnson published her first award-winning book about her boyfriend Jack, *Minor Characters*, shortly after the conference, and has continued to explore his legacy with *Door Wide Open* and *The Voice Is All* in the years since, as well as writing several novels, all while being a working editor and college professor.
You can find her at — JoyceJohnsonBooks.net

Ronna Johnson went on to co-found the Beat Studies Association and the *Journal of Beat Studies*, and has never stopped digging the archeology and expanding the universe of Beat studies, including a passionate emphasis on the unjustly unrecognized Beat women.
You can find out more at — BeatStudies.org

Faye Kesey and Ken continued their high school sweetheart love affair until Ken passed away in 2001. She kept teaching Sunday school and managing his legacy, and then in 2011 ended up marrying an old family friend of theirs, the *Lonesome Dove* writer Larry McMurtry.

Kit Knight continued to partner with Arthur in their indispensable *The Unspeakable Visions of The Individual* (tuvoti) publications until his passing in 2012, and took care of the archives after that.

Paul Krassner *still* kicks ass and takes names, continuing to publish *The Realist* until 2001, and since then remains his rabble-rousing self — publishing books, articles, doing appearances, and as of this pressing finishing his first novel — about a contemporary Lenny Bruce-type performer (since he knew the original n all).

Richard Lerner first made the *What Happened To Kerouac?* documentary at Boulder, then to the gratefulness of all, oversaw the 2-disk re-release in 2012 that doubled the length of the movie and the size of the gift this doc is for all who've seen it.
You can find him at — RichardLernerProductions.com

Lewis MacAdams was Lerner's co-director on *What Happened to ...?* and has since gone on to release a half-dozen books of poetry, as well as co-found the Friends of The Los Angeles River organization, and has been a practical activist and award winning conservationist for a slew of environmental causes.

Michael McClure has continued to write, publish and perform his metaphysical environmental poetry, releasing dozens of books and CDs, and eventually teaming up with Doors' keyboardist Ray Manzarek for many years of touring and recording together.
You can find him at — Michael-McClure.com

Dennis McNally continued to bridge the worlds between The Beats and The Dead, first becoming the band's official historian in 1980, then their publicist by 1984. After touring with them through Jerry's demise, he then wrote the band's official history, the nearly 700-page *A Long Strange Trip*, and in 2014 *On Highway 61*

about "music, race the evolution of cultural freedom" in America.
You can find him at — DennisMcNally.com

Gerald Nicosia had his epic Jack biography *Memory Babe* come out shortly after the conference, and thereafter has been a fixture on the Kerouac scene, including releasing a Jan Kerouac tribute/biography in 2009, and one of the only LuAnne Henderson interviews, *One And Only*, in 2012.
You can find him at — GeraldNicosia.com

Randy Roark continued to work with Allen annotating and indexing his poetry from before the conference until his passing in 1997, and along the way also published 15 books on everything from the Grateful Dead to Jean Cocteau, founded the literary magazine *Friction*, all while assembling one of the world's largest collections of psychedelic artwork.
You can find him at — RandyRoark.com

Doug & Judi Sharples continued to shoot footage and conduct interviews for years for their consummate documentary on Jack, *Go Moan For Man*, and have continued to tweak it all these years since and are still planning on a theatrical and DVD release.

Gary Snyder was not at the conference in person, but was in spirit, and has lived on thusly championing The Earth, The Spirit, The Soul, The Journey, winning numerous major awards while simultaneously living true to everything Japhy Ryder was about.

Sue and I remained together in a pretty amazing formative relationship until 1985 when she met another guy like me but a little more like her, and they lived happily ever after.

John Tytell & Mellon are still together and have continued to produce great works — both prose and photographic — about the Beats and a wide range of other similarly beatific subjects like The Living Theater, Robert Frank and New York City.
You can find fresh Mellon at — MellonTytell.com

Anne Waldman has continued to run the Jack Kerouac School of Disembodied Poetics at Naropa ever since the conference 30 years ago, and has still found time to publish over 30 books of poetry, teach classes, give readings, mentor young voices, and has kept the flame alive in Boulder and beyond since Allen's passing.
You can find her at — AnneWaldman.org

George Walker has remained an active Merry Prankster, and along with Kesey & Babbs was the Power Trio turning The World's Mightiest Home Movie into a releasable version, and has also written a (still unpublished) book about his time On The Bus.

Regina Weinreich went on to shepherd Jack's *Book of Haikus* into print, and published another book on *Kerouac's Spontaneous Poetics,* and is teaching and writing about the Beats and the arts, and is active in New York City to this day.

You can find her at — ReginaWeinreich.com

Ed White gave Jack the idea of "sketching" that changed his approach to his art, and Ed went on sketching and designing buildings for the rest of his life, becoming a renown architect of things that last, and also preserving what already was — much like his good friend from New York.

The Five Documentaries
Shot at The Summit

As part of the production of the event, we had to deal with not one, not two, but *five* documentary film crews shooting and interviewing everybody they could. There may be no books about Boulder '82 until this one, but there are five films that were shot almost entirely or mostly at the conference. And pretty much all of them are still considered to this day to be the best Jack docs ever made.

This Song For Jack — directed by Robert Frank — 26 minutes, B&W — first screened in 1983, and occasionally since, but never released commercially in any format. It's home-movie-like footage shot almost entirely on the Chautauqua lodge porch — the unofficial conference clubhouse — featuring Allen Ginsberg, William Burroughs, John Clellon Holmes, Gregory Corso, Herbert Huncke, Michael McClure, Edie Kerouac, Carl Solomon, Kens Kesey & Babbs, Abbie Hoffman, Dave Amram, Ann Charters, Joyce Johnson, Jack Micheline, Andy Clausen and others.

Allen's idea for the conference, besides celebrating a great man of letters and bringing old friends together again, was that new art would be created. Everywhere you saw people scribbling secret scatological thoughts in notebooks, as Jack instructed, but the Beats' unofficial official filmmaker was also capturing the images from his unique and insider perspective. One funny aspect — Robert is known to have been a lifelong smoker of the sacred herbs, and okay maybe it was a constant at the conference, but there's about a half a dozen different joints seen being smoked in this 20 minute film! :-)

Like all great documentarians including the Maysles brothers and D.A. Pennebaker the cameraman/filmmaker has the ability to disappear in a small crowd. Thankfully there were also the other documentaries made, with the principals sitting down for expository interviews, but here we get the behind-the-scenes home-movie honest footage of everybody just hanging out, telling jokes, being giddy, comfortable, feet up. This is what the Beats are like when they're not on stage, and more the way I remember the conference than any of the other docs.

Thanks to Tracy from the Robert Frank Collection at The Museum of Fine Arts in Houston for making my recent screening possible.

What Happened To Kerouac? — directed by Richard Lerner & Lewis MacAdams — 96 minutes — first released theatrically in 1986 (see photo p. 403); DVD re-

release in 2012 with fully two hours of extras — Boulder '82 Conference interviews with Gregory (his best ever captured on film), Jan Kerouac, Carolyn Cassady, Edie Kerouac Parker, John Clellon Holmes, Allen, Burroughs, Ferlinghetti, McClure, Creeley, Abbie Hoffman, Fran Landesman; plus additional off-site interviews with Gary Snyder, Ed White, Father 'Spike' Morissette, Ann Charters and Joyce Johnson.

The new second DVD of "extras" includes: 17 minutes of the "Beat & Politics" panel with Allen, Burroughs, Abbie and Leary, with Paul Krassner moderating; 12 minutes of Abbie Hoffman's rousing speech; then various previously unreleased interview clips with: Allen, Burroughs, Gregory, Huncke, Jan, Carolyn, Snyder, McClure, Creeley, Steve Allen, the actor Paul Gleason (with some priceless stories about the Florida years), Ann Charters and Father Spike.

Especially with this second disk added to the DVD, and maybe even without it, this is the best doc on Jack, and certainly the Conference, that you can buy. Lewis and Richard get it, big time. They're "one of us" and A) bring out the best in their interview subjects, and B) have the best sensibility to what's interesting about the whole thing.

The Beat Generation — directed by Janet Forman — 86 minutes — first theatrical release 1987; first video release 1998 — Conference interviews with Jan, Allen,

Gregory, Huncke, Ferlinghetti, Creeley, Diane di Prima, Carl Solomon, Ray Bremser, Anne Waldman, Abbie Hoffman, Tim Leary, Clark Coolidge, Larry Fagen; plus additional interviews with Burroughs, Amiri Baraka, Hettie Jones, Steve Allen and Dave Amram. Regina Weinreich was also involved as a writer.

Very much Big Picture '40s / '50s era and overall Beat Generation more than about Jack per se. Lots of exploration of writing in general, and mental illness and how it was (mis)treated back in those days, and the paths those who didn't fit in took, and how it expanded into the protest movements of the '60s. Lots of stock footage of the '40s, '50s and '60s depicting the eras as the interviewees voiceover what was happening then.

This is the *one* doc on the Beats that Carolyn Cassady actually liked!

Jack Kerouac: *King Of The Beats* — directed by John Antonelli — 78 minutes — released theatrically in 1985 — has been repackaged a few times with different titles including "*Kerouac,*" "*Kerouac, the Movie*" and "*On The Road with Jack Kerouac*" — it's most recognizable because of the distinctive Peter Coyote narration, and for its dominant use of dramatizations of Jack's life set to biographical narration or voiceover readings from his books, including *Maggie Cassidy, Visions of Gerard, Doctor Sax, Vanity of Duluoz, The Town And The City,*

On The Road, Visions Of Cody, Desolation Angels, The Dharma Bums and *Big Sur*. All the roles were played by unknown actors, except for the guy who's Neal, David Andrews, in about his third role ever, but he went on to have a successful work-a-day career in television dramas with guest appearances in everything from *Law and Order* to *Dawson's Creek*.

Conference interviews with Allen, Burroughs, Holmes, Ferlinghetti, McClure, Huncke, Creeley, Carolyn, Edie, Carl Solomon, Joyce Johnson, and both Ann & Sam Charters, all with the editorial guidance of John Tytell; plus additional interviews with Seymour Krim in his living room, Father 'Spike' Morissette in a bar near his church, Stanley Twardowicz in his art studio in Northport, and Gilbert Millstein in his apartment office.

Go Moan For Man — directed by Doug & Judi Sharples — 2 hours — limited theatrical release 1999-2001; DVD planned to be available "soon" — The film was birthed at the '82 conference. Director Doug said, "We just had to go once we'd heard about it. All the surviving Beat figures were going to be there, all these characters out of American literary history, out of Kerouac. It seemed like a once-in-a-lifetime opportunity to document Kerouac characters in the flesh, so we ordered as much film as we could ... and headed to Boulder."

And interestingly, he went on to say something that

comports exactly with my own experience: "What was so amazing at Boulder, when I first saw many of Kerouac's characters for the first time, was that they were exactly as he described them — the patterns of speech, the physical characteristics and peculiarities."

And he also came to the same conclusion I did with — "The importance of the material from Boulder was that it documented many of the real-life characters from the Duluoz Legend talking about Kerouac a mere 13 years after his death."

The film is divided into three segments: it opens with a dramatization of Jack's life; followed by general interviews with all the Beat luminaries, many of whom have since passed away; there's fully 25 minutes of interviews and clips from Camp Kerouac in '82, including some of the panel discussions, and interviews with Ginsberg, Burroughs, Ferlinghetti, Snyder, Corso, John Clellon Holmes, John Montgomery, Ken Kesey, Edie Kerouac-Parker, Stella Sampas, Jan Kerouac, Carolyn Cassady, Joyce Johnson, Ann Charters, Doug Brinkley, Dennis McNally, John Tytell, Sterling Lord, Gerald Nicosia, Ed Sanders, Roger Brunelle, John and Jim Sampas, and others. It also includes interesting location shots of Kerouac sites in Lowell, New York, North Carolina, Florida, New Orleans, Mexico, Tangier, Desolation Peak, and even Shelton, Nebraska!

Renown Beat scholar Dave Moore — who is definitely

not prone to hyperbole — calls it "the definitive Kerouac documentary."

With Henri Cru
at the "What Happened to Kerouac?"
opening on Bleecker Street

There wasn't a bridge between the Beats and
the Pranksters — it was just a loving embrace.
Merry Prankster Anonymous
with Big Al Hinkle
at The Beat Museum in S.F., 2015

The Birth of The Book

You wake up one day and your whole life changes just by a chance seeing of a picture.

Much the way it might with a chance spotting of a poster on a bookstore wall.

As Jack says, "My books are my children." And as Mama always preached — pregnancy can happen in an instant.

Unlike most books, this one had a precise Birth Day.

I had no plans to become a parent when I got up on Tuesday, February 19th, 2013, but it was then that I saw a photograph posted to an online Beat group that featured a bunch of the Founding Fathers of the Beat Generation hanging out on a porch at a gathering I went to in 1982.

Peter Orlovsky, Lawrence Ferlinghetti, William Burroughs, Gregory Corso, John Clellon Holmes, Allen Ginsberg, Carl Solomon, with Robert Frank seated, on the front porch of Allen's house in Boulder, July 1982.
Photo courtesy Jerry Aronson from "The Life and Times of Allen Ginsberg" 8 hour DVD set.

It was just like that inexplicable flash vision of seeing the conference poster in the sixth bookstore that prompted the entire adventure. You never expect your future to show up in front of you, but BAM! there it is!

Everyone in the online group was agog at this large gathering of giants, and how everybody looked so young, and that they were all together, and what an amazing collection of spirits this was.

To me it was just an old picture of my summer vacation. As it turned out, not a single one of these myriad scholars or fans in the online group had attended this legendary Woodstock.

A flow of online comments ensued, and since I'd been to it, people started saying, "I bet you've got some great stories, Brian!" And "I hope you brought a camera!"

"Well, now that you mention it ... " I hadn't looked at those pictures or thought about this thing in years. But being a conscientious contributor I thought I'd chime in with some memories.

"This'll just take a few minutes to write," I thought.

I started fresh the next morning — "I'll just whip this off then go run these errands I gotta do" — even though I didn't even have an "E" key on my new but broken MacBook! Had to push the little knobby thing down below!

Somehow I didn't get it finished that first day. So, "For sure I'll just finish it up tomorrow. Gawd, I can't believe this is taking so long." I started in that second day, but as it kept rolling down the road more and more memories kept coming into focus — and I was transported back to that time, as happens when you write — you begin to live in that world and not the physical one you're sitting in.

The next day I thought, "For sure it'll be done by tonight, damn it." But more photo albums and cassette tapes and notebooks and such kept tumbling off the mountain onto the path, more doors to open, more surprises, more memory boxes, more road going, until . . . "Well, for sure I'll have this done in a week." Then . . . "Well, make sure you're finished in 10 days. It *can't* take more than that!!" And this daily delusion of finishing it "tomorrow" went on for eleven daze, every single one of them thinking it would be done the next for sure. But it took eleven for the arc to be told from inception to curtain.

Of course, all sorts of other memory triggers and picture painting and fact checking and fine tuning and stuff continued for weeks, ... and then months, and then ... wait a minute ... sheesh!

But I had no concept of telling this Adventure Tale when I woke up that February morning, and after eleven time-traveling days in labor this baby was bouncing. And boy, they grow up fast!

The Sources

On The Road in Nashville, shortly after the conference

Some of the ingredients in the kitchen:

Two different road notebooks from the trip; three hitchhiking logs; typed post-trip LogNotes; multiple cassette recordings made at the conference and *on the road;* an inch-thick folder of papers from the conference including schedules and newspaper clippings and to-do lists; other Beat folders full of gems; my 1982 datebook; my Grateful Dead set lists and show notes; photo albums; Cliff Miller's photos and memories; letters and postcards home; letters to friends during and after it; recent conversations and emails with fellow attendees.

An incomplete list of some of the works relished while on this book's road, all by people I owe an enormous debt to for preachin' and teachin' and makin' life worth livin' quite frankly:

Jack Kerouac's *On The Road, The Dharma Bums, Desolation Angels, Visions of Cody, Lonesome Traveler, Old Angel Midnight, Scripture of The Golden Eternity, Windblown World, Good Blonde & Others*, and his *Book Of Haikus* that Regina Weinreich put together; Allen Ginsberg's *Howl and other Poems*; the *Kerouac – Ginsberg Letters*; Allen's *Deliberate Prose* collection of essays; John Clellon Holmes' *Go, The Horn*, and his book of biographical essays *Representative Men*; the Charters' excellent Holmes-Kerouac biography *Brother-Souls* especially Sam's vivid chapter on the Boulder conference; Gregory Corso's *Gasoline & Vestal Lady*; Michael McClure's *Scratching The Beat Surface*; *The Herbert Huncke Reader*; the Kerouac–Burroughs collaboration *And The Hippos Were Boiled In Their Tank*; Dave Moore's *Neal Cassady Collected Letters*; Carolyn Cassady's *Off The Road;* Jan Kerouac's *Baby Driver*; Edie Kerouac's *You'll Be Okay*; Gifford & Lee's oral biography *Jack's Book*, and Gifford's *Kerouac's Town*; Dennis McNally's *Desolate Angels* Kerouac bio and *A Long Strange Trip* Grateful Dead history; Holly George-Warren's richly diverse *Rolling Stone Book of The Beats*; Ann Charters' *Kerouac* biography; Gerald Nicosia's *Memory Babe;* Tom Clark's *Jack Kerouac* bio; Tim Hunt's *Kerouac's Crooked Road*; Clark Coolidge's *Now It's Jazz: Kerouac & The Sounds*; Carole Tonkinson's *Big Sky Mind: Buddhism and The Beat Generation*; John Leland's *Why Kerouac Matters*; John Tytell & Mellon's *Paradise Outlaws*; Jane Kramer's *Allen Ginsberg In America*; Isaac Gewirtz's beautiful

Beatific Soul with all the stuff from the NYPL collection; Steve Turner's Beat family scrapbook *Angelheaded Hipster*; Fred McDarrah's *Kerouac & Friends* and *Beat Generation: Glory Days In Greenwich Village*; Chris Challis's *Quest For Kerouac*; Bill Morgan's *I Celebrate Myself: The Somewhat Private Life of Allen Ginsberg*; Simon Warner's rockin' *Text and Drugs and Rock 'n' Roll*; Joyce Johnson's *Minor Characters*; Brenda Knight's *Women of The Beat Generation*; Hettie's *How I Became Hettie Jones*; Arthur and Kit Knight's *The Beat Road* with loads of photos from the conference; the *Moody Street Irregulars* conference issue; the *Kerouac Connection #28* conference remembrance; *The Review of Contemporary Fiction* Summer of '83 Kerouac issue with the killer John Clellon Holmes Boulder conference reflections in it; the 2013 *Journal of Beat Studies* with the Naropa essays; Randy Roark's historic small-press *Friction* magazine about the conference; John Montgomery's little collection *The Kerouac We Knew* printed especially for the conference; Sam Kashner's hatchet job *When I Was Cool* about being the first student at the Jack Kerouac School of Disembodied Poetics; tons of old and new copies of Kevin Ring's excellent *Beat Scene* magazine; *The Beat Papers of Al Aronowitz*; Robert Niemi's *The Ultimate, Illustrated Beats Chronology*; Mike Evans' *The Beats: From Kerouac to Kesey*; *Electric Kool-Aid Acid Test*; Ken Kesey's *Demon Box* and *Further Inquiry;* Kesey & Babbs' *Spit In The Ocean* "Cassady" issue; Babbs & Paul Perry's *On The Bus*; the Jerry Garcia interview book *A Signpost To New Space;* Phil Lesh's *Searching For The Sound*;

The Complete Annotated Grateful Dead Lyrics; Oliver Trager's *The American Book of The Dead* and his Lord Buckley bio *Dig Infinity!*; Sam Cutler's *You Can't Always Get What You Want*; Rock Scully's *Living With The Dead*; Blair Jackson's *Garcia* biography; Steve Silberman & David Shenk's *Grateful Dead Skeleton Key*; Jerilyn Lee Brandelius' *Grateful Dead Family Album; The Rolling Stone Interviews* book (2007); the entire *Rolling Stone* magazine digital archives; Bob Dylan's *Chronicles*; Sam Shepard's *Rolling Thunder Logbook*; Sean Wilentz's *Bob Dylan In America*; the Barry Miles' McCartney book *Many Years From Now*; Doug Brinkley's *Majic Bus*; Eric Burdon's *Don't Let Me Be Misunderstood*; Mezz Mezzrow's *Really The Blues* for the jazz language reminder; Dave Barry's *Greatest Hits* for the lightness of being; Jerry Levitan's memory-proving remembrance of meeting John Lennon in 1969, *I Met The Walrus*; *Huck Finn* for the road of it; *Treasure Island* for the adventure of it; *Catcher In The Rye* for the voice of it; and *Leaves of Grass* for the Celebrating of it.

Not to mention watching the Beat masterpiece *Pull My Daisy;* the documentaries *This Song For Jack* by Robert Frank, *What Happened To Kerouac?* by Richard Lerner and Lewis MacAdams, including the excellent two hours of "Extras" on the Deluxe Edition DVD, *The Beat Generation* by Janet Forman, *Kerouac* by John Antonelli and *Go Moan For Man* by Doug & Judi Sharples, all filmed largely at the conference; also ... the brilliantly edited collage and definitive Beat doc masterpiece *The Source*; the *One Fast Move Or I'm Gone* doc about Kerouac's *Big Sur;* the National Film Board of Canada's *Jack Kerouac's Road* largely about his francophone roots; the Hollywood dramatization of part of Carolyn Cassady's book, *Heart Beat*; and then the later kinda better one *The Last Time I Committed Suicide*; Walter Salles's loving adaptation of *On The Road;* Michael Polish's beautiful mostly voiceover telling of *Big Sur*; the Columbia years dramatization *Kill Your Darlings*; James Franco's channeling of Allen in *Howl;* David Cronenberg's successfully surreal collage *Naked Lunch;* the *Neal Cassady* docudrama starring Tate Donovan; the Naropa documentaries *Fried Shoes Cooked Diamonds* (1979) and *Crazy Wisdom* (2011); *Wholly Communion* about the 1965 International Poetry Incarnation at the Royal Albert Hall; *The Life & Times of Allen Ginsberg* by Jerry Aronson; *Burroughs: The Movie* from 1983 (that I attended the New York premiere of on Edie's arm); the Granada Television doc *It's So Far Out It's Straight Down* about the mid-sixties London underground scene; Laki Vazakas' insider and brutally revealing *Huncke & Louis;* Francois Bernadi's honest late-life portrait *The Original Beats: Corso and Huncke* doc, plus the outtakes; *Gregory Corso Reads From The U.S. Constitution and Bill of Rights*; Chris Felver's lovingly assembled *The Coney Island of Lawrence Ferlinghetti;* Ron Mann & John Giorno's 1982 *Poetry In Motion* doc with Allen, Anne, Gary, Amiri, Burroughs, McLure, Berrigan, Creeley, Sanders et al; Marie Beatty's 1989 collage of contemporary voices *Gang of Souls: A*

Generation of Beat Poets where John Giorno looked me straight in the eye and told me to publish myself; Doug Brinkley's great talk on Jack at the University of Texas in Austin; the 2005 Michael Bowen interviews from Amsterdam about the Human Be-In; the Pranksters' movie avec Neal *North To Madhattan,* and the other Key-Z production *The Acid Test*; the British Channel 4 *Ken Kesey: Tripping* documentary; the movie *Magic Trip* with all the original Neal and bus footage; the priceless inside interviews in the German doc *Edge City: The Story of The Merry Pranksters;* the PBS Oregon *Ken Kesey* doc.; Kevin Alexander's *Rebels: A Journey Underground*; the British-made *Grateful Dead – Dawn Of The Dead & The Rise Of The San Francisco*; *The History of Rock n Roll* documentary and raw footage; The Silicon Valley Historical Association's Jerry Garcia interview, the last he ever gave on camera; the *Sunshine Daydream* docu-concert about the Dead's show at Kesey's Creamery in '72; *Revolution* (the Summer of Love documentary); the power-of-music movie featuring the Dead *The Music Never Stopped* (thanks to The Mighty White Horst!); *Billy Connolly's Route 66* BBC road doc, and numerous episodes of the original TV series.

Plus listening to the Naropa audio tapes of various conference events; Rhino's 1990 *Kerouac Collection* of Jack's recordings (especially the solo sans music disc), as well as their 1992 box set *The Beat Generation,* and their invaluable *Holy Soul Jelly Roll* Ginsberg collection; BBC Radio 4's *Burroughs at 100*; recordings of the Grateful

Dead's 1982 Red Rocks shows; the Dennis McNally / Bob Weir interview at the 50th anniversary of *On The Road* Lowell show August 12, 2007; and tons of mindful music from Jerry Garcia, David Crosby, Johnny Clegg, Aaron Copeland, Ludwig Van and such.

And then there's internet's ability to produce memory-generating images and info on things otherwise uncaptured, especially Dave Moore's amazing The Kerouac Companion, Levi Asher's endlessly rich LitKicks.com, Peter Hale's encyclopedic Allen Ginsberg Project, and David Wills' Beatdom.

Acknowledgements and Gratitude To:

With Furthur at Yasgur's Farm in 2014

Marie-Laure Dagoit for first posting the photo of the
Beats gathered on the porch in Boulder that was the key
that started the car on this whole road trip;
Beat group members Jeanne Masanz, Mary Jo Hicks-

Sullivan and Richard Marsh for being the first ones to say
they wanted to read my Tales of Boulder, and then Jeanne
especially for being such an invaluable early reader;
and Ken Morris for all of the same but also reminding me I
might have taken pictures!
and all the others on the Facebook Kerouac and Beat
Generation groups who have been so enthusiastic and
passionate about keeping the flame alive;
and to all the various characters involved in the storyline
who proofed their sections or their loved one's — you know
who you are — and Thanks!
all the other early readers, including Al Robinson, Thomas
Kauertz, Sion Lidster, Sarah Benton, Andrew Geltzer and
the late great June King (RIP) in particular;
my first love Susan Howard for giving me the foundation
my life was built on, and to her whole family — without
Beth having a birthday in June, none of this would have
happened;
my old buddy Cliff Miller for giving me the landing strip to
shoot for that let the plane take off in the first place;
my surrogate mother Carolyn Cassady and surrogate
siblings John and Jami for adopting me into their lives and
being such heartful handfuls;
my friend, and friend to Edie Kerouac and Henri Cru, Tim
Moran, for everything he did for them while they were alive
and for honoring their voice and spirit in their afterlife,
including proofing my writings about them;
my British Beat brother Dave Moore for creating many
online worlds of endless facts and being a human
encyclopedia;

my American Beat brother Levi Asher for an eternity of
partnership and an essential early reading;

my savior in the Art Dept., David Wills, for swooping in to
save the day on the cover and book formatting;

my professor cum laude friend Walter Raubicheck for
guiding my spinning top into the sacred sanctuary of
books and history;

"my childhood friend" Walter Salles for making me fall in
love with the blank canvas again, which directly led to this
book being painted;

my Somerset Soulmate Noemie Sornet for first suggesting
I should publish this;

my left coast poet partner S.A. Griffin for being a freight
train engine of truth and spirit barrelling through the
center of town and shaking the walls;

my Neil Young / Jerry poet brother Dan Barth for sharing
his colorful firsthand memories and being a super valuable
late early reader;

my favorite living Jerry in San Francisco, Cimino, for
fulfilling The Beat Museum dream and fanning the flames
of my own;

The Mighty White Horst and The Leaning Tower of Gisa
for the early reading, encouragement and guardian angel
watching;

The Wizard of Wonder for being the doctor who told me
the due-date;

my globetrotting Beat brother Barry Floch for taking the
classic Kettle of Fish photo and allowing me to use it on
the cover;

my fellow Winnipeg BH, Brian Humniski, for his early

reading and constant encouraging;

Peter Hale at Allen Ginsberg's for helpfully answering all sorts of questions;

my literary agent Janet Rosen for seeing the vision and helping develop the picture;

all the original Merry Pranksters including Ken Babbs, George Walker, Mountain Girl & Anonymous for their support, encouragement and fact-checking;

Zane Kesey and all the next-gen Pranksters for reigniting The Bus and championing The Spirit;

Jerry Aronson for taking the historic photo of the gang on Allen's front porch that spawned this whole book being written, and for giving me permission to include it;

Randy Roark for putting together that amazing issue of *Friction* right after the Conference happened with so many fresh accounts, including the letters of regret from Gary Snyder and others;

my Woodstock confreres Raymond Foye, Rhoney Stanley, Shiv Mirabito & Maryanne Asta for their welcoming inclusiveness;

Dale "Gubba" Topham for his early support, and all the catches he caught and mysteries he solved;

my neighbors Chris & Sarah for enthusiastically cheering on my Tales Of The High Seas;

And for ... everything — Jack, Jerry, Keez, Allen, Abbie, John Clellon Holmes, John Lennon, David Crosby, Robert Hunter, Aretha, Vincent, Mark Twain, Henry David Walden, Uncle Walt, Lenny Bruce and all the cats that got crucified one way or another on the path to enlightenment.

421

Photo Credits

Cover photo - author at the Kettle of Fish — by Barry Floch
Taken fall of 1982, and wearing the S.S. Doric t-shirt of an
oceanliner I stowed away on in 1981. But that's a whole other
book.

John Cassady at the Hollywood sign (p. v) — by author
Sue (p. 2) — by author
Original conference poster (p. 4) — by author
Hitchhiking notes (p. 8) — by author
Author's self-portrait in notebook holding same sign as in
photograph (p. 15) — by author
Author, Cliff & friend, with Denver/Boulder hitchhiking sign (p.
17) — unknown
Arthur & Kit Knight's inscription in book (p. 29) — by author
Conference nametag (p. 30) — by author
Allen Ginsberg at Kesey's car (p. 33) — by author
Political Fallout panel (p. 68) — by Phyllis Segura
Staff button (p. 74) — by author
Notebook (p. 84) — by author
Kesey multiple exposure (p. 105) — by author
Kesey press conference (p. 109) — by Lance Gurwell
Author & Kesey (118) — by Allen Ginsberg using author's camera
Red Rocks Grateful Dead t-shirt (p. 128) — by author
Acid Test 1965 poster with Ginsberg, Cassady, the Dead etc. (p.
134) — by author
Six Gallery postcard announcement (p. 140) — unknown
Author & Cliff sitting on his Cadillac (p. 150) — unknown

Walking up to Kesey's farm (p. 336) — by author
The front of Furthur (p. 351) — unknown
Neal's wheel (p. 352) — by author
Interior back of bus (p. 353) — by author
'78 bus photo with Cowpokes (p. 354) — by unknown camper
Author in Furthur bus mirror (p. 355) — by author
"Home to Vancouver" Kesey hitchhiking sign (p. 366) — by author
Author & Sue in Vancouver post-trip (p. 371) — unknown
Author & Sue in 2015 (p. 372) — Greg Krantz
Carolyn Cassady & author in Amsterdam (p. 383) — by John Cassady
Henri Cru and author at movie (p. 403) — unknown
Anonymous and Al Hinkle (p. 404) — by author
Allen's front porch grouping (p. 406) — by Jerry Aronson (from "The Life and Times of Allen Ginsberg" 8 hour DVD set)
Author at typewriter in Nashville (p. 409) — by Albert Kaufman
2 Boulder notebooks (p. 410) — by author
Brian at Furthur bus 2014 (p. 417) — by Chris Foster
Cassette tapes (p. 421) — by author

Back Cover Photographs:

with hitchhiking sign in Denver – by Cliff Miller
with Ken Kesey in Boulder – by Allen Ginsberg
Halloween Steal Your Face in NYC – by Brother Tom
the Furthur bus in Oregon – by the author
with Edie Kerouac in her living room in Detroit –by Susan Wright
with Carolyn Cassady on her back porch in England – by Sam Hammond
with Sue in Vancouver – unknown
with the Furthur bus at Woodstock – by Chris Foster

All photos used by permission.
Every effort was made to contact the copyright holders and credit images appropriately.

Cover design and book production: the mighty David Wills

Index

427

Made in the USA
Lexington, KY
12 April 2017